# PUNJAB

## A Tale of State Terrorism, Persecution, Econocide, and Genocide

## Bakhshish Singh Sandhu, MD

NEWMAN SPRINGS PUBLISHING
320 Broad Street
Red Bank, NJ 07701

First originally published by Newman Springs Publishing 2022

ISBN 978-1-63881-235-7 (Paperback)
ISBN 978-1-63881-236-4 (Digital)

Printed in the United States of America

To all those who struggled for freedom and justice, and fought for the rights of others and their own.

# Contents

# Foreword

This book chronicles the long chain of abuses and usurpations by successive governments of India, since its independence in 1947, against its captive Sikh nation. Its author, a practicing physician in Philadelphia, having tasted freedom himself, describes the deep feeling of ongoing pain of the oppressed Sikh people being held as hostages in their erstwhile country of Punjab. The author, being a medical doctor, has diagnosed the primary source of this chronic pain (subjugation) and prescribes the curative medicine (freedom) in an easily understandable narrative. I myself, being an engineer, can understand the direct cause and effect of the convoluted social, psychological, and anthropological explanations of tyranny by the majority. The persecution, unspeakable tortures, and extrajudicial killing of Sikhs by the Indian police and army have been an ongoing process under different Indian regimes.

Under the grand political design to keep Sikhs under absolute despotism, India has remained steadfast in its policies of oppressing them since 1947. After the savage invasion of Darbar Sahib (Golden Temple Amritsar) by the Indian Army in 1984, the entire Sikh nation expressed outrage over this naked aggression and extremism by Indira Gandhi's government. During the November 1984 Sikh Genocide, over thirty thousand Sikhs were massacred in cold blood all over India, with the support and connivance of the Indian government. Justice has been elusive.

The truth about these events has been kept hidden behind the veil of India's false democracy. Censorship of the press along with broadcasting misinformation and fabrication of false news has been the primary mode of keeping the world unaware of how India has been carrying out massacres of innocent people in Punjab and the rest of India.

The conduct of the various governments installed by different political parties since 1947 has confirmed my belief that Sikhs will never be treated as equals to the majority community in India, and their differences shall remain irreconcilable. The author provides plenty of reliable and objective data in this book as the basis for this increasingly popular belief among all Sikhs, particularly among the five million or so diaspora Sikhs.

Countless peaceful struggles and attempts by Sikhs to resolve issues deliberately created by India's ruling parties in Punjab over the last seventy-five years—covered in this book—have brought vicious retribution and further oppression. In 1947, at the time of the partition of the Indian subcontinent between India and Pakistan, Sikhs decided to go with India based on promises of religious freedom and political autonomy. As these promises have been broken, and India has carried out the Sikh genocide, Sikhs now must withhold their consent to be governed by India to regain their lost sovereignty, dignity, and honor.

Bakhshish Singh Sandhu, MD, and I wholeheartedly supported Dr. Gurmit Singh Aulakh, the first president of the Council of Khalistan (whose primary objective is the independence of Punjab), until he passed away on June 21, 2017. Dr. Sandhu took over this mantle and has served ably in that position ever since. Having seen him in action for many years, I know Dr. Sandhu is dedicated to bringing freedom to Punjab peacefully and lawfully. Interested readers should find his book an excellent read and a good source of historical data on Sikh sacrifices and their pursuit of liberty and justice.

It is important to mention that extremism in the defense of liberty is no vice, and moderation in the pursuit of justice is no virtue. I have enjoyed reading this book and recommend it to all the people who love sovereignty, justice, religious freedom, and human equality.

Dr. Hardam Singh Azad, PhD
Houston, Texas, USA, 77024
March 12, 2021

# Preface

There has been an unfulfilled need, for decades, to expose the genesis and execution of genocidal violence against Sikhs in India. This genocide has been hidden behind the veil of India's questionable democracy. Most of the world has been oblivious to India's false claims of being the world's largest democracy, based simply on its population's massive size. Questions arise whether the masses in India are free. The answer lies in the facts on what transpired in Punjab after 1947, when the British handed over its control to India, which is detailed in this book. Sikhs, in specific, and the people of Punjab, in general, are suffering from the discriminatory policies of successive Indian governments. Sikhs have been the target of the Indian governments' incessant policies to weaken the Sikh community by denying their religion, state of Punjab, identity, and language. The facts contradicting India's claims of being a democratic, peaceful, and nonviolent country have been outlined in the chapters that follow.

What happened after 1947 and how the successive Indian governments trampled the Sikhs and forced them to consider their choices is the subject matter of this book. This book describes the Sikh struggle for freedom and justice. Its purpose is to show the Sikhs a glimpse of what has been transpiring in Punjab since 1947. It is to give them, and the rest of the people of Punjab, insight into the reality and the extent of Punjab politics controlled and manipulated by India and a much-needed jolt to wake them up to the choices they have in shaping their future. This book is to apprise them about what the future holds for them and why they need to be proactive rather than being reactive and defensive. Its purpose is to raise awareness among all the people of Punjab about how they are being manipulated and discriminated against based on their religion, and the whole world about how India has not left any stone unturned to subjugate them.

Beginning from the time of Guru Nanak[1] (the first Sikh guru and founder of Sikhism, 1469–1539) till now, Sikhs have experienced recurrent periods of tremendous upheaval while never losing sight of their goal of freedom, justice, and human equality, even under the most excruciating circumstances. Throughout their journey, despite many setbacks, they have never lost hope and instead chose to feel triumphant with Guru Nanak's message of an ever-rising spirit and Guru Gobind Singh's (the tenth Sikh guru, 1666–1708) creation of *Khalsa*,[2] with the doctrine that one must be ready to die for one's faith and righteous causes, and the war against tyranny must be won. Despite a great deal of adversity, and in many instances, with odds heavily stacked against them, Sikhs have been unwavering in their faith and willing to make ultimate sacrifices for worthy causes. They have thrived because of their commitment to hard work, sharing with, and caring for others.

Sikhs' distinct identity and concept of human values stand in sharp contrast to Brahmanism's inherent values and practices. For Sikhs, human equality is fundamental to their faith. In contrast, Brahmanism's lifeline concept promotes human inequality by dividing society into a caste system (annexure 8) in which people belonging to different castes have different rights and privileges or a lack thereof. Starting from 1947, the Indian system of governance, created by the Congress Party and followed by all the successive Indian governments, has been anti-Punjab and anti-Sikh. The system is designed to subjugate Sikhs and make them weak and keep them deprived and repressed so that they would never be strong enough—politically, economically, and religiously—to ask for their rights. India has been under the constant fear that, one day, Sikhs may take

---

[1]  Guru Nanak's teachings, see footnote.

[2]  Khalsa: Guru Gobind Singh created Khalsa in March 1699, a formidable force to promote human equality and fight injustice. Khalsa is a concept of saint-soldier; one should behave like in saint in times of peace and a soldier in times of oppression and injustice.

over India, so it is best to keep them repressed. To accomplish this goal, India's governments, with the help of its state-controlled news media, have turned non-Sikh Punjabis against the Sikhs. India's governing bodies have misunderstood the religious element of Sikhs that keeps them awake at night. However, the Sikhs have never entertained an idea to run over India and rule this country.

The Sikh's struggle for sovereignty of Punjab is not against a religion or a political party or anyone—person or a group of individuals. It is to reestablish the sovereignty of Punjab. It is to thwart the existential threat to Sikhs in India. It is to prevent repression, persecution, and unforeseen repeat of the future genocide of Sikhs.

Guru Nanak created a new system of belief in which the prevailing thoughts are one God, human and gender equality, and one has a direct connection with God without any intermediary. Nanak advocated intolerance toward injustice, and he encouraged his followers to speak up and speak out against tyranny. He discarded the doctrine of reincarnation and the Hindu caste system. Guru Ram Das (the fourth Sikh guru) laid down the foundation of Darbar Sahib, the Golden Temple in Amritsar, which was completed around 1574. It has four entrances, one from each direction, signifying access and welcome to all from any direction, with a further affirmation of human equality and dignity. People of all backgrounds, religions, and castes can eat, bathe, and worship together. Guru Arjan[3] (the fifth Sikh guru) collected and compiled Sikh scriptures into *Adi-Granth* in 1604, giving his followers written rules of conduct, helping them organize, and providing them with a distinct structure to the Sikh religion. Guru Hargobind (the sixth Sikh guru) bestowed the doctrine of Miri-Piri around 1609, which posits the coexistence of politics and spirituality, and created a Sikh state within the Mughal Empire by arming Sikhs for an eventual showdown on the battlefield. On the Vaisakhi day of March 29, 1699, Guru Gobind Singh created Khalsa, a formidable force to fight oppression and injustice. He bestowed upon Sikhs a distinct identity and political existence and a desire to be socially

---

[3] "All are coequal partners in this commonwealth with none looked down upon as alien" (Guru Arjan, the fifth Sikh Guru).

17

free and politically independent. Guru Gobind Singh stated in the *Zafarnama* (*the victory letter sent by Sri Guru Gobind Singh in 1705 to Aurangzeb, the Mughal emperor of India, after the Battle of Chamkaur*) that life could be meaningful only if one has honor. When one's honor is stolen, he declared, the very continuance of one's life is shameful. How India's political machinery has methodically and persistently attacked Sikh identity and dignity has been outlined.

The teachings and practices of the ten Sikh gurus compiled as the eleventh guru (eleventh being the virtual living guru, Sri Guru Granth Sahib, the Sikh Holy Scripture) have shaped the Sikh identity and culture. These scriptures promote the universality of equal rights. Sikhs believe in social and gender equality and that all people are created equal, and altruistic society. Such principles contrast sharply with Brahminism, which promotes human inequality by maintaining a caste system and its dominance over minorities. The differences between Sikhism and Hinduism, and the desire to exploit Punjab's natural resources, have been the driving forces behind the Sikh Genocide, persecution, repression, and unspeakable tortures of the Sikhs in India. Thus all the Indian governments, since securing independence from the British rule in 1947, regardless of their makeup or political affiliations, have remarkably similar, highly reproducible, and tyrannical behavior toward the Sikhs.

Following 1947, Sikhs quickly recognized that they had been betrayed by India's first prime minister, Jawahar Lal Nehru, who reneged from his promise to create an autonomous state in the north of India where Sikhs could enjoy the glow of freedom. Mahatma Gandhi repeatedly assured Sikhs that the Congress Party would make no such laws that would disappoint any citizen, much less entire communities. One of the first major blows to the Sikhs under the newly established Indian government was the fact that the Sikh religion was not recognized as a stand-alone religion in the Indian Constitution enacted in 1950. The following chapters will further highlight the decades of systematic attacks on Sikhs and their values by successive Indian governments.

## Notes

Sikhism is a monotheistic, divinely revealed egalitarian religion. Guru Nanak proclaimed, "As the Word of the forgiving Lord comes to me, so do I express it, O Lalo." The teachings of the ten Sikh gurus and some other revered persons belonging to different religions and regions are compiled in Sikh Holy Scripture, Sri Guru Granth Sahib (SGGS). Sikhism originated in Punjab, located in the northwest of the geographical region now called the Indian subcontinent, about the end of the fifteenth century. It is the fifth-largest religion in the world and among the youngest of the major world religions. The fundamental beliefs of Sikhism articulated in the sacred scripture SGGS include faith and meditation on the name of one creator of the universe, equality of all humankind, engaging in selfless service, striving for social justice, gender equality, and honest conduct while living a householder's life. Sikhism is a monistic religion with the basic concept that one supreme entity controls the entire universe. This entity is referred to as Ik Onkar (one God). Guru Nanak strived to build altruistic humanity and traveled far and wide to achieve this goal. A Sikh has five identifiers: Kesh (unshorn hair), Kanga (wooden comb), Kara (iron bracelet), Kashera (lengthy shorts), and Kirpan (sheathed sword).

Sikhism is based on the spiritual teachings of Guru Nanak and successive ten gurus, Sri Guru Granth Sahib (SGGS) being the last. The Sikh Holy Scripture (SGGS) is considered the last virtual living Sikh Guru. Guru Nanak established Kartarpur (creator's town) around 1520 and gathered the original core of Sikh Panth (community).

Before his death, Guru Gobind Singh (the tenth Sikh guru) bestowed the guruship (Gur-Gadhi) to the SGGS. Thus the SGGS became the literal embodiment of the eternal impersonal guru, where the scripture's word serves as the spiritual guide for Sikhs. Sikhism rejects claims that any one religion has a monopoly on the Absolute Truth (God). Guru Gobind Singh ordained all Sikhs to follow Sikhism according to the teaching described in the SGGS and not to follow any other scripture or religion.

In his teachings, Guru Nanak emphasized three main messages: Kirat Karo—work hard honestly, do not cheat, be truthful, and you shall live; practicing it, you shall enjoy peace. Naam Japo—remember Waheguru (God) by reciting Naam silently or spoken while keeping in mind that Waheguru is always with you. Vand Ke Chhako—share what you have with others, especially those who need help. We all should remember these three golden rules.

Guru Nanak taught that living an active, creative, and practical life of truthfulness, fidelity, self-control, and purity is above the metaphysical truth. That ideal person is one who "establishes union with God, knows his will, and carries out that will." The essence of Sikh teachings is summated by Guru Nanak, "Realization of truth is higher than all else. Higher still is truthful living." Followers of Sikhism are called Sikhs. Sikhism is derived from the Punjabi word *Sikhi* (Sikh faith), with its roots in Sikhna (to learn). Guru Hargobind (the sixth Sikh guru), after the martyrdom of his father, Guru Arjan (the fifth Sikh guru), established the concept of political (Miri) and spiritual (Piri), both to be mutually coexistent.

Sikhism has evolved in times of religious persecution. After they refused to convert to Islam, two Sikh gurus—Guru Arjan and Guru Tegh Bahadur—were tortured and executed by the Mughal rulers. Guru Gobind Singh's two elder sons were killed in war at Chamkaur Sahib, and the youngest two (ages seven and nine) were bricked alive, their heads chopped off when the wall reached their shoulders, for their refusal to accept Islam. The persecutions of Sikhs triggered the founding of the Khalsa as an order of saint-soldiers to protect freedom of religion and oppose the tyrants. Thus the concept of Sant Sipahi, a saint-soldier, was born (a Sikh is a saint in peace and warrior in the time of war). Sikhism now has more than twenty-eight million followers spread all over the world. Sikhs inhabit all corners of the world, primarily in the UK, the USA, Canada, Australia, and the Middle East, beyond their home state of Punjab.

# Acknowledgments

My heartfelt gratitude goes to the martyrs and their families, who supported the peaceful and, when no choice left, armed struggle for freedom and justice and told their warriors never to quit and never to be shot in the back.

I wish to thank:

- Late Sant Jarnail Singh Bhindranwale, who raised his voice against injustice and jolted the Sikh nation to wake up to reality and defend their faith and identity.
- All Sikh Jathebandies, who endeavored for the single goal of independence of Punjab-Khalistan and willingly took all the risks.
- Punjab Human Rights Organizations, People's Union for Civil Liberties, People's Union for Democratic Rights, Citizens for Democracy, Amnesty International, Human Watch Asia, and all other organizations that brought out the truth about Punjab.
- Authors Cynthia Keppley Mahmood, Gurdarshan Singh Dhillon, R. N. Kumar and Georg Sieberer, Ranbir Singh Sandhu, Joyce Pettigrew, Barbara Crossette, Mary Ann Weaver, Inderjit Singh Jaijee, Zuhair Kashmiri and Brian McAndrew, Lt. Col. Partap Singh, Jaskaran Kaur, and Pav Singh, and all those who impartially described the Sikh struggle for freedom and justice in their publications, and some of them had traveled from abroad and risked their lives for this purpose.

- My wife, Charanjit Kaur Sandhu, and my brother, Karj Singh Sandhu, for their inspiration and support.
- Gurpatwant Singh Pannun, the legal adviser to the Sikhs for Justice, for his vision and ironclad will to liberate Punjab from Indian occupation; the entire Sikhs for Justice team, for reviving and bring to the forefront the struggle for independence of Punjab and recognition of Sikh massacre in Delhi and all over India in 1984 as the Sikh Genocide.
- Dr. Gurmeet Singh Aulakh, the former president of Council of Khalistan, who dedicated his life to drum up the political support for the independence of Punjab on the Capitol Hill from 1986 to his last breath on June 21, 2017, and incorporated the Sikh struggle for Khalistan in congressional records under the title US Congress on Sikh Struggle for Khalistan.
- And all others who, in any way, shape, or form, supported the Sikh cause for freedom and justice.

# Introduction

Ever since the creation of the country of India by the partition of the Indian subcontinent on August 15, 1947, by dividing it into Hindu-dominant India and Muslim-dominant Pakistan, the erstwhile country of Punjab (now Indian-Punjab) has been colonized by India. The dividing line of partition passed through the middle of Punjab, leaving a large number of Sikh institutions of significance and highly fertile land in the Pakistan Punjab. A once self-governing sovereign, Sikh Empire (Sikh state) was occupied and subjugated first by The East India Company and then the British Raj. In 1947, it was handed over to the newly independent India. The promises of self-governance and autonomy made by the leaders of the Indian Congress Party during the struggle for independence have been broken. The Sikh state remains occupied and colonized.

The process of alien subjugation, domination, and exploitation of the Sikh state that began with the British colonization of Punjab in 1849 continues under the Republic of India. India not only diverted Punjab's land and its resources for itself but also proceeded to destroy the Sikh national, religious, and cultural identity. The carving up of Sikh territory, diversion of its key economic resources, denial of religious freedom, violation of fundamental civil and political rights, and regular pogroms on Sikh communities and holy sites across India demonstrate Sikh subjugation, domination, and exploitation by India.

With its state-controlled media, India has repeatedly tried to conceal the facts and has withheld information about the Sikh Genocide in November 1984, in Delhi after the assassination of then-Prime Minister Indira Gandhi by her Sikh bodyguards on October

23

31, 1984. As highlighted later in this text, there has been a long history of discrimination, political treachery, and phony negotiations which resulted in repression, persecution, and unspeakable tortures of Sikhs since 1947.

In June 1984, the Indian Army invaded Darbar Sahib (Golden Temple Amritsar) under the attack code-named Operation Blue Star. This attack was planned on one of the holiest days (the Martyrdom Day of Guru Arjan) in Sikh history, when a rather large number of Sikhs gather there. More than ten thousand Sikhs—mostly pilgrims and volunteers—were killed in this operation. Punjab was virtually cut off from India and the rest of the world by rigid censorship of the press, cutting off lines of communication, and suspending all modes of transportation. A large majority of the journalists covering this event were packed in a bus and hauled to the adjoining state of Haryana to keep the operation hidden from the world.

In April 1985, Citizens for Democracy, a human rights organization, sent a fact-finding team of five persons to Punjab under the leadership of a prominent social worker Amiya Rao. They determined that in Punjab, democratic rule was replaced by a rule of the army and police. They described a terrible tale of torture, ruthless killings, falsified encounters with police, and deliberate ill treatment of women, including assault and rape. Their report showed that a large number of persons subjected to preventive detention or arrests under the antiterrorist laws were innocent.[4] To implicate ordinary citizens of Punjab, the government of India enacted several new black-draconian laws in the 1980s in addition to the preexisting laws like the Unlawful Activities Prevention Act (UAPA), Maintenance of Internal Security Act (MISA), and National Security Act (NSA).

According to India's State Reorganization Act of 1956, the demarcation of the boundaries of the states was based on the language of its residents. To justify the denial of the statehood of Punjab, the government of India denied Punjabi as an official language, a language spoken by more than one hundred million people, and the

---

[4] *Oppression in Punjab: Citizens for Democracy Report to the Nation*, US ed. (Sikh Religious and Educational Trust, 1985), Foreword.

tenth largest in the world. Sikhs led by Akali Party carried out several peaceful demonstrations between the mid-1950s and early-1960s for the creation of the state of Punjab and recognition of Punjabi as the state language. While the agitations were secular and demanded the rights of all the people of Punjab, the Hindu community in Punjab vehemently opposed these demands. The Sikhs alone had to launch peaceful protests for basic constitutional rights, the kinds of which are never denied to the majority community of India. All successive Indian governments since 1947, regardless of their political makeup, have pampered the Hindu communal sentiment. In the meantime, Punjab has been allowed to bleed and burn.

Following the assassination of Prime Minister Indira Gandhi on October 31, 1984, the then-ruling party of India (Indian National Congress), also known as Congress (I), organized and orchestrated attacks targeting Sikhs throughout India. The personalized attacks were wide, ranging on the lives, homes, businesses, personal property, and places of worship of Sikhs. This was accomplished with the connivance of the ruling party politicians who provided logistic support, incendiary materials, petroleum, money, and alcohol. These attacks were carried out in a meticulous, highly reproducible, and malicious manner resulting in the loss of thousands of lives. More than thirty thousand Sikhs were killed in this brief yet tragic period. A large number of the victims were helpless and burnt alive in front of their family members and neighbors. Thousands of Sikh women were raped. Countless Sikh gurdwaras were burnt to the ground. Sikh properties, homes, and businesses were looted, ransacked, and destroyed. Over three hundred thousand Sikhs were uprooted and displaced during the melee. The perpetrators of horrible crimes have not been punished and enjoy impunity.

By enacting black-draconian laws, India gave its army and police oppressive powers without any liability and awarded them with cash and promotion for the heads of Sikhs. India's state terrorism fomented insurgency, which led to further oppression and massacres of Sikhs.

India is now engaged in the econocide of farmers. It is worth noting that a vast majority of Sikhs in Punjab are farmers. India controls Punjab's natural resources and institutions, religious and political. The passing of the three farm laws in 2020 is designed to control the small landholding of farmers. These farm laws are: Farmers Produce Trade and Commerce (Promotion and Facilitation) Bill 2020, Farmers (Empowerment and Protection) Agreement on Price Assurance and Farm Services Bill 2020, and the Essential Commodities (Amendment) Bill 2020.[5]

These laws remove the restrictions on food hoarding. The restriction on food hoarding was enacted in 1955 to prevent price manipulation, which benefited a few controlling the food supply chain. This removal of restrictions of food hoarding is a favor to the political allies of the ruling party at the cost of the poor.

India is not a democracy for all its citizens, particularly religious minorities. This is evidenced by the suppression of free speech and the right to assembly, use of water cannons with filthy water, blockade of roads with big boulders, cutting off internet and electric supply, the ruling party's thugs attacking peacefully protesting farmers, and beating of unarmed farmers by police during the ongoing protests against the newly enacted farm laws since November 2020.

The Sikhs have endured discrimination, brutality, and attacks on their religion and identity for centuries by various ruling parties, including Mughals and the British Raj, and now the Indian regime. To control Punjab with an iron-fisted rule, India created the Fifty-Ninth Constitutional Amendment Act (1988)[6]. Empowered by this amendment, India proclaimed a state of emergency in Punjab in 1988. Indira Gandhi had declared an emergency in 1975 that applied to all of India. However, the distinction was that this time, the emergency declaration applied only to Punjab. The explanation given was the fighting between Sikh militant organizations and India's Army, along with its police and paramilitary forces. The newly promulgated acts were draconian in nature that gave police, army, and paramili-

---

5   https://prsindia.org/billtrack/the-essential-commodities-amendment-bill-2020.
6   https://www.india.gov.in/my-government/constitution-india/amendments/
    constitution-india-fifty-ninth-amendment-act-1988.

tary officers unlimited powers to shoot, kill, torture, detain, arrest, incarcerate, or create terror with total impunity.

Historically the Sikhs fought Mughals and the British for centuries for sovereignty. They had created independent Punjab from 1709–1716, under Banda Singh Bahadur, and then from 1799–1849, under Maharaja Ranjit Singh. Since the loss of their sovereignty in 1849 to the British, they have never given up the idea of regaining their independence. Punjab fell to the British in 1849, after several bloody battles, only because of the betrayal by some top non-Sikh generals in Maharaja Ranjit Singh's regime, who made clandestine deals with the British for their personal gains. For about a century, from 1849–1947, Punjab remained a semi-autonomous state under the British.

During the prepartition negotiations before 1947, the British were dealing with three religious entities: Hindus, Muslims, and Sikhs. The Sikhs, even having known clearly that neither Muslims nor Hindus would be a good choice for them, did not push astutely and aggressively enough for their sovereign state. They had not forgotten the massacres and the indescribable tortures by the Mughals. The memories of how the Hindus had played a role in the martyrdom of the Sikh gurus (Guru Arjan Dev and Guru Tegh Bahadur) and two younger sons of Guru Gobind Singh (Zorawar Singh and Fateh Singh) were fresh in their minds. They also had not forgotten the Hindu hill kings' attacks on Guru Gobind Singh[7] and their betrayal of Banda Bahadur during his battles with the Mughals. Guru Gobind Singh, at the age of nine, had convinced his father, Guru Teg Bahadur, to sacrifice his life to protect the religious freedom of Kashmiri Hindus in 1675.

The Sikhs did not want to become a minority in a Muslim state. They decided to go with mainstream India on the promises and the assurances, made repeatedly by the congress leadership of Mahatma Gandhi and Jawaharlal Nehru. They were assured by Mahatma Gandhi that no constitution will be passed that does not

---

[7] https://www.quora.com/Why-did-Hindu-Kings-fight-more-battles-with-Guru-Gobind-Singh-and-his-Sikhs-comparative-to-Muslim-Kings.

protect their rights.[8] Jawaharlal Nehru promised them of setting up a state in the north of India where the Sikhs could enjoy the glow of freedom. It was based on these assurances that the Sikhs chose India versus Pakistan.

Starting in 1947, in a preplanned fashion, Congress Party's behavior toward the Sikhs and the state of Punjab took a 180-degree turn. Jawaharlal Nehru, when asked about the sudden change in the attitude of the Congress Party toward the Sikhs, answered boldly that things are now different, and the Sikhs had missed the freedom train.

Beginning in 1948, India started to carve areas out of Punjab. Finally the remainder of Punjab was trifurcated in 1966, creating two new states, Himachal and Haryana, thus reducing Punjab to a fraction of its original size before 1947. It is important to mention that these two new states had never pressed for statehood. When Punjabi Suba was created after a decade of struggle, certain Punjabi-speaking areas were excluded from the new state. Chandigarh, the state's capital, was not handed over to Punjab in violation of the Reorganization of the States Act of 1956.

India's Constitution, passed in 1950, labeled Sikhs as Hindus. For this reason, the Sikh representatives, Bhupinder Singh Maan and Hukum Singh, refused to append their signatures to the Indian Constitution.[9] Hukum Singh, a devout Sikh lawyer and later Lok Sabha speaker, was one of the most dynamic members of the Constituent Assembly of India. Singh had refused to sign a draft of the constitution as he felt it failed to address equal rights and religious freedom. He said, "Let it not be misunderstood that the Sikh community has agreed to this Constitution. I wish to record an emphatic protest here... The minorities and the Sikhs have been ignored and completely neglected."[10] Drawing authority from the Article 25(b) of India's Constitution, which labels "Sikhs" as "Hindus," the minority Sikh community is being denied many legal and religious rights,

---

[8]   Inderjit Singh Jaijee, *Politics of Genocide: Punjab, 1984–1995* (Baba Publishers, 1995) 1.

[9]   https://theprint.in/forgotten-founders/sardar-Hukum-singh-a-minority-rights-champion-in-constituent-assembly/132147/.

[10]  Ibid.

including freedom to follow its family law and by forcing the Sikh community to follow "Hindu Personal Laws." The legislation promulgated in India has, for the last several decades, clubbed Sikhs with Hindus so that Hindu Personal Law applies to Sikhs under the following statutes that govern the everyday life of Sikhs living in India: Hindu Marriage Act of 1955, Hindu Succession Act of 1956, Hindu Minority and Guardianship Act of 1956, and the Hindu Adoption and Maintenance Act of 1956.

When Sant Jarnail Singh Bhindranwale, head of the Damdami Taksal, a Sikh religious organization, protested the injustice and attacks on Sikh institutions, he was called a terrorist and a separatist. Indian government propagated the idea of Khalistan (independent Punjab) by first promoting its demand by infiltrating different Sikh organizations, supplying weapons to Sikh separatists, and then waging a war against them. By that time, neither Sant Bhindranwale nor any other Sikh organization was demanding Khalistan. Sikhs were simply asking for the establishment of Punjabi Suba (Punjab State), which was denied to them during the formation of other states. The states were reorganized on a linguistic basis. To justify the denial of the formation of the Punjab State, India denied the official status of Punjabi as a language.

India imported ammunition from Afghanistan, like rocket-propelled grenade launchers to attack Hindu temples, and blamed the Sikh freedom fighters for the same to win Hindus' sympathy and their votes and turn them against the Sikhs. In May 1988, a *Frontline* segment reported that "in Punjab, it is an accepted view that at least some of the death squads had been unleashed by the government." This freelance journalist's story also indicated that RAW (Research and Activities Wing) was using imported AK-47s and RPG-7 anti-tank rocket-propelled grenades in Punjab to justify the addition of the Fifty-Ninth Amendment to the constitution, by which the government could impose an emergency on the state and "suspend the right to life."[11]

---

[11] Joyce Pettigrew, *Sikhs of the Punjab* (London, 1995), 133.

Indian government passed several black and draconian laws to suppress the Sikhs. These included Armed Forces (Punjab and Chandigarh) Special Powers Act, December 1983 (annexure 7); Punjab Disturbed Areas Act, 1983 (annexure 6); and the National Security Act (1980). Under these laws, Sikhs could be arrested, imprisoned, tortured, extrajudicially killed or jailed for an undetermined time without due access to legal process. Their only fault was that they were Sikhs. During the 1980s and early 1990s, they were taken away overnight or during the day, their families not knowing about their whereabouts. They were moved from one police station to another and another. Often there were no records of their arrest or any case against them. The police, army, and paramilitary forces enjoyed full impunity for their actions, including torture and extrajudicial killings.

During Operation Blue Star, the Indian Army deployed tanks and helicopters and poisonous gas, killing about ten thousand Sikhs. This attack was preplanned two years in advance and rehearsed extensively to make it an astounding success. Simultaneously thirty-seven other Sikh gurdwaras were attacked. Though initially, it was presented as a necessary step to capture Sant Jarnail Singh Bhindranwale, the Indian government later admitted that the attack was carried out to break the Sikhs physically and mentally so that they would never again ask for their rights.

Before Operation Blue Star, Akali Dal, and subsequently Sant Bhindranwale, tried to negotiate with Indira Gandhi on multiple issues involving Punjab statehood, demand for Chandigarh as Punjab State's capital, the inclusion of Punjabi-speaking areas into Punjab, which were deliberately left out at the time of trifurcation of Punjab in 1966. However, every time, the negotiations broke down at the last moment. Indira Gandhi negotiated in bad faith. She projected herself as the country's guardian and portrayed Sikhs as anti-nationals who were intent on ripping the country apart. In reality, however, the Congress government reneged on a deal in February 1984, at the behest of the chief minister of the neighboring state of Haryana, not risking the Hindu vote. According to the journalist and part-time political consultant Kuldip Nayar, the Congress leader took an intransigent stand on Chandigarh's status and was in no mood to compromise. Soon after the talks were aborted, violence against Sikhs flared up in two major cities in Haryana, Panipat, and Jagadhari, resulting in nine dead and three gurdwaras destroyed. Reports suggested that authorities did little to protect Sikhs.[12]

Indira Gandhi's government deliberately pitched the Hindu community against Sikhs. Whenever a Hindu died a violent death, the government was in a hurry to announce that the killers were Sikhs, without any evidence.[13] The intention was to scare Hindus, pretend to be their protector, and win their sympathy by massacring Sikhs.

Operation Blue Star was followed by Operation Woodrose, Operation Black Thunder I, Operation Black Thunder II, killing thousands of Sikhs. Operation Blue Star was a blow to the Sikh psyche, and an attack on their hearts; thousands innocent pilgrims were massacred just to capture a few so-called hardcore militants. Other methods to capture militants in the Golden Temple complex were ignored because the real reason for this attack was not to capture some militants but to deal a devastating blow to Sikhs physically and mentally so that they would never again demand justice and equal rights. Indian Army invasion of Golden Temple Amritsar was well planned and rehearsed more than two years in advance.

Out of denial of justice, religious freedom, Sikh religious identity, first denial and then trifurcation of the state of Punjab, and denial of Punjabi as a language was born the armed uprising in Punjab. Bhai Dhana Singh, a member of the original Panthak Committee claims:

> Armed struggle was not our choice; it was forced on us. Even in the declaration of Khalistan on 29 April 1986, we appealed to all the peace and justice-loving people in the world to help us get liberated from the yolk of this tyrannical

---

[12]  Pav Singh, *1984: India's Guilty Secret* (2017), 57.

[13]  Pritpal Singh, "The Times of Sant Baba Jarnail Singh Jee Khalsa Bhindranwale: Saint-Soldier in the Finest Tradition," *Sikh Unity*, January 4, 2014.

regime. We are the believers in Guru Nanak, we believe in working for the good for all, we believe in equality and justice. In that declaration, we appealed to all the people to come and join us in our struggle.[14]

Indian government criminalized the Sikh demand for justice, religious freedom, and Punjabi Suba (state). Most of the time, criminal elements were created and operated by the Indian government who infiltrated the Sikh organization. They were provided with weapons and logistic support to carry out their mission of creating a disturbance and demand for Khalistan.

In July 2019, India banned Sikhs for Justice, a New York-based human advocacy group for propagating the cause of independence of Punjab through a nonbinding referendum vote named Punjab Independence Referendum. Subsequently in July 2020, the Ministry of Home Affairs (MHA) declared nine wanted men, including Gurpatwant Singh Pannun, of Sikhs for Justice (SFJ), who was designated as an individual terrorist under the Unlawful Activities (Prevention) Act (UAPA). The others designated as individual terrorists under UAPA include: Paramjit Singh of Babbar Khalsa International, Hardeep Singh Nijjar of Khalistan Tiger Force, Gurmit Singh Bagga of Khalistan Zindabad Force, and Ranjeet Singh from the same outfit, among others.[15] Several Sikhs for Justice supporters have been arrested, tortured, and imprisoned for distributing literature on Khalistan.

During the November 1984 Sikh Genocide, more than thirty thousand Sikhs were killed in Delhi and all over India, in eighteen Indian states, and about one hundred Indian cities after the assassination of Indira Gandhi. The assassination was a revenge killing for the massacre of Sikhs during the Indian Army attack on Darbar Sahib,

---

[14]  Cynthia Keppley Mahmood, *Fighting for Faith and Nation: Dialogue with Sikh Militants* (Philadelphia: University of Pennsylvania Press, 1996) 148.

[15]  https://www.hindustantimes.com/india-news/under-uapa-govt-declares-nine-terrorists-including-gurpatwant-singh-pannu-as-designated-terrorists/story-PH2mRLtw2mE1jCfP5HkpKJ.html.

ordered by Indira Gandhi. During the Sikh Genocide, frenzied mobs butchered Sikhs, others were decapitated and necklaced by placing tires around their necks and setting them ablaze by pouring gasoline over them. In many areas, murder squads were supplied phosphorous to incinerate their victims. Women were violently gang-raped, their breasts were cut off, police batons were thrust into their vaginas. Hundreds of dead and many actively dying Sikhs were burnt in bonfires at the local intersections, thus obliterating any evidence of their identity and death. All done with the connivance of the government officials and politicians.

After thirty-seven years of impunity for perpetrators of the carnage, survivors have expressed feelings of injustice and hopelessness. In his address to the United States Congressional Committees on the topic of genocide, titled "The Cost of Denial," Dr. Gregory Stanton, president Genocide Watch, and 2007–2009 president of International Association of Genocide Scholars, touched on the mental implications of the genocide and the effects of the ongoing denial of justice and recognition of victims. He stated:

> It is actually a continuation of the genocide because it is a continuing attempt to destroy the victim group psychologically, and culturally, to deny its members even the memory of the murders of their relatives…studies by genocide scholars prove that the best predictor of future genocide is the denial of a past genocide coupled with impunity for its perpetrators.[16]

India's policy to deprive Punjab of its hydel power and water by diverting 70 percent of its waters to nonriparian states has caused maximum damage to the state. And instead of its hydel power, Punjab is forced to use expensive and highly polluting thermal power with daily dependence on coal hauled from distant states. The control and management of Punjab's river waters and hydel power lie

---

[16] http://genocidewatch.net/about-us-2/cost-of-denial/.

under the Indian government, compared to other states who are in charge of their river waters and dams. During negotiations, Indira Gandhi negotiated in bad faith, only to renege from the agreements at the last moment before the planned press announcement of these negotiations.

According to *Max Arthur Macauliffe (1903)*:

> It (Hinduism) is a boa constrictor of the Indian forests. When a petty enemy appears to worry it, it winds around its opponent, crushes it in its folds, and finally causes it to disappear in its capacious interior... Hinduism has embraced Sikhism in its folds; the still comparatively young religion is making a vigorous struggle for life, but its ultimate destruction is, it is apprehended, inevitable without state support.[17]

Initially the Sikhs did not want Khalistan; they simply wanted religious freedom, which was seriously curtailed by the Indian government. When questioned on the issue of Khalistan, Bhindranwale answered how a nation would want to break up the country for the freedom of which it had sacrificed so much, referring to more than 80 percent of the sacrifices made by Sikhs for the independence of India. Now after having been subjected to slavery, denial of their religion and language, attacks on the Sikh religious institutions, 1984 Sikh Genocide, econocide by diverting Punjab's natural resources, and deploying Sikh soldiers merely as weapons to win wars, the Sikhs have reached the milestone that independence of Punjab is their only option.

Mahatma Gandhi, before 1947, made the following promise to Sikhs:

> I ask you to accept my word and the resolution of Congress that it will not betray a sin-

---

[17] https://www.azquotes.com/quote/798400.

gle individual much less a community. Let God be the witness of the bond that binds me and the Congress with you (Sikhs). When pressed further, Gandhi said that Sikhs would be justified in drawing their swords out of the scabbards as Guru Gobind Singh had asked them to if Congress would renege on its commitment. Sikh friends have no reason to fear that the Congress Party will betray them. For, the moment it does so, the Congress would not only thereby seal its doom but that of the country too.[18]

That prophecy has come true; the Congress Party is no longer in power, and India is falling apart, cracks have started to appear along the religious and linguistic lines, several regions are pursuing their sovereignty, and Sikhs are pressing on for independence of Punjab.

---

[18] Mohandas Karamchand Gandhi, *Young India*, March 19, 1931.

# The 1947 Mass Migration and Massacre of the People of Punjab

## *More Than Half a Million Sikhs Died within a Few Days of India's Independence*

In August 1947, when the British hastily left, the Indian subcontinent was partitioned into two independent countries: a Hindu-majority India and a Muslim-majority Pakistan. The subcontinent was divided based on religion, and the line of separation was drawn based on the religious majority in the areas of Bengal and Punjab. This was one of the greatest mass migrations and massacres of the twentieth century. This partition led to unprecedented migration which was poorly planned and executed without adequate safeguards to protect people from being slaughtered. The British, Muhammed Ali Jinnah, leader of the Muslim League, and Mahatma Gandhi and Jawaharlal Nehru, the two prominent leaders of the Hindu-dominated Congress Party, being well aware of the impending doom, deliberately failed to act to prevent the unprecedented human suffering.

As a result of this partition, more than twelve million, and according to some estimates as many as twenty million people were displaced, leading to unprecedented refugee crises. There was large-scale violence leading to the death of up to two million people. The numbers mentioned vary widely. However, according to most estimates about six hundred thousand Sikhs were slaughtered within a few days of the creation of the two independent countries.

The plan to divide the Indian subcontinent was declared in June 1947. However, no thought-out process regarding the migration of the massive population was established. People were waiting and wondering concerned as to what will become of them. They had unanswered questions as to where they would go, where would they end up, how would they reach their destination. Widespread violence was expected. People were afraid. The Congress Party failed to address the issues, nor did it show any desire to defend or protect these people. People were concerned about their land and homes. They were concerned about their elderly, debilitated, frail, and young children. Could it have been that the Congress Party was overly anxious and wanted to have their country in a hurry and let the majority government rule the minorities? It was the people of Punjab and Bengal, the most industrious and revolutionary of all the Indians, thrown under the bus. They were simply abandoned to be on their own. It was particularly hard for the farmers to leave their highly fertile land behind, which they had rehabilitated with great efforts, sweat, and toil. It was equally hard for merchants who would abandon their businesses, having no idea if they would ever be able to start a new one.

It appeared that neither the Congress Party nor the Muslim League nor the British government anticipated that there would be such a massive exchange of population in such a short time and create unprecedented human crises in the history of mankind. While the discussions and negotiations were going on about the partition of the Indian subcontinent, the violence had already begun. Major violence erupted in Rawalpindi, now in Pakistan Punjab, in March 1947, resulting in thousands dead. This early warning signal was ignored by the three main negotiating parties who were more concerned about where the partition line would be drawn.

Retrospectively it appears quite logical that the Congress Party had an insidious plan for Punjab and Bengal. This played out as the occupation of Punjab and subjugation of its people following 1947. Bengal was divided into Hindu-majority West Bengal and Muslim-majority East Bengal (East Pakistan). In 1971, India invaded East Pakistan and created a new country of Bangladesh.

I was born in 1947, in the Amritsar District of Punjab, in a village near the border of Pakistan. While growing up, I asked my father about the two large mounds of earth near my village. It was the leftover of the destroyed Muslim villages, he answered. I also questioned him about the increasing violence and theft in the region. He emphatically answered that there was much better law and order in the British Raj as compared to that time.

Historian Patrick French, in his book *Liberty or Death*, describes how it came to the personalities among the politicians of the period, particularly among Muhammad Ali Jinnah, and Mahatma Gandhi, and Jawaharlal Nehru. All three men potentially could have been close allies. But in the early 1940s, their relationship had deteriorated to such an extent that they could barely be persuaded to sit in the same room.[19]

Before the partition of the subcontinent, the British government was negotiating with three separate parties: Muhammad Ali Jinnah, representing Muslims, the Congress Party representing Hindus, and Master Tara Singh representing the Sikhs. Muslims got Pakistan, Hindus got India, but the Sikhs could not reclaim Punjab and its sovereignty. They finally decided to go with India based upon several promises made to them by the Congress Party leaders, assuring them of religious freedom and an autonomous state in the north of India where they could enjoy the glow of freedom.

Punjab was an independent country until 1849, when it came under British rule. At that time, India was not a single country but a conglomeration of more than five hundred autonomous princely states. During the partition of this subcontinent, in August 1947, the country of Punjab was not reestablished as an independent state as it existed in 1849 as a result of improper decolonization. The British divided this subcontinent solely based on two religions—Hinduism and Islam—leaving the other religious minorities at the mercy of their new masters. These minorities, Sikhs in particular, not only lost their empire, but they have also been subjected to genocide, econocide, and religious persecution.

---

[19] https://www.theculturediary.com/stories/great-divide-violent-legacy-indian-partition-william-dalrymple.

Throughout the negotiations, the Sikh leaders made their demands clear. They also made it clear that they would resort to violence if the award went against the interests of their community as they saw it coming. They stressed three main objectives: First, maintenance of solidarity and integrity of the Sikh community. Second, the retention of Sikh-owned land in rich agriculture tracks that their ancestors had settled and developed. Third, the important Sikh historical gurdwaras and shrines be included in Indian Punjab. However, despite the emphasis on these demands, the holiest Sikh shrines, namely Nankana Sahib, Panja Sahib, and Kartarpur Sahib, and a large mass of their highly fertile land went to Pakistan Punjab.

The deliberate acts of violence, massacre, rape, and abduction to force migration of people from one side to the other were carried out by all parties involved—Muslims, Hindu, and Sikhs. While Sikh groups carried out violence at the regional level, they were far from being alone in engaging in these activities. Such acts were carried out extensively also by Muslim groups and gangs in West Punjab who attacked Hindus and Sikhs, and by Hindu groups and gangs in East Punjab who attacked the Muslim population in East Punjab.

Sir Cyril Radcliffe, a British lawyer who never set a foot in India, was appointed to draw the boundaries between the would-be countries of India and Pakistan.[20] Pakistan consisted of two parts: East Pakistan, which later became Bangladesh, and West Pakistan. These two being about 1,300 miles apart, this system was destined to fail.

When extensive negotiations failed, the new boundaries were formally announced on August 14, 1947, the day before the independence of the two new countries, Pakistan and India.[21] Fourteen million people, who went to sleep in their countries the night before, woke up being in the wrong country. This partition would go down as one of the most traumatic man-made events in world history.

---

[20] Larry Collins and Dominique Lapierre, *Freedom at Midnight*, new ed. (London, Harper Collins, 1997), 171.

[21] Dalrymple, "The Great Divide: The Violent Legacy of Indian Partition," *The New Yorker*, 2015.

Some fourteen million people crisscrossed to their new countries, not knowing where and when they would end up, if at all they did survive.

Both sides carried out violent attacks against the other. The lack of troop deployment along the new borders to maintain law and order shall forever remain on the British Empire's conscience because half a million troops stood by idly while the massacre was going on. As Nisid Hajari wrote in his book, "Gangs of killers set whole villages aflame, hacking to death men and children and the aged while carrying off young women to be raped. Some British soldiers and journalists who had witnessed the Nazi camps claimed that the partition brutalities were worse."[22]

The British simply didn't want to get their hands dirty in this business of keeping Indians from going at one another's throats, with the result that the British military did not actually try to prevent people from massacring one another or abducting one another or taking possession of the property, according to Professor Ayesha Jalal, an acclaimed Pakistani historian.[23] This has been disputed by Anthony Matthews, a former British officer, who claimed that plans were made and properly executed with Indian troops, with both British and Indian officers deployed to control the situation. They were far too few, but they were not any more available.

---

[22] Nisid Hajari, *Midnight's Furies: The Deadly Legacy of India's Partition* (Boston, Mariner Books, 2016), 134.

[23] https://www.npr.org/templates/story/story.php?storyId=98529513.

# How India Usurped the Sikh Religious Identity

## Denial of Separate Religious Identity to Sikhs under the Constitution of India

Founded in the fifteenth century by Sri Guru Nanak Dev Ji, Sikhism is the world's fifth largest religion with over twenty-eight million followers, a distinct set of faith and principles, religious scripture (Sri Guru Granth Sahib), rituals, and practices. Sikhs in India comprise 1.8 % of the total population, with the majority living in Indian-occupied Punjab. It is the undisputed historical fact that since its inception, Sikhism has been recognized as a separate religion in its standing, except in post-colonial India, where Article 25 of the Indian Constitution labels Sikhs as Hindus.

Despite the historically unchallenged status of Sikhism, after the partition, the constitution of India was drafted and promulgated, in the face of Sikh members of the constituent assembly, with provisions that dealt a fatal blow to the separate religious identity of Sikhism.

Explanation II to Article 25 of the constitution of India provides that "the reference to Hindus shall be construed as including a reference to persons professing the Sikh, Jaina or Buddhist religion, and the reference to Hindu religious institutions shall be construed accordingly."[24]

---

[24] Article 25(2b) in the Constitution of India 1949.

## Consequences of Labeling Sikhs as Hindus in the Indian Constitution

*Sikhs are subjected to Hindu personal laws in India.* Relying on Article 25 of the constitution, several other laws were promulgated to subjugate the Sikh community by forcing them to follow the Hindu religious laws which violate freedom of religion. In the legal system of India, personal law means legislation governing matters of personal nature in a manner particular to a religious community based on the distinct religious and faith-based practices of a community. Such legislation includes the laws and customs as to marriage, succession, adoption, and other family relations of a particular religious community. The importance of family laws under the Indian legal system is paramount as it governs the everyday life of a religious community.

Drawing authority from the Article 25(b) Constitution, which labels Sikhs as Hindus, the minority Sikh community is being denied many legal and religious rights, including freedom to follow its family law and by forcing the Sikh community to follow Hindu personal laws. The legislation promulgated in India for the last several decades has clubbed Sikhs with Hindus so that Hindu personal law applies to Sikhs under the following statutes that govern the everyday life of Sikhs living in India:

- Hindu Marriage Act of 1955
- Hindu Succession Act of 1956
- Hindu Minority and Guardianship Act, 1956
- Hindu Adoption and Maintenance Act, 1956

Section 2(b), common to these acts, provides that these acts apply to *"to any person who is a Buddhist,* Jaina *or Sikh."*

Consequently Sikhs in India are forced to register their marriages, inherit their properties, and adopt children by classifying themselves as Hindus and by following the rules of Hindu personal laws. The Sikhs have a serious grievance that in India, Hindu law is applied to them when they are not Hindus. Such wrong labeling and classification violate fundamental principles of religious freedom and solidifies the denials of the separate religious identity of Sikhs. It is unjust on the part of a state claiming itself to be secular, to compel a minority community to accept a label that affects its independent and distinct nature.

## Multiprong Attacks on Sikhs

The Sikhs have been under incessant attacks in every imaginable form since the independence of India from British rule. It is quite comparable to the proverb "Out of the frying pan, into the fire." Their worst fears came true immediately after the August 1947 Partition of India into Muslim Pakistan and Hindu India. They quickly realized that while the Muslims and the Hindus got freedom, the Sikhs had simply exchanged one master for the other. While the British departed, their new master, the Indian political system, proved to be their worst nightmare. They not only lost the sovereignty for which they had paid the heaviest of the prices, but they now had to also defend themselves from the attacks against their religion, identity, mother tongue, and natural resources. These attacks have taken different forms and shapes over time but have occurred in a well-planned and organized fashion to ultimately subsume Sikhism into the folds of Hinduism. All peaceful attempts by Sikhs to rebuff these attacks have been answered with bullets, unspeakable tortures, and genocidal violence. Some forms of these attacks are described below:

a.  Violent attacks against Sikhs and Sikh gurdwaras
b.  Systematic attacks on Punjabi economic resources
c.  Systematic attacks on Sikh religious freedom
d.  The systematic denial of justice to Sikh victims
e.  Systematic attacks on Punjab's political autonomy
f.  The 1984 Sikh Genocide
g.  Denial of religious freedom, Sikh identity and the language (Punjabi)

Sikh identity is inextricably linked to Sikhism—a monotheistic religion that originated in Punjab in the late-fifteenth century and is practiced by twenty-eight million followers globally.[25] Article 25 of the constitution of India appears to subsume Sikhism as a sect of Hinduism as opposed to recognizing it as a separate religion in its own right.

Punjab has thus been reduced to a colony occupied by India. The independent Sikh Empire had attained all the internationally accepted criteria of sovereign statehood—it was a Sikh state. It was attacked, occupied, and subjugated by foreign powers—initially the East India Company, then the British Raj—before being handed over to India. Promises of self-governance and autonomy by leaders of the Indian Congress Party during the struggle for independence have been broken. A process of annihilation of Sikh national identity that began with the British colonization has been accelerated under the Republic of India. The Sikh state effectively swapped subjugation at the hands of one foreign power for domination and exploitation by others.

Through concentrated attacks on Sikh speech, assembly, and association, the government of India has demonstrated that it does not afford Sikhs the fundamental guarantees given to all citizens by the Indian Constitution.[26] As set forth below, attempts to express the desire for self-determination by peaceful means and within the constitutional framework have been met with violence and suppression. Those arguing for self-determination have been labeled as terrorists, gagged, and jailed. The Union government regularly imposes media blackouts and repressive censorship over "sensitive" issues such as the 1984 Sikh massacres. In 2018, India came 138th (out of 180) in the World Press Freedom Index[27] and was labeled as the fourth most dangerous country for journalists in the world.[28] In the 1950s and 1960s, tens of thousands of Sikhs were detained on this basis. Detention and ill treatment escalated in the 1980s and continues to

---

[25] William H. Mcleod, *Exploring Sikhism* (New Delhi: Oxford University Press, 2000).

[26] Constitution of India, Article 19.

[27] Reporters Without Borders, "India," https://rsf.org/en/india.

[28] International News Safety Institute, "Causalities Database: 2018," https://newssafety.org/casualities/2018/.

the present. In World Press Freedom Index 2020, India ranked 142 out of 180 countries,[29] indicating further deterioration of the freedom of the press in India.

According to Human Rights Watch, international human rights organizations and global civil society appealed to international leaders and the Indian government to bring justice to the victims of the human rights abuses of 1984, to no avail.[30] Many of those implicated have served in government positions and are being shielded from prosecution.[31] Notwithstanding Dr. Manmohan Singh's (former prime minister of India) apology for the massacres of 1984, there has been a continued refusal to accept state responsibility or commit to justice.[32] According to Judge Dhingra who presided over the cases associated with the 1984 massacres, a system that permits the legitimized violence and criminals through the instrumentalities of the state to stifle the investigation cannot be relied upon to dispense basic justice uniformly to the victims.

Successive governments have failed to prosecute those responsible for the killings and human rights abuses of 1984. Two government-appointed commissions and further eight committees were given the mandate to investigate the attacks on the Sikh population. The results ranged from a complete and unapologetic whitewash (Misra Commission) to a more sophisticated exoneration of implicated congress leaders (Nanavati Commission). Of 3,163 arrested suspects, the cases against the Congress Party and police officers were blocked and dropped through blatant political interference and corruption.[33] There have been no prosecutions for rape. This highlights

---

[29] https://rsf.org/en/ranking.

[30] Amnesty International, "India: Punjab—Twenty Years on Impunity Continues," 2004.

[31] Amnesty International, "India: Government Has Failed Victims of 1984 Sikh Massacre," April 15, 2009.

[32] Human Rights Watch, "Joint Letter to President Obama Re: the 30th Anniversary of Anti-Sikh Attacks in India," November 4, 2014.

[33] Pav Singh, *1984: India's Guilty Secret* (Kashi House, 2017), 127–151.

a comprehensive failure of the Indian legal system to provide Sikh victims with a semblance of justice.[34]

India's treatment of Sikhs has worsened with the election of Narendra Modi as prime minister of India. The recent events of state violence against Sikhs, coupled with historical legal subjugation of the community, show how the state terrorism against Sikhs not only continues but has also escalated under Modi's rule, states Gurpatwant Singh Pannun, legal adviser to the Sikhs for Justice.

---

[34] Human Rights Watch, "India: No Justice for 1984 Anti-Sikh Bloodshed," October 29, 2014.

# How India Diverted Punjab's Natural Resources

---

## *Use of Punjab Waters as a Weapon Against Sikhs*

Water is a lifeline for humans, animals, and birds. While water is essential for creating and sustaining life, too much or too little water can be equally dangerous. The state of Punjab has an agricultural economy. As per Agriculture Census 2015–2016, 86.2% of the farmers own less than five acres of land and a majority of them own less than two acres falling in the category of small marginal farmers. The livelihood of the large majority of Punjabi people is dependent upon agriculture. Punjab is a state of five rivers, hence the name Punjab (Punj "five", aab "river"). Punjab has an abundance of water supply, the lifeline for farmers. However, the Indian government, over the last several decades, has diverted more than 70 percent of this precious commodity to adjoining states, leaving Punjab with an arid land. The strength of the Sikhs lies in the religious moral orientation of the Punjab peasantry.

When a truncated Punjabi Suba (state) was created in 1966, it was made politically and administratively an ineffective substate virtually under the direct administrative control of the Indian government. This is evident from the fact that not only the basic subjects of hydel power and irrigation were kept in central government hands, but also the central institutions of Planning Commission, UGC (University Grants Commission), etc. were used to see that nothing worthwhile, even in their field of functioning, could take place in Punjab without the prior approval of central government.

Political, administrative, and constitutional arrangements were made to subdue and dwarf Punjab as a state. Agriculture is the lifeblood of farmers of Punjab as well as of its people. Landownership gives the farmers a sense of independence and strength, no matter how small the landholdings. Even marginal farmers who own a few acres of land feel financially secure because they can grow three crops a year and have enough food supply for the family. It is because of the hardworking Punjab farmers that it still supplies about 40 percent of the food reserves of India.

The state of Punjab was created in 1966, under the Punjab Reorganization Act of the same year. Even though the much-fought-for Punjab State was finally created, it was not only much smaller, but also the key controls of its administration stayed under the power of the Indian government. Water and the generation and distribution of hydel power remained under the control of India as well. This Punjab Reorganization Act of 1966 was in serious violation of the Indian Constitution and international law concerning riparian rights. There are two important aspects of this constitutional violation. Firstly, it was practically directly governed by the Indian government. Secondly, it violated the riparian rights of Punjab concerning its water resources. It was discriminatory because the control of the river waters of other states was under their control. For example, the control of the waters of the Yamuna river remained under the state government of Haryana, an agricultural state adjoining Punjab. However, the control of Punjab waters remained under the direct control of India. Thus Punjab has been reduced to administratively a state, subjugated and enslaved.

The policy to deprive Punjab of its hydel power and water by diverting more than 70 percent of its waters to nonriparian states has caused maximum damage to the state. And instead of its hydel power, Punjab is forced to use expensive thermal power with daily dependence on coal hauled from distant states with resultant pollution. This has been having a damaging effect on the progress of all agriculture and industry in the state. The groundwater level in Punjab has been dropping steadily. Additionally consistent economic measures have been adopted through banks, financial institutions, licensing, and pricing policies to inhibit the economic and agricultural production and growth in the state. The farmers have been given excessive amounts of loans beyond their capacity to make payments on these loans as agricultural income can be variable, unpredictable, and is highly dependent upon the quantity of rain and adverse weather conditions. Suicide rates among farmers in Punjab are among the highest in the world, secondary to their inability to pay back loans and fear of losing their land.

It is important to note that the questions regarding territory, the population formula, and their water and hydel power were constitutional issues and could have been easily resolved and settled. But these issues were kept hanging for decades. Instead, ancillary communal law and other issues were promoted and raised so that the real issues may get sidetracked. The constitutional issue regarding water and hydel power, pending before the supreme court, was withdrawn by the Punjab government under pressure from the Indian government, and the matter was prolonged and complicated.

Thus the deliberate diversion of Punjab water has proved disastrous for the Punjab farmers. Farmers have been forced to use electrically operated tube wells. The water level in Punjab has dropped to a dangerously low level, requiring submersible pumps as the water level keeps dropping further. This is happening in the face of Punjab's water being diverted to nonriparian adjoining states. India followed a multifold strategy of exploitation rule through the meek ministries of Punjab. Whenever the legislative assembly of Punjab has acted on behalf of its constituents that seems to be contrary to the grand scheme of things of the ruling party in Delhi, Indian governments have responded with the dissolution of the elected Punjab State government and its replacement with the president's rule. Since 1947, Punjab legislative assemblies have been dissolved nine times, resulting in more than 3,500 days of central rule in Punjab.

Three major human rights groups of Punjab, namely Punjab Human Rights Organisation (PHRO), Lawyers for Human Rights (LFHRI), and Sikhs for Human Rights (SFHR), organized a discussion on Punjab's water crisis on the Sixty-Eighth International Human Rights Day on Saturday, December 10, 2016, at People's

Convention Hall, Sector 36B, Chandigarh. While linking up the issue of Punjab's water crisis with human rights, the discussion was held on the topic of "Water Crises of Punjab and Solution." At this meeting, while referring to sections 78, 79, and 80 of the Punjab Reorganisation Act, 1966, Dr. Gurdarshan Singh Dhillon said that no other state in India was subjected to such a situation where the constitutional and legal rights of a state are so blatantly violated. He said that unlike the present chief minister of Karnataka, the political leaders of Punjab lack the guts to take a strong political stand on the issue of Punjab waters.[35]

## The 1988 Punjab Floods—Using Water as a Weapon

In 1988, Punjab had its most disastrous floods when all the rivers in Punjab overflowed, killing and displacing thousands of people. In four days, from September 23–26, 634 mm rainfall fell in the Bhakra area. People lost their crops. Beas Bhakra Management Board was accused and held responsible for triggering off the flood by releasing the waters from the dam, which burst the banks. B. N. Kumar, chairman of Bhakra Beas Management Board, was shot dead by militants as revenge for Beas Bhakra Management Board's role in floods. Nine thousand of Punjab's 12,989 villages were flooded, of which over 2,500 were completely marooned or simply washed away. This was the biggest flood in Punjab's history, as it disrupted the lives of over thirty-four lakh (a lakh is 100,000) people. As people were trying to survive and manage, the Union Agriculture Minister Bhajan Lal infamously said that the floods were a blessing in disguise—his logic being that it would increase Punjab's groundwater level. This flooding is considered to be deliberately set, releasing vast amounts of water too quickly, resulting in an incalculable loss of human and animal life. Experts believe that the water should have been released slowly over a longer period.

---

[35] https://www.sikhsiyasat.com/2017/01/20/pritam-singh-kumedan-tells-the-story-of-loot-of-punjab-river-waters/.

## *Satluj Yamuna Link (SYL) Dispute; Blatant Violation of Riparian Rights of Punjab*

Satluj Yamuna Link Canal or SYL, as it is popularly known, is an underconstruction, 214-kilometer-long (133 mi.) canal to connect the Sutlej and Yamuna rivers. It is meant to divert a large amount of much-needed water from Punjab to the adjoining state of Haryana. Over 75 percent of Punjab's waters are being diverted to other states with impending prospects of Punjab land becoming barren. SYL and other canals are being dug and water drained out of Punjab, which itself needs every drop of it.

To prevent the further drain of Punjab waters, Akali Dal (a Sikh political party) started their campaign under the banner of *Dharam Yudh Morcha* ("righteous campaign"). The Dharam Yudh Morcha was a political movement launched on August 4, 1982,[36] by the Akali Dal, in partnership with Jarnail Singh Bhindranwale, with its stated aim being the fulfillment of a set of devolutionary objectives based on the Anandpur Sahib Resolution.[37]

The basic issues of the Dharam Yudh Morcha were related to the prevention of the digging of the SYL Canal deemed unconstitutional, the redrawing of Punjab's boundaries following the Punjabi Suba movement to include left-out Punjabi-speaking areas, the restoration of Chandigarh to Punjab, the redefining of relations between the central government and the state, and greater autonomy for the state as envisioned in the Anandpur Sahib Resolution. The Akali Dal had demanded what was constitutionally due Punjab. The main thrust of the Morcha was against the economic erosion of the state of Punjab, with the most important demand was the restoration of the state's river waters as per constitutional, national, and international norms based on riparian principles. More than 75 percent of the state's river waters were being drained from the state to Rajasthan and

---

[36] Major Gurmukh Singh (retd. 1997), *Jarnail Singh Bhindranwale*, 3rd ed., ed. Singh, Harbans, (Patiala: Punjab University, 2011), 352–354.

[37] https://www.satp.org/satporgtp/countries/india/states/punjab/document/papers/anantpur_sahib_resolution.htm.

Haryana, which were nonriparian states, along with its accompanying hydropower potential powered by Punjab's only natural wealth. The construction of the Haryana side of the canal was completed by June 1980,[38] but the construction on the Punjab side has been repeatedly challenged as it violated the riparian right of the state of Punjab.

After the Indian National Congress came to power in Punjab in 1980, an agreement on river waters of Punjab was reached on December 31, 1981, between Punjab, Haryana, and Rajasthan, which were all under Indian National Congress rule, with Darbara Singh being the chief minister of Punjab and Indira Gandhi being the prime minister of India. Following this agreement, Akali Ministry filed a case in the supreme court about the sole constitutional rights of Punjab to its waters and hydroelectric power, challenging the validity of this agreement. However, Darbara Singh, under pressure from Indira Gandhi withdrew the case from the supreme court of India. Pointing to the arm-twisting of Darbara Singh's government in 1982, Dr. Dharamvir Gandhi said, "Punjab had to withdraw its case challenging the controversial sections of the Punjab Reorganisation Act, 1966, from the Supreme Court and was forced to sign an unjust and illegal agreement for parting with its water to Haryana and Rajasthan."[39] However, when the Akali Dal came back to power in Punjab, in October 1985, the newly elected Punjab Legislative Assembly repudiated the 1981 agreement.

The construction of the canal on the Punjab side was started but was stopped in July 1990, after a chief engineer associated with its construction was shot dead by militants. The canal remains uncompleted to date due to disputes over the issue. In 1999, Haryana filed a suit in the supreme court seeking construction of the canal.[40] In 2002, the supreme court directed Punjab to complete its part of the

---

[38] "Sutlej-Yamuna Link Canal issue: Field of dreams," *The Indian Express*, March 21, 2016, retrieved November 15, 2016.

[39] https://www.tribuneindia.com/news/archive/features/cong-sad-lying-on-syl-says-gandhi-220619.

[40] John R. Wood, *The Politics of Water Resource Development in India: The Case of Narmada* (SAGE Publications India, 2007), 74.

SYL Canal within a year. Punjab refused to do so and petitioned for a review of the court order which was rejected. In 2004, the supreme court directed the Union government to get the canal completed through a central agency. The Central Public Works Department was appointed on July 2, 2004, to take over the canal construction work from the Punjab government. However, on July 12, 2004, the Punjab Legislative Assembly passed the Punjab Termination of Agreements Act, 2004, which abrogated all its river water agreements with neighboring states. The president of India then referred this bill to the supreme court in the same year.

The court began hearings on the bill by the Punjab Assembly on March 7, 2016. On March 15, 2016, the Punjab Legislative Assembly unanimously passed the Punjab Satluj Yamuna Link Canal Land (Transfer of Proprietary Rights) Bill, 2016, proposing to return the land that had been taken from owners for building the SYL Canal. On March 18, the supreme court ordered the Punjab government to maintain the status quo on the land meant for the construction of the canal. On November 10, the court gave its opinion that the Punjab government's 2004 bill, which terminated river water agreements, was illegal. On November 15, the Punjab government passed an executive order, denotifying the land meant for the digging of the canal, and returned it to its original owners through a notification issued by Punjab's financial commissioner of revenue K. B. S. Sidhu, utilizing revenue powers that rest with an IAS officer. Punjab's Legislative Assembly also passed a resolution on the next day, demanding royalties for river water supplied to its nonriparian neighbors Haryana, Rajasthan, and Delhi. All of the denotified lands were returned by November 20. A status quo was, however, again ordered by the supreme court relating to the land on November 30.[41]

SYL dispute is mired in controversy over the application of riparian rights to Punjab river waters. India has been trying all means to steal the water resources of Punjab despite its blatant violation of international law and its constitution. There has been a clear prece-

---

[41] "Supreme Court Orders Status Quo on Sutlej-Yamuna Link Canal Land," *Times of India*, November 30, 2016.

54

dent described below in which the Narmada River Dispute put the riparian states of Madhya Pradesh, Maharashtra, and Gujarat versus the nonriparian state of Rajasthan, a potential beneficiary of irrigation water, in opposition to one another. Narmada River Water Dispute Tribunal was set up to resolve the dispute whose final order is described as below:

> Final Orders The Narmada Water Dispute Tribunal issued their "Final Orders" in terms of Section 5(3) of the Inter-State Water Disputes Act, 1956, on August 16, 1978, reproduced as Appendix "B" to this chapter. Evaluation of the Verdict of the Tribunal 1. Significant Features of the Verdict While dealing with the claim of Rajasthan for allocation of 2500 cusecs of the excess flow of Narmada water, the Tribunal observed: "We are of the opinion that such a claim cannot be entertained. As we have pointed out in our Order dated 8th October 1974, the right of Rajasthan to share Narmada Water is based on the Agreement between the parties, dated 12th July 1974. Otherwise, Rajasthan, being a non-riparian state, is not entitled as a matter of law to any share in the Narmada waters of the interstate river Narmada. The claim of Rajasthan must therefore be based on the Agreement of the Chief Ministers dated 12th July 1974."[42]

The tribunal thus made it clear that Rajasthan had no locus standi or any rights to Narmada River waters.

---

[42] http://14.139.60.114:8080/jspui/bitstream/123456789/678/22/Narmada%20River%20Water%20Dispute.pdf.

# How India Attacked the
# Punjabi Language

## Denial of Punjabi by Punjabi Hindus

While earlier in June 1948, Punjabi and Hindi were both made official media of educational instruction, the Municipal Committee of Jalandhar, in February 1949, resolved to make Devanagari Hindi the sole media in its schools, and the senate of Panjab University refused to use Punjabi in any script; both were strongholds of the Arya Samaj, which, supported by its Jan Sangh and Hindu Mahasabha allies, had never accepted the formula or implemented it in its schools.[43] To undercut the linguistic basis of the demand, the Arya Samaj embarked on a newspaper propaganda campaign to encourage the Hindus of even the Punjabi-speaking area to disown Punjabi entirely and select Hindi in census beginning in early 1951.[44] This repudiation of Punjabi was repeated in the 1961 census, ten years later,[45] and half of the demographic would continue to select Hindi even after the movement in the 1971 census. After failed efforts to absorb the Sikhs, and with the slogan of "Hindi, Hindu, Hindustan," Hindu organizations opted to spurn the Punjabi language so that the

---

[43] J. S. Grewal, *The New Cambridge History of India II.3: The Sikhs of the Punjab*, rev. ed. (Cambridge: Cambridge University Press, 1998), 187.

[44] Ibid., 188.

[45] Harnik Deol, *Religion and Nationalism in India: The Case of the Punjab (Routledge Studies in the Modern History of Asia*, 1ˢᵗ ed. (New York City: Routledge, 2000), 94.

Sikhs would be considered a linguistic minority as well as a religious minority, and thus prevent the formation of a state which would be Sikh-majority.

While every area in the country was fighting for its linguistic demarcation and autonomy, the Sikhs alone had to fight for the Punjabi-speaking areas and their welfare. The Punjabi-speaking Hindus had openly started working against their autonomy and interests. While every Maharashtrian fought for the interests of Maharashtra, every Bengali fought for the interests of Bengal and every Gujarati for the interests of Gujarat; it was ironic that the Sikhs alone were left to struggle for the interests of Punjab—all of it— including the areas dominated by Punjabi speaking Hindus who disowned their mother tongue.

### Hindu Politicians and Religious Leaders' Campaign against Punjabi

During the 1951 census, Hindu ministers and leaders influenced Hindus to declare Hindi as their mother tongue instead of Punjabi.[46] The result, though ridiculous, became evident because the public in Punjab declared their mother tongue purely on a communal basis. In the towns and cities, where Hindus were a predominant majority, the returns showed Hindi as their language, with surrounding rural areas where Sikhs were in majority returns revealed Punjabi as their language. It became evident to everyone that the returns have been communalized, and Prime Minister Jawaharlal Nehru deprecated its evidence falsely. He further accentuated the tragedy by stubbornly refusing to form Punjabi Suba. If the Punjabi Suba had been formed in 1956, along with other linguistic states, the integration between Hindu and Sikhs would have been promoted without any subsequent communal problems. When a news correspondent asked Nehru as to why he was against Punjabi Suba, he answered, "How

---

[46] Ram Narayan Kumar and George Sieberer, *The Sikh Struggle* (Delhi, 1991), 177.

can I give power in the hands of my enemies (Sikhs)." Jawahar Lal Nehru, who had promised an autonomous state of Punjab before 1947, the year of independence of India, had another face which came into light immediately after the partition of Indian subcontinent. So quick was the change in his behavior that it clearly exposed his treacherous plan to woo the Sikhs into his folds and then strangulate the Sikh nation.

### Punjabi Excluded from J-K Languages Bill

Punjabi is not only one of the main languages in Punjab, but it is also popular in all adjoining states like Jammu and Kashmir, Haryana, Rajasthan, Himachal Pradesh, and Delhi. The Union Cabinet has approved a bill under which Kashmiri, Dogri, and Hindi, apart from the existing Urdu and English, will be the official languages in the union territory. The Punjabi language has been specifically excluded. On September 3, 2020, Punjab Cabinet minister Charanjit Singh Channi stated:

> Punjabi was popular among a large population of Jammu and Kashmir and the move has hurt sentiments of lakhs of Punjabi-speaking people there, terming it as an attack on the federal structure of the country. By excluding the Punjabi language, the Government of India has taken an extreme step which has caused resentment among minorities not only in Jammu and Kashmir but amongst all Punjabi-speaking populations of the country, said the minister.[47]

The minister stated that Punjabi has been part and parcel of the constitution of Jammu and Kashmir, and even countries like Canada

---

[47] https://www.outlookindia.com/newsscroll/exclusion-of-punjabi-from-jk-languages-bill-an-attack-on-federal-structure-punjab-minister/1928990.

and the UK have given due recognition to the Punjabi language at the international level, but in its own country, the BJP-led government has done this "shameful act."[48]

---

[48] https://www.punjabnewsexpress.com/national/news/exclusion-of-punjabi-from-jk-languages-bill-another-attack-on-the-federal-structure-of-the-country-channi-118762.

# How India Trifurcated Punjab

## A Crippled Punjab State Formed in 1966

*History of Punjab*—Punjab is the name of the country to Northwest India and Northeast Pakistan. Its history can be traced as far back as 326 BC. Its name is derived from five rivers (Panj "five"-aab "river") running through this land. These five rivers—Beas, Sutlej, Ravi, Chenab, and Jhelum—merge into the Indus River, which discharges into the Indian Ocean. Punjabi civilization is one of the oldest on earth, with its distinguished language, culture, food, attire, script, folklore, and people.

Punjab was an independent country until 1849, when the British conquered it and loosely attached it to the region now called India. When Punjab was a sovereign nation, India was not; it was then a conglomeration of hundreds of princely states under British control. However, when the British left, the whole region was divided into two regions, one for the Hindus (India also called Hindustan) and the other for the Muslims (Pakistan), by an inappropriate and imperfect decolonization process that was ill conceived, leading to the massacre of more than six hundred thousand Sikhs and the displacement of millions more in a few days, following August 15, 1947. A large number of Muslims and Hindus also lost their lives in the same process. The naive Sikh leadership of the time was very suspicious of the majority Hindu rule and their assurances, but upon the persuasion by the Congress leadership, eventually decided to go with mainland India despite the warning of Mohammad Ali Jinnah. Jinnah had told Mater Tara Singh, head of Akali Party (political party representing Sikhs), that they have seen Hindus as coslaves but not as their masters. This stern forewarning was ignored by the Sikh leadership to its peril, only to repent later when they were denied their religion, region, state, and language. The prophecy of Jinnah had come true immediately after August 15, 1947.

## Sikhs Establish Their Rule

Bandha Singh Bahadur established Sikh Rule in 1709. Shortly before Guru Gobind Singh (the tenth Sikh guru) merged with the Almighty God in 1708, he commissioned Banda Singh Bahadur and sent him to Punjab with a small number of Sikhs to carry the Khalsa mission of establishing Sikh political sovereignty and to liberate Punjab from the oppressive Mughal rule.

Banda, upon entering Punjab, organized his army by collecting his soldiers from different parts of Punjab. He started conquering small villages and towns. In this process, he won several small towns one by one. The land under the control of the Mughals was possessed and distributed to the cultivators of the land. This was a revolutionary process in which the feudal system was abolished. Thus the Sikhs established their rule. During the fierce battle, at Chappar Chirri (near Landran and Mohali), Wazir Khan, commander in chief of the Mughal forces, was killed, and his army was defeated. This historic battle was fought in May 1710, in which the mighty Mughal Army lost to the Khalsa force under the command of Banda Singh Bahadur.

The fighting between the forces of Banda Singh Bahadur and the Mughal rulers continued. The Mughal forces drove Banda Singh Bahadur and the Sikh forces into the village of Gurdas Nangal, Gurdaspur, Punjab, and laid siege to the village.[49] The Sikhs defended the small fort for eight months under conditions of great hardship. In December 1715, the Mughals broke into the starving garrison and captured Banda Singh and his companions. He was taken to Delhi,

---

[49] Kenneth Pletcher, *The History of India* (The Rosen Publishing Group, 2010), 200.

along with a caravan of about seven hundred[50] other Sikh prisoners who were brutally tortured and ruthlessly killed one by one.[51] They could have saved their lives by accepting Islam. However, out of about seven hundred Sikh prisoners of war, not one accepted Islam. Banda's son was killed, and his heart was taken out and thrust into Banda's mouth. Banda's body was cut into pieces with pincers. Such was the determination of the Sikhs that they refused to adopt Islam under any circumstances.

Following the death of Banda, Sikhs were almost wiped out. The Mughal emperor Farrukhsiyar issued an edict according to which every Sikh was to be arrested and offered only one option— either Islam or the sword. With the death sentence on their heads, Sikhs withdrew to Punjab hills, where they sought refuge in jungles. In these inaccessible jungles, they happily sang Raj Karega Khalsa (the Khalsa shall rule) to fulfill their aspirations.

Multiple invasions from the north by the dreaded Nadir Shah and his general, Ahmad Shah Durani, caused the gradual and total collapse of the Mughal rule in Punjab. Following this, the Khalsa (order of baptized Sikhs) hiding in the jungle on the hills descended into the plains. They formed independent principalities, called Misls, over the ashes of the Mughal Empire. They exercised sovereignty in Punjab and propagated Khalsa Raj. Maharaja Ranjit Singh united these twelve Misls into one single kingdom and invaded Lahore in 1799 and firmly establish Sikh Raj, with Lahore being its capital.

### The Sikh Empire

Sikh Empire (also referred to as Sikh Khalsa Raj, Sarkar-i-Khalsa, or the Punjab Empire) was a federal monarchy, established in 1799 by Maharaja Ranjit Singh, as a union of twelve previously inde-

---

[50] Surinder Johar, *Guru Gobind Singh* (The University of Michigan: Enkay Publishers, 1987), 208.

[51] Gurbaksh Singh, *The Khalsa Generals* (Canadian Sikh Study & Teaching Society, 1927), 12.

pendent states (or Misls) of the Sikh Confederacy.[52] At its peak in the mid-1830s, it covered an estimated five hundred thousand km sq and was the home to 3.5 million people; its territory spanning from Khyber Pass to western Tibet, along its west-east axis, from Kashmir to Mithankot along its north-south axis. Punjab was the empire's heartland, with Lahore as its capital. Numerous contemporaneous accounts and artifacts confirm that the Sikh Empire minted its own money and maintained diplomatic relations and trade links with the British and French Empires, among others. Before its annexation by the British, the Sikh Empire attained all four internationally accepted criteria of sovereign statehood, namely (a) permanent population, (b) defined territory, (c) government, and (d) the capacity to enter into relations with other states.[53]

After the creation of the country of India, successive Indian governments systematically started dismantling Punjab. Punjab was denied the status of a state when other states were created. When Punjab State was finally created in 1966, after many lengthy and peaceful demonstrations by Sikhs, it was a truncated crippled state. At that time in 1966, the Indian government had no choice but to create the state of Punjab, ten years after the other states were recognized in 1956. However, the newly created state was about one-tenth of the size of the original Punjab at the time of the partition of India. Not only was Punjab reduced to a small size, but it was also deprived of its capital of Chandigarh, which was converted into a union territory and became the shared capital of Punjab and Haryana. Several Punjabi-speaking areas were awarded to the newly created state of Haryana, which should have been part of Punjab. There was an unconstitutional and ruinous drain of Punjab's river waters in violation of the riparian rights.

The demand to create Punjab State was so intense that Indira Gandhi had to buckle under the pressure put on by the Sikhs

---

[52] J. Grewal, "Sikh Empire (1799–1849)," *The New Cambridge History of India: The Sikhs of Punjab* (Cambridge: Cambridge University Press), 99.

[53] Uio Faculty of Law, "Montevideo Convention on the Rights and Duties of States of 1934," Article 1, http://www.jus.uio.no/english/services/library/treaties/0/1-02/rights-duties-states.xml.

despite her fierce resistance to such demand. She stated that her father, Jawaharlal Nehru, was against the formation of Punjab State. Jawaharlal Nehru turned anti-Sikh when his father, Motilal Nehru, told him that Guru Gobind Singh had solidified the concept of human equality by creating Khalsa on March 29, 1699, which cuts the lifeblood of Brahminism's concept of human inequality.

### Carving Up Punjab

In 1948, the province of Himachal Pradesh was created out of twenty-eight princely states controlling the foothills of the western Himalayas, with a further four southern hill states carved out of East Punjab. The further territory was reallocated from Punjab to Himachal Pradesh in November 1956, when the latter became union territory under the 1956 States Reorganisation Act.[54]

In 1966, approximately half of the remaining territory was carved out of Punjab under the Punjab Reorganisation Act to create the state of Haryana. Under the same legislation, Chandigarh, the new capital of Punjab, became the shared capital of Punjab and Haryana States and was transferred under New Delhi's control as a union territory. Aside from the loss of over half of its territory, Punjab lost access to over two-thirds of its most important economic resource—the waterways that irrigated its agricultural land (see an attack on the economic resources section below).

### Punjab under the British East Indian Company and the British Raj

The Sikh Empire was one of the last territories on the Indian subcontinent to lose its sovereignty and be annexed by the British East India Company. The British assumed full control of its territories in 1849, following several Anglo-Sikh battles.

---

[54] See States Reorganisation Act, 1956, under part II, section 15, https://indiacode.nic.in/bitstream/123456789/1680/1/195637.pdf.

During the British occupation, Punjab remained semiautonomous. After World War I, the people of Punjab started protests and civil disobedience for independence. The British government responded with brutal force to suppress these protests. The most notable was the Jallianwala Bagh massacre in Amritsar in 1919, where up to one thousand civilians were killed. This massacre was well planned and carried out on April 13, 1919. The people were first entrapped into an enclosed area, exits closed, and then fired upon. This drew outrage from the people of Punjab and India, further strengthening the struggle for sovereignty. This led to the enactment of the Government of India Act 1919. Under this act, responsibility for agriculture, health, education was transferred to elected members of the Punjab Legislative Council.[55] The Punjab Legislative Assembly and the first autonomous provincial government took power in 1937.[56] Thus although subsumed into the British Raj, the territory, population, and power structures of the Sikh Empire persisted throughout the colonial period, representing a form of Punjabi national identity and self-governance.

The British did create a system of canals improving the irrigation system spurring an agro-industrial revolution in the region. Large parcels of the land which were previously barren now became fertile. However, the majority of the population of Punjab remained poor and uneducated.

### Sikhs' Objection to the Truncated Punjab State Formed in 1966

When Punjabi Suba was finally created in 1966, it was never accepted by the Shiromani Akali Dal (the elected Sikh body) in its existing form because Chandigarh was to be the capital of Punjab to compensate it for Lahore (the capital of the Sikh Empire), which

---

[55] The Government of India Act 1919, https://archive.org/stream/govtofindiaact 19029669mbp/govtofindiaact19029669mbp_djvu.txt 52.

[56] J. Grewal, "The Sikh Empire (1799–1849)," *The New Cambridge History of India: The Sikhs of the Punjab* (Cambridge: Cambridge University Press), 170.

was lost to Pakistan in 1947. However, it was retained as a union territory. Several Punjabi-speaking areas in districts such as Ambala, Kurukshetra, Karnal, Hisar, Fatehabad, and Sirsa region were given to Haryana. In the hill region, areas like Nalagarh, Una, and Kangra, Lahul-Spiti, and Shimla, which were earlier part of Punjab, were given away to Himachal Pradesh. The control of Bhakra Dam, Nangal Dam, Nangal Hydel Channel, and hydropower stations and headworks associated with the main river were given to the Bhakra Beas Management Board, under the Indian government control.

It took ten years (1956–1966) for the Sikh political parties to pressure and finally convince the Congress Party to create Punjabi Suba. However, Akali leadership again felt that there was deception and manipulation at every political level in the planning of the formation of the newly created Punjabi Suba. Sant Fateh Singh, who was spearheading the Punjabi Suba Morcha (campaign) in 1966, gave another call to all to prepare for another long-drawn agitation to have the Punjabi-speaking areas left in Haryana and Chandigarh transferred to Punjab, besides seeking the control of Bhakra Dam and other hydropower projects and headworks.

Sant Fateh Singh announced that he would immolate himself on December 27, 1966, at the Akal Takht where he had started fast-unto-death in the third week of December. His announcement rocked the union government. The then-Prime Minister Indira Gandhi invited Sant Fateh Singh for a meeting, but he declined. She and the president of India appealed to him to end his fast. When Sant Fateh Singh refused to yield, Indira Gandhi sent Hukum Singh, a respected Sikh leader, to convince the sant that there was no reason why Chandigarh should not go to Punjab.

Hukum Singh was an influential Sikh leader who had contributed to the formulation of the Indian Constitution. He was elected to the Constitution Committee and became speaker of the Parliament in 1962, the first Sikh to hold that position. He convinced Sant Fateh Singh to end his fast. Sant Fateh Singh called off his immolation, scheduled on December 27, 1966, just in the nick of the time. Despite the commitment made by Hukum Singh to Sant Fateh Singh on behalf of Indira Gandhi, Chandigarh and the

Punjabi-speaking areas were never transferred to Punjab. The control of Punjab river waters rests with the Bhakra Beas Management Board (BBMB), controlled by central government.

Even though Punjabi Suba was created in 1966, after innumerable agitations and loss of lives of hundreds of peacefully protesting farmers, it was indeed a trifurcated state. The Akalis declared it as a betrayal of the Sikhs by the Congress Party because what they got in the form of Punjabi Suba was a truncated state.[57]

---

[57] https://www.tribuneindia.com/news/archive/comment/punjabi-suba-what-s-there-to-celebrate-292265.

# How India Turned Punjab into a Garrison State

Violence which destroys homes and buildings
is serious, but violence directed against the
dignity of Man...if we remain silent, the
clamor of violence will stifle the cry of the
people, who call for justice and peace.
                                    —Pope John Paul II

India carried out a massive buildup of the army and paramilitary forces to prepare for the invasion of Golden Temple Amritsar in 1984. Mary Ann Weaver, a British correspondent, in her report to *Sunday Times London*, June 17, 1984, stated that about fifteen thousand troops took part in the invasion. According to some estimates, more than seventy thousand troops were deployed in Punjab. They were spread all over Punjab to prevent any uprising in the villages. Punjab, being an agricultural state, most of its population lives in the villages. The Sikh regiments were moved away from Punjab, and the non-Sikh regiments were diverted to Punjab to prepare for the assault.

Before the Indian Army invaded Golden Temple Amritsar, Punjab was cut off from the world, and there was rigid censorship of the press. The people of Punjab and the rest of India heard only what was relayed by the state-owned Indian news media. Several stories of large-scale atrocities perpetrated on the Sikhs were circulating in Delhi and other places, but they were not confirmed. By blocking the news media and the nongovernmental organizations during the 1980s and the 1990s, India very successfully kept the rest of the world oblivious of the facts of genocidal violence against the Sikhs. To suppress and persecute the Sikhs and to further prevent them from ever asking for their fundamental human rights, the successive Indian governments enacted barbarian and draconian laws. These laws gave the police and other law-enforcing agencies sweeping powers and made the judiciary so weak that no independent country can defend or justify.

## The Black-Draconian Laws and the People of Punjab

To suppress the genuine demands of the people for justice, the government of India passed black laws that gave extraordinary powers to police, army, and paramilitary forces in Punjab. These acts were widely used in depriving the people of Punjab of their civil liberties and fundamental rights and have given sweeping powers to the police and other paramilitary forces to torture and harass the simple village folks for ulterior purposes. No democracy has such draconian laws targeting its citizens, especially during a time of peace. These acts gave the government, the police, and the army even to take away the right to life from its people. These laws are enlisted below:

- Unlawful Activities Prevention Act (UAPA) enacted in 1967
- Maintenance of Internal Security Act of 1971
- National Security Act (NSA) of 1980
- Punjab Disturbed Areas Act of 1983
- Armed Forces (Punjab and Chandigarh) Special Powers Act of 1983
- The Terrorist Affected Areas Act (Special Court Act) of 1984
- Terrorist and Disruptive Activities (Prevention) Act 1985–1995 (TADA)[58]

---

[58] Inderjit Singh Jaijee, *Politics of Genocide: Punjab 1984–1994* (1995), 140.

## *Unlawful Activities Prevention Act*

Unlawful Activities Prevention Act (UAPA) was passed by the Indian government in 1967, aimed at effective prevention of unlawful activities associations. Its main objective was to make powers available for dealing with activities directed against the integrity and sovereignty of India.

Passage of this act empowered Parliament to impose, by law, reasonable restrictions on:

1. Freedom of speech and expression
2. Right to assemble peaceably and without arms
3. Right to form associations or unions

This law has been further strengthened by subsequent amendments several times as follows:

1. The Criminal Law (Amendment) Act, 1972
2. The Delegated Legislation Provisions (Amendment) Act, 1986
3. The Unlawful Activities (Prevention) Amendment Act, 2004
4. The Unlawful Activities (Prevention) Amendment Act, 2008
5. The Unlawful Activities (Prevention) Amendment Act, 2012
6. The Unlawful Activities (Prevention) Amendment Act, 2019[59]

The law contravenes the requirements of the International Covenant on Civil and Political Rights.[60] The last amendment was enacted in July 2019, when its power was expanded. This time it

---

[59] The Unlawful Activities (Prevention) Amendment Bill, 2019 (PDF).
[60] "OHCHR" International Covenant on Civil and Political Rights," www.ohchr.org.

was amended, allowing the government to designate an individual as a terrorist without trial. Under this act, Gurpatwant Singh Pannun, legal adviser of Sikhs for Justice, was declared a terrorist without trial. On Wednesday, July 1, 2020, India declared nine individuals, including Gurpatwant Singh Pannun, as terrorists under the Unlawful Activities (Prevention) Act (UAPA).[61]

The others who have been designated by the Ministry of Home Affairs (MHA) as *individual terrorists* under the UAPA include Paramjit Singh (Babbar Khalsa International), Hardeep Singh Najjar (Khalistan Tiger Force), Gurmit Singh Bagga (Khalistan Zindabad Force), Wadhawa Singh Babbar (Babbar Khalsa International), Lakhbir Singh (International Sikh Youth Federation), Ranjeet Singh (Khalistan Zindabad Force), Paramjit Singh (Khalistan Commando Force), Bhupinder Singh Bhinda (Khalistan Zindabad Force).[62]

## Maintenance of Internal Security Act of 1971

The Maintenance of Internal Security Act (MISA) was a controversial law passed by the Indian Parliament in 1971, giving the administration of Prime Minister Indira Gandhi and Indian law enforcement agencies very broad powers: indefinite preventive detention of individuals, search and seizure of property without warrants, and wiretapping.

## The National Security Act of 1980

The National Security Act[63] was promulgated on September 23, 1980. The objectives and the reasons proclaimed by this act were that in the prevailing situation of communal disharmony, social tensions, extremist activities, industrial unrest, and increased tendency on the part of various interested parties to engineer agitation on different

---

[61] https://www.tribuneindia.com/news/nation/gurpatwant-singh-pannun-among-nine-designated-as-terrorists-under-uapa-107197.

[62] Ibid.

[63] "NSA, A Weapon of Repression," www.pucl.org, retrieved October 10, 2015.

issues, it was considered necessary that the law and order situation in the country is tackled in a most determined and active way. However, similar laws already existed in the books, and these additional laws were to repress and intimidate the people to such an extent that they dare not speak up or speak out against any unreasonable activities of the police or the government officials.

## Amendments in the National Security Act

The National Security Amendment Ordinance No. 5 was issued in April 1984, by which a detainee may remain in jail for fifteen days without knowing the reason for his/her arrest.[64] Furthermore, the procedure for submission in the case of the detainee was amended in such a way that a detainee will undergo imprisonment for six months before his detention could be found unjustified by the advisory board. Under this act, innocent persons were arrested and detained under fabricated charges. The following are a few examples of persons arrested, released, and rearrested under cookbook charges.

Giani Puran Singh, a Granthi (Sikh priest) at Akal Takht, was arrested under FIR (first information report) number 263/84 on September 30, 1984, under section 124 and 153A, and was released on bail after three months. He was again arrested after one month and remained in jail for an unknown period. He was involved with ten others in the said case, but none of them were mentioned in the said FIR.

Another example is of Mrs. Rajinder Kaur, president of Sri Akali Dal. She made a speech on September 14, 1984, in a Gurdwara in which she said, "We want a place where Sikhs could have a breath of freedom." She then asked people to raise their hands if they approved of such a place. One lady, Mrs. Harbhajan Kaur Khalsa, raised her hand. Harbhajan Kaur was arrested under the National Security Act,

---

[64] *Oppression in Punjab: Citizens for Democracy Report to the Nation*, US ed. (1986), 90.

though Mrs. Rajinder Kaur was not arrested. Khalsa was able to get bail in February 1985, after spending six months in jail.[65]

## The Punjab Disturbed Areas Act, 1983, Act No. 32 of 1983 (The Eighth Day of December 1983)

Under this act, the Punjab government was given the power to declare the whole or a part of the district of Punjab as a disturbed area. This act gave any magistrate or police officer not below the rank of subinspector or havildar (a rank in India equivalent to a sergeant) extraordinary powers to shoot and kill any suspect with total impunity.

Any designated officer, if he believes that it is necessary to do so for maintenance of public order, after giving a due warning as he may consider necessary, may fire upon or use force, even to the cause of death, against any such person who is acting in contravention of any law or order. It prohibited the assembly of five or more persons or the carrying of weapons or things capable of being used as weapons, firearms, or explosives.

This act gave powers to—any magistrate or police officer not below the rank of a subinspector may, if he thinks that it is necessary so to do—destroy any arms dump, prepared or fortified position or shelter from which armed attacks are made or are likely to be made or are attempted to be made or any structure used as a training camp for armed volunteers or utilized as a hideout by armed gangs or absconders wanted for any offense (for details, see annexure 6).

## Armed Forces (Punjab and Chandigarh) Special Powers Act of 1983

Under the special powers of the Armed Forces Act of 1983[66] (see annexure 7), any commissioned officer, warrant officer, non-

---

[65] Ibid., 91.

[66] "Black Laws and the People: An Enquiry into the Functioning of Black Laws in Punjab," Peoples Union for Democratic Rights, April 1985, p. 12.

commissioned officer, or any other person of equivalent rank in the armed forces may, in a disturbed area:

a) If he is of opinion that it is necessary so to do for the maintenance of public order, after giving such due warning as he may consider necessary, fire upon or otherwise use forces, even to the causing of death, against any person who is acting in contravention of any law or order for the time being in force in the disturbed area prohibiting the assembly of five or more persons or the carrying of weapons or of things capable of being used as weapons or firearms, ammunition or explosive substances.

b) If he is of opinion that it is necessary so to do, destroy any arms dump, prepared or fortified position or shelter from which armed attacks are made or likely to be made or are attempted to be made, of any structure used as a training camp for armed volunteers or utilized as a hideout by armed gangs or absconders wanted for any offense.

c) Arrest, without a warrant, any person who has committed a cognizable offense or against whom a reasonable suspicion exists that he has committed or is about to commit a cognizable offense, may use such force as may be necessary to effect the arrest.

d) Enter and search, without a warrant, any premises to make any such arrest as aforesaid or to recover any person believed to be wrongfully restrained or confined or any property reasonably suspected to be stolen or any arms, ammunition, or explosive substances believed to be unlawfully kept in such premises, and may for that purpose use such forces as may be necessary, and seize any such property, arms ammunition or explosive substances.

e) Stop, search and seize any vehicle or vessel reasonably suspected to be carrying any person who is a proclaimed offender, or any person who has committed a non-cognizable offense, or against whom a reasonable suspicion exists that he has committed or is about to commit a non-cognizable offense, or any person who is carrying any arms, ammunition or explosive substance believed to be unlawfully held by him, and may, for that purpose, use such forces as may be necessary to effect such stoppage, search or seizure, as the case may be.

f) Every person making a search under this Act shall have the power to break open the lock of any door, almirah, safe, box, cupboard, drawer, package, or another thing if the key thereof is withheld.

g) Any person arrested and taken into custody under this act and every property, arms, ammunition or explosive substance or any vehicle or vessel seized under this act, shall be made over to the officer in charge of the nearest police station with the least possible delay, together with a report of the circumstances occasioning the arrest, or as the case may be, occasioning the seizure of such property, arms, ammunition or explosive substance, or any vehicle or vessel.

h) No prosecution, suit, or other legal proceedings shall be instituted, except with the previous sanction of the central government, against any person in respect of anything done or purported to be done in exercise of the powers conferred by this act.

For more details on this act, see annexure 7.

## Terrorist Affected Areas (Special Courts) Act July 1984

The intended purpose of the Special Courts Act was speedy trials of certain offenses in the terrorist-affected areas.[67] Several offenses

---

[67] *Oppression in Punjab: Citizens for Democracy Report to the Nation*, US ed. (1986), 93.

listed in this act as scheduled offenses were already covered by the Indian Penal Court. These include the Explosives Act, the Arms Act, the Telegraph Act, the Railway Act, the Unlawful Activities Act, the Anti-Hijacking Act, and the Prevention of Damage to Public Property Act. The offenses such as waging war, sedition, abetting mutiny or attempting to seduce a member of the armed forces from his duty, creating communal hatred, the threat of injury to a public servant, harboring offender, defiling or injuring a place of worship with intent to insult a religion, intentional act of such an insult, murder, attempt to murder, serious hurt, wrongful confinement, kidnapping, robbery, and dacoity were already provided and punishable under the Indian Penal Code. The government resorted to these drastic measures to make ordinary people live in fear to such an extent that it became hard for them to carry out their daily activities.

According to section 167 of the Criminal Procedure Code, magistrate can give police remand only for fifteen days, but in Special Courts Act, this period has been extended to thirty days. Moreover, according to the Criminal Procedure Code, on the expiry of sixty or ninety days, as the case may be, the accused is bound to be released on bail. But the Special Courts Act has extended this period to one year. The result is that the police have been empowered to deprive an innocent person of his liberty for one year without even bringing charges against him. There have been several cases in which a person was already arrested by the police to harass and torture him, and after the expiry of a seven-to-eight-month period in jail, the police had just withdrawn the case on the ground that no material could be gathered against the detainee. Though the accused is released in such cases, during the period of detention, the family of the accused stands broken and his means of livelihood deprived.

Following are the illustrative cases to show how the police have been making use of this act to deprive innocent persons of their civil liberties:

- Randhir Singh s/o Harbans Singh Ghuman: Resident of village Ghuman Kalan, age twenty, was arrested in Gurdaspur on August 16, 1984, in FIR 80/84, dated April 2, 1984, under section 302 of Indian Penal Code of Police Station Dera Baba Nanak. After torturing him for several days and keeping him in jail for three months, the police withdrew the case against him.

- Amrik Singh was arrested on July 3, 1984, and a case planted on him that he was making provocative slogans at a gathering of one-hundred-men audience. In April 1985, police furnished names of two witnesses, i.e., Kashmir Singh and Shri Seva Singh. However, when contacted, these two witnesses told the family of Amrik Singh that they had not seen any such incident, but the police had told them that they were witnesses in the case. These two persons filed their affidavits in the court alleging that they had not seen any such incident and based on the same, Amrik Singh was released on May 3, 1985.

## Terrorist and Disruptive Activities (Prevention) Act 1985 (TADA)

The primary objective of TADA was to deny the citizens their right to judicial review. It gave the police unlimited time to interrogate the prisoners by third-degree methods. The prisoners were tortured repeatedly to extract confessions and extort money. The confession made by the prisoner before a police officer became admissible as evidence. The identity of the witness was not required to be revealed. The prisoners were tried in places far away from the occurrence of the alleged crime, thus making it impossible for the defendant to prepare for his defense.

When the people of Punjab and other Indians were carrying out their campaign and struggle for independence from the British, they were arrested, tortured, and many of them spent extended periods in prisons facing harsh conditions. Some of them paid the ultimate price and gave their lives without hesitation. It is hard to perceive that they could have ever imagined that they would have to face again the same kind of repressive or even more drastic laws in free India. It is important to note that the same kind of repressive laws that were condemned as the Charters of Slavery during the British rule are being enacted in one form or the other in India after independence. Besides this act was also used against political parties, trade union workers, and innocent activists.

## False Accusations against Sikhs of Waging a War against the Government of India

It was claimed by the government that 1,592 civilians/terrorists were captured from inside the Golden Temple and 796 from other gurdwaras. A great majority of them were innocent civilians. The government captured a large number of pilgrims and charged them with waging a war against the state. The government thus inflated the numbers to justify the invasion of Darbar Sahib. According to some reports, Bhindranwale's men were only 140–150, and about 80 percent of them had run away from the Golden Temple at the start of the Blue Star Operation. Therefore, charges of waging a war were foisted by the government on thousands of innocent civilians apprehended during the operation to justify the government's action. Therefore, to justify that these innocent accused do not get any relief entitled to them in ordinary courts, the National Security Act was amended in June 1984, and Special Courts Ordinance proclaimed. The following is an example to show the types of so-called terrorists captured from the Golden Temple:

Kanwaljit Singh:[68] He was a twenty-year-old student at Khalsa College Delhi (evening) whose father, Satnam Singh, ran a provision store at Lawrence Road, Delhi. He had visited Golden Temple on June 2, and wanted to return to Delhi but found that all outgoing trains were canceled, and therefore, both of them were forced to stay at the Golden Temple at Guru Ram Das Sarai. Kanwaljit had to miss his interview at Delhi with the Institute of Bank Management on the morning of June 3, and his examination with the State Bank of India

---

[68] *Oppression in Punjab: Citizens for Democracy Report to the Nation*, US ed. (1986), 86.

the same afternoon. He was captured by the army, along with other pilgrims, and sent under detention to Jodhpur Jail.

Other civilians who happened to be at the Golden Temple complex for various reasons, like villagers staying at the rest house to seek medical treatment, were captured, charged, and sent to detention centers. They were charge-sheeted with the same offenses of waging a war against the state on prefilled cyclostyled papers.

## *Jail, Not Bail*

"Bail, not jail" is the general rule that has been adopted in criminal trials which begin with the presumption of innocence in favor of the accused. The idea behind this is that if the accused is detained before and during the trial, then it has grave consequences for the accused. Though he is presumed to be innocent until his guilt is proven, yet he would be subjected to psychological and physical deprivations of jail life. The jailed accused loses his job and is prevented from contributing effectively to the preparation of his defense. Moreover, the burden of his detention falls heavily on the innocent members of his family. Therefore, to grant bail is the rule than the exception. But in Punjab, this rule has been changed into "jail, not bail." The Special Courts Act has been framed in such a manner that it is almost impossible for the accused to be released on bail under it.

One of the most obnoxious effects of the act is the denial of the rights guaranteed under section 438 of the Criminal Procedure Code. Section 438, usually called the provision for the anticipatory bail, empowers the high court and court of sessions to grant anticipatory bail, i.e., direction to release a person on bail even before the person is arrested. According to the forty-first report of the Law Commission on the Code of Criminal Procedure Code, the necessity for granting anticipatory bail arises because sometimes, influential persons try to implicate their rivals in false cases to disgrace them for other purposes by getting them detained in jail for some days. Apart from false cases, where there are reasonable grounds that a person accused of an offense is not likely to abscond, or otherwise misuse his liberty while on bail, there seems no justification to require him to first submit to custody and remain in prison for some days and then apply for bail. This section is a salutary provision that enacts the mandate of Article 21 of the constitution of India, but the people of Punjab have been deprived of this salutary provision. The numerous cases mentioned in the report elsewhere show how the deletion of section 438 of the Criminal Penal Code for the people in Punjab has brought misfortune and havoc for innocent persons. The case of Paramjit Singh Sidhu, advocate at Jalandhar, is also illustrative of this: Though this advocate has been daily practicing in Jalandhar Court, there is no likelihood of him absconding, yet the police have raided his houses several times in his absence and tried to arrest him on false charges. His only crime was that he was valiantly fighting for justice for several innocent citizens who have fallen victims to the police rapacity.

### Everyone Guilty until Proved Innocent

Section 20 of the Special Courts Act puts everybody in jeopardy, and the dreaded sword of Damocles hangs on their head. According to this section, if an accused person is shown to have been at a place declared as a disturbed area at a time when firearms or explosives were used, then the presumption is there, unless the contrary is shown that "such a person had committed such an offense." This section applies to offenses under sections 121, 121A, 122, or 123 of the Indian Penal Code, which relates to waging of war against the government of India, conspiracy to wage war to overawe the government of India, collecting arms to wage war, and concealing with intent to facilitate design to wage war. Thus any law-abiding and innocent person can be roped in with the help of these draconian principles. Such brutal laws have no place in a society that calls itself democratic and civilized.

### Avoiding the Public: Trial on Camera

Section 327 of the Criminal Procedure Code provides for an open trial to which the public generally may have access because the public trial in open court acts as a check against judicial caprice or vagaries, and serves as a powerful instrument for creating confidence in the public in fairness, objectivity, and impartiality of the criminal justice. But the Special Courts Act offends this basic norm of a fair trial. Subsection (1) of section 12, under the pretext of protection of witnesses, provides that all proceedings before special courts shall be conducted on camera. This provision serves as a cover for hiding governmental incompetence, insufficiency, and police brutality.

To justify the existence of special courts, the police have been hauling up a large number of innocent persons, mostly in Arms Act. More than 80 percent of cases pending in various courts in Punjab were under Arms Act because it is easy for the police to implant a knife or a pistol on anyone. Due to trial in the camera, the public has been deprived of the benefit of seeing with its own eyes as to what kind of terrorists the special courts try. Since under the Special Courts Act, accused can be detained for one year without charges being brought against him, and it may take another couple of years in detention if the trial begins, most of the accused, despite being innocent, admit their guilt on the advice and pressure from police. The police do so to justify the arrests to make up numbers to their credit. Convictions in cases under Arms Act generally range from seven to eight months, and the accused, therefore, after passing seven to eight months in jail, deem it better to admit the guilt as the judge of the Special Courts Act sentences them to imprisonment already served and releases them. If these poor fellows do not admit guilt, then they will have to wait to face trial for two to three years and remain in jail, which period will be far longer than they are going to get in the sentence which they have already served.

### Who Is the Terrorist?

At the time of the promulgation of the Special Courts Act, the people of India were led to believe that the objective of this act was to deal with the terrorists only. But the act was framed in such a way that even petty crimes, family disputes, individual offenses that had no element of terrorism in them were tried under the Special Courts

Act. This made life miserable for innocent people who were charged as terrorists.

One example is the case of *State v. Girdhari Lal* in the Jalandhar Special Courts Act. Girdhari Lal was only sixteen years old and was working in a shop for surgical instruments. His proprietor had a dispute with his neighbor over the shop building. The other party, with the help of the police, got Girdhari Lal implicated in a false case under Arms Act. A small knife was implanted upon him. The police usually implant a knife on a Hindu and a pistol or a barcha (long stick with a sharp-pointed knife at the end) on a Sikh. Girdhari Lal could come out only following his confession to the supreme court after remaining in jail for eight months.

The Special Courts Act has been worded so vaguely that even the offenses of a purely private nature like murder or injury in a domestic quarrel that does not have any element of terrorism are being tried by special courts with the sole purpose of harassing the public.

It is important to note that before deciding not to extend the term of Terrorist Affected Area (Special Courts) Act beyond July 1985, the government armed itself with another repressive measure, i.e., the Terrorist and Disruptive (Prevention) Activities Act (TADA) in May 1985, which contained the similar draconian provisions as in the former act. In the latter act, the special courts are going to function under the label of the National Security Act, which still hangs over the heads of the people like the sword of Damocles.

## An Investigation by the People's Union for Democratic Rights

The People's Union for Democratic Rights sent a fact-finding team to Punjab in March 1985, to investigate the torture and the killing of the people of Punjab. The investigation revealed that not only were the laws ineffective concerning stated purposes, but worse, helping to further the communal alienation and creating a favorable climate for communal terrorism. This is a consequence of the antidemocratic nature of the laws and the wide scope they provide for their arbitrary and indiscriminate application.

This report documented that after the Indian Army's attack on the Golden Temple in June 1984, combined operations were undertaken in the rural areas, and those arrested from the Golden Temple and the rural areas were placed in army camps. These included women and small children. After the army was removed, the police continued its search for terrorists, making indiscriminate arrests. While some of those arrested were released, the rest were transferred to different jails and placed under the jurisdiction of various special courts. The information collected points to the widespread use of torture, fabrication of evidence, severe harassment of the families of which the male members were missing/absconding. It also reflects upon the mindless and arbitrary use of laws often either to settle personal scores or to teach a lesson to anyone who dares to voice any protest against antidemocratic laws and procedures.

PUDR revealed that their inquiry points to the serious and widespread violation of the fundamental rights of the people through both the use and the misuse of black laws enacted in Punjab. The extraordinary powers bestowed on the army, the police, and courts have resulted in alienating the people, breeding resentment, and creating discontent. As the principal target in the implementation of these laws are members of the Sikh community, this has very harmful implications given the communal situation.[69]

---

[69] "Black Laws and the People: An Enquiry into the Function of Black Laws in Punjab," Peoples Union for Democratic Rights, April 1985.

# How India Carried Out
# Extrajudicial Killing of Sikhs

---

When Sikhs asked for their simple rights—which were never denied to other people of India—they were labeled terrorists, antinationals, and separatists. To justify its behavior toward them, India started the indiscriminate persecution and extrajudicial killings of Sikhs. India staged fake police encounters (a false claim that the detainee started shooting at the police and tried to run away) and promulgated draconian laws to break them mentally, physically, and economically so that they would never again ask for their rights. The following is a brief description of these activities.

The tiny state of Punjab covers barely 1.54 percent of India's landmass, and Sikhs comprise about 1.8 percent of India's total population. However, it has the dubious honor of hosting more troops, paramilitary, and police than ever maintained by foreign rulers, Mughals, and the British during peacetime. More Sikhs have been killed in free India than during some two hundred years before the fourteenth day of August 1947, comprising all communities.

An estimated 150,000 Sikhs have been arrested, tortured, and tens of thousands extrajudicially killed by the police and the security forces since 1947. Prisoners have been kept in detention for months or years without trial under special legislative provisions, suspending normal legal protections. Some of them are languishing in jails for a lifetime since the 1980s, not knowing their fate. Their families have given up hope. Arrests and detention of some of these persons were never recorded. In many cases, the police reported that they were killed in police encounters, even though their arrests were witnessed. In other cases, police acknowledged the arrests but stated that the detainees had escaped. Often police raided the houses at night and took away the suspects, their families not knowing their whereabouts, wondering where to look for them.

Punjab police are notorious for their use of excessive force, arresting innocent people, keeping them in custody for several days before producing them in court. Often many of the detainees are never charged with any crime. Frequently there is no record of their arrest or any charges filed against them. The first information report (FIR), a formal record of arrest with a description of wrongdoing, is either delayed or not filed at all. Frequently while in police custody, detainees are bound, stripped, beaten, abused, and tortured. Some of the detainees are sexually assaulted. They are forced to confess guilt under the threats of torture and harm to his/her family members.

The police often get away with torture and extortion. The police share the extortion proceeds with their superiors or among themselves. Although major international human rights organizations have protested the abuses experienced by the people of Punjab, much of the world remains oblivious to the scale of atrocities committed there. The threat of militant secessionists provided the excuse for draconian security efforts that targeted the entire Sikh population. People were abducted from their homes in the dead of night, taken into custody, and charged with crimes they never committed, often tortured and raped, and sometimes killed outright.

The Punjab government has been a partner in the crime of pardoning several convicted police officers. In several high-profile cases, the police officers have not been arrested by the state, even in the light of judicial inquiries in which they were proven guilty. Several human rights organizations and a group of lawyers have criticized the Punjab government for recommending the premature release of several convicted cops who were out on bail or have spent few months in jail even if they were sentenced to life imprisonment.

On October 6, 1993, Harjit Singh was kidnapped by Punjab police. He was killed by the Uttar Pradesh (another state in India) Police on October 12, the same year. The police claimed that he was killed in a fake encounter. Uttar Pradesh superintendent of police

Ravinder Kumar, Inspector Brij Lal Verma, Constable Onkar Singh, and Punjab police inspector Harinder Singh were all sentenced to life imprisonment by a special CBI court in Patiala (Punjab). Punjab governor VP Singh Bhadnore pardoned all four police officers after recommendations by the state government of Punjab's Captain Amrinder Singh. Sukhpal Singh Khaira, a member of the Punjab Legislative Assembly, condemned the Punjab governor, Chief Minister Captain Amarinder Singh, and DGP Dinkar Gupta for granting pardon and described their actions as a mockery of the judicial system and murder of the constitution.[70]

Another example is that of Jaswant Singh Khalra, a human rights activist, who was picked up from his home in broad daylight in 1995. He was brutally tortured and died in police custody as a result of the injuries during the torture. The police denied his arrest and refused to provide his whereabouts.

The guilty police officers were eventually identified, tried, and sentenced. Kalra has been recognized for uncovering thousands of disappearances, unlawful killings, and secret cremations of Sikhs by the Punjab Police. *It took ten years to bring his killers to trial.* Six police officers were convicted. In 2007, the Punjab and Haryana High Court upheld five convictions, enhancing all sentences to life imprisonment. The sixth official was acquitted. For more details, see the under the section "Extrajudicial Killing of Jaswant Singh Khalra, a Human Rights Activist."

### Gurdev Singh Kaunke (Akal Takhat Jathedar), Tortured to Death

Jathedar Gurdev Singh Kaunke (acting Jathedar of Akal Takhat) was illegally arrested from his house by the then-SHO (station house officer) Jagraon, on December 25, 1992. Later he was extrajudicially

---

[70] https://www.ndtv.com/india-news/punjab-government-grants-pardon-to-cops-convicted-in-fake-encounter-case-2057485.

murdered by the Punjab police following intense torture. His body was never returned to his family.[71]

The resolution of independent Punjab Khalistan was passed on January 26, 1986, by Panthak Committee, following the Sarbat Khalsa gathering at Darbar Sahib. At the gathering, Sarbat Khalsa appointed Jasbir Singh Rhode as the Akal Takhat Jathedar. Since Rode was in prison, Gurdev Singh Kaunke was appointed as the acting Jathedar of Akal Takhat. The declaration of independence of Khalistan was made on April 29, 1986, from Akal Takhat.

Police inspector Gurmeet Singh arrested Gurdev Singh Kaunke from his home on December 25, 1992, in his village, Kaunke Kalan. His wife, Gurmail Kaur, on December 28, went to see him at the police station. She was told that he was moved from Sadar Police Station Jagraon to Criminal Investigative Agency (CIA) interrogation center, also at Jagraon. When Kaunke's wife told police that she had brought some food for him, she was informed that he was in no condition to swallow anything due to torture. This information was corroborated by a youth released on December 30, 1992, from the same prison and a doctor who had seen him in custody.

Later on, on the thirty-first day of December, Gurmail Kaur was informed that Mr. Kaunke was removed from the interrogation center and that his whereabouts were unknown. Following this, police stated that Kaunke had escaped from police custody on January 2, 1993. Gurdev Singh Kaunke was tortured to death, and his body was made to disappear and not given to his family.

The Committee for Coordination of Disappearance in Punjab (CCDP) investigated Mr. Kaunke's case. It acquired conclusive evidence of Mr. Kaunke's inhumanely performed tortured from the twenty-fifth day of December 1992, to the first day of January 1993. CCDP also acquired irrefutable evidence that Mr. Kaunke was tortured to his death.

Ram Narayan Kumar of the Committee for the Coordination of Disappearance in Punjab confirmed the deposition of a serving

---

[71] Balpreet Singh, "First Hand Accounts of the Murder of Jathedar Gurdev Singh Kaunke," World Sikh Organization of Canada, retrieved November 2, 2016.

SSP of the Punjab Police. They gave eyewitness reports of the torture and death of Mr. Kaunke. They searched wherever they wanted without warrants and without any requirement to present them before the court for up to one year.

The Punjab Police is known for its distinction of being one of the most brutal in the world. Interrogation centers of Punjab Police present a touching scene of human misery. Each police station in Punjab is a torture center on its own. Those arrested for even a minor misdemeanor are at the mercy of the police. The torture may be endless unless the suspect admits being guilty or pays bribery. Failing these two, his family members, including females, are at risk of meeting the same fate.

Some of the gruesome methods of torture are outlined as follows:

1. Laying prostrate on the ground and moving heavy rollers over the body until the muscles are crushed
2. Application of electric shocks to the genitals
3. Gouging eyes and pulling out fingernails
4. Inserting hot iron rods into the rectum to disguise injury
5. Pulling apart legs until the hip joints come out of the sockets
6. Pulling apart legs with intent to tear the body into two halves
7. Hanging the body upside down
8. Inserting chili powder into eyes, nostrils, and rectum
9. Spraying salt and red pepper into fresh wounds created with sharp instruments
10. Dipping the body in deep water after putting it into a gunny bag. This treatment is more excruciating on winter nights.
11. Beating the victims until the skin comes off
12. Sexual abuse of women relatives in the prisoner's presence

The following statement is from a Hindu doctor working in rural areas of the Amritsar district:

> The police torture people very cruelly.
> Firstly, they begin by savagely beating them.

Secondly, they bend their hands and arms backward and upward toward the ceiling and tie them there (Kachcha Fansi or half-baked hanging). Thirdly, they then administer an electric shock. In Tarn Taran, an electrically generated belt is used. Fourthly, they use wooden weapons on the body and crush the legs. I see fifty to one hundred per year in such like condition within a five to ten-kilometer radius. If a boy looks as though he is dying in the police station, they plan an encounter some kilometers away, the day before. It is very meticulously planned. Encounters are always 100% bogus.[72] This is evidence of one of the thousands of extra-judicial killings of Sikhs by Indian authorities. Images of Sikhs killed by police torture and fake encounters may be accessed under reference number 73.[73]

### Army Rule in Punjab

According to Jaijee, at peak deployment, army[74] personnel involved in curbing militancy in Punjab ranged between two to three hundred thousand. They were drawn mainly from the corps based in Ambala, Bathinda, and Jalandhar. The army was extensively deployed in Punjab to counter the armed struggle for the independence of Khalistan. Before Operation Blue Star, the army was brought in to help police, which the government felt was ineffective in controlling the freedom movement's uprising, an estimated sixty thousand army personnel were spread throughout Punjab, mostly in the Amritsar district.

---

[72] Joyce Pettigrew, *Sikhs of the Punjab* (London, 1955), 69.
[73] http://shaheed-khalsa.com/genocide.html.
[74] Jaijee Inderjit Singh, *Politics of Genocide: Punjab 1984–1994* (1995), 215.

For months before Operation Blue Star, it was an undeclared army rule in Punjab.[75] That civil authorities had ceased to function will be clear from the following instance: An accused with eyes tightly bandaged was produced before the chief judicial magistrate, Shri Cheema. The court ordered the bandage to be removed. His orders were not obeyed. After hearing the case, the court ordered that the accused be sent to jail and not returned to army custody. At once, the junior commissioned officer in the army entered and told the magistrate in Hindi, which all heard—"Goli khayega or remand dega" (you want to be shot or issue the remand)—in the retiring room the order of the court, sending the accused to jail was torn up and replaced by remand order.

Shri Cheema complained to the sessions judge and the district magistrate, who brought the matter to the brigadier's notice. The brigadier expressed regret but took no action to address the issue.

Indian government deployed a massive amount of army and paramilitary force in Punjab and seventy-thousand-strong Punjab Police to suppress the freedom movement. The government finally decided to use the ultimate weapon in Punjab, with the undeclared aim of putting down militancy, which amounted to introducing martial law from the backdoor. The civil authorities had never requisitioned army support; it operated unlawfully. All Sikh political parties and human rights organizations condemned this deployment. No modern civilized country has used its armed forces in such an unabashed manner against its people.

Sikhs considered Operation Woodrose in 1984 as the second war the Delhi government started against Punjab, after Operation Blue Star. Sikhs decided to face it with bravery and self-confidence. It reflected on the Sikh tradition of never bowing to repression and injustice reminiscent of the tyrannical reign of the Mughal governor of Lahore Mir Mannu. Sikhs then coined the phrase "the more they cut us, the more we grow."

---

[75] *Oppression in Punjab: Citizens for Democracy Report to the Nation*, US ed. (A Sikh Religious and Educational Publication, 1986), 33.

## Punjab and India Are a Police State

The Indian government controls the police in Punjab. The Punjab government has little control over the police. The police keep the detainees in their custody and torture them to extract evidence and/or extort money. Such evidence has been admissible in a court of law. The police often obtain remands from the court to extend the detention of those in custody by falsifying records. This gives the police more time to torture the victims. If the detainee is seriously hurt by torture and not expected to survive, he/she may be killed by police, stating that the detainee absconded or denying that the police ever made such an arrest. Family members of the suspect, including women and children, are rounded up and interrogated by police. The detainees are threatened with harm to their family members for failure to confess guilt.

The Punjab Police are notorious for arresting innocent people, torturing and forcing them to plead guilty. According to a report in the *Hindustan Times*, September 22, 1990, the BSF had arrested more than 160 young men the previous fortnight and taken them to various interrogation centers. Many of them were given ten to fifty lashes each day. Some of them were given electric shocks, had heavy logs rolled over their legs, and were hung upside down. According to medical reports, two of them, named Dilbagh Singh and Prem Singh, suffered brain hemorrhages. Hardev Singh, twenty years old, suffered multiple fractures on his left arm. [76]

Under the Children Act 1960 and the East Punjab Children Act 1976, boys younger than sixteen years old and girls below the age of eighteen cannot be detained either at a police station or in a regular jail, but the authorities paid no heed to these laws. CBI officers view children as future freedom fighters (which they call terrorists) and treat them accordingly and brutally. An officer confessed, "These are all fine ideas for newspapers and preachers. We had on our hand

---

[76] "India: Human Rights Violations in Punjab: Use and Abuse of the Law."

suspected terrorists and would-be terrorists."[77] Human rights organizations brought these acts of inhumanity to the notice of senior-
most administrators, including the governor. However, no relief was
granted till Kamladevi Chattopadhyay, the well-known social worker,
finally approached the supreme court about the detention of several
Sikh children in Ludhiana Jail, which ordered their release. However,
there were more children in the Ludhiana jail than Kamladevi knew
about, and got released. To avoid the knowledge of their illegal detention, the superintendent of jail transferred them to the Nabha jail,
where already a few such children had been kept, thereby increasing
their number to eight. Their fate remains unknown.[78]

Barbara Crossette, in her book *India: Facing the Twenty-First
Century*, observed that under Indira Gandhi's regime, spies and agent
provocateurs operated extensively, infiltrated opposition groups, and
staged acts of violence intended to appear as the handiwork of the
militants.

The erstwhile director general of police Julio F. Ribeiro stated
that police accountability is to itself in Punjab. This same state of
affairs was highlighted collectively by the senior-most civil servants,
commissioners, and the administrative secretaries at a meeting in the
Punjab capital. They told Chief Secretary Tejinder Khanna[79] that
there was total police rule, and they were irrelevant and humiliated.
However, they were too scared to have their statements recorded in
the proceedings of the meeting.

Prime Minister Gandhi appointed J. F. Ribeiro (September
1985), Punjab director general of police, a man known for his
brutality, to pursue the iron-fisted policy. Ribeiro pursued the bullet-for-bullet policy and ruled the state with direct instructions from
the Indian government. Illegal detentions and nonjudicial killings
were the order of the day.

[77] Gobind Thukral, "Atrocities on Sikh Children," *India Today*, September 30,
1984.
[78] Ram Narayan Kumar and Georg Sieberer, *Sikh Struggle* (Delhi, 1991), 291.
[79] Inderjit Singh Jaijee, *Politics of Genocide* (Chandigarh, 1995), 195–196.

Ribeiro, in his policies and programs, recognized neither the Indian Constitution nor the state ministry. He stated that in Punjab, the police were accountable to no one. He had the blessing of Prime Minister Indira Gandhi, thus bypassing the state government of Punjab. He prepared a hit list of top militants of category A, and another category B, to be eliminated without the due process of law. He issued an order to all district police superintendents, promising financial rewards ranging from Rs. 25,000 to Rs. 100,000 (one lakh) for liquidation of the listed men described as "terrorists."

Under his authority, SSP Azhar Alam had created the killer squads of his own, called Alam Sena (army), which killed thousands of Sikhs with total impunity. Ribeiro, in total disregard for the law, employed persons with criminal records in his police force. These police officers had indulged in murders, robberies, and other criminal activities like extortion. The organizations like Black Cats, Alam Sena, or vigilante groups were carrying on criminal activities disguised as police officers. *Hindustan Times* reported that undercover agents continued to operate in the state and were using weapons provided by the police to kidnap local people and extort money from them.[80]

The fate of Sikhs in other states of India is equally ominous, if not more. They are virtually treated as hostages and intimidated. There are numerous occasions when they have been massacred, their women dishonored, properties looted, and destroyed. The beating of Sikhs, pulling or cutting their beards or hair are frequent occurrences. Human rights organizations like Amnesty International, Asia Watch, and the UN Human Rights Committee have condemned human rights abuses in India with particular reference to Punjab. Many other non-Sikh organizations in India, like Peoples Union for Democratic Rights (PUDR), Peoples Union for Civil Liberties (PUCL), Committee for Information and Initiative on Punjab, have investigated and documented numerous cases involving extrajudicial killings, torture, and disappearances.

---

[80] *The Hindustan Times*, December 12, 1990.

## *K. P. S. Gill and Police Terror*

K. P. S. Gill was appointed as a replacement for Ribeiro when in 1988, Ribeiro was elevated to the rank of adviser to the governor of Punjab, S. S. Ray. Ribeiro was attacked by Sikh militants and had a narrow escape. It is conceivable that after the direct attack on him by Sikh militants, he no longer had the spine to go on killing Sikhs. Under Gill, police and secret hit squads became the state's chief organs and could indulge in any illegalities or brutalities without hindrance or criticism. He was reported to have prepared the hit lists of his own.

Simranjit Singh Mann, while submitting his resignation from the Indian Parliament, drew his attention to the hit squads called Black Cats and Indian Lions, who were clandestinely operating in the state and were responsible for murdering and pillaging.[81] He brought out the fact that the state is actively involved in killing and murdering Sikh leaders by the Indian Lions, which is also known as Vaidya Commando Force (VCF) and Lala Jagat Narayan Tiger Force.[82]

All India Hindu Shiv Sena also trained its commandos to carry out clandestine activities. *Current Weekly*, in its issue dated August 5–11, 1987, brought to light a story that described a camp somewhere in Amritsar district where All India Hindu Shiv Sena was training about one thousand of its young followers in the use of arms and commando tactics. The boys let their hair and beards grow and assumed the appearance of Sikh youth. The plan was to train these young men to act as agent provocateurs. They would attack Sikhs, thereby creating an aversion among Sikhs for the militants.

Ribeiro recruited in his police force individuals with criminal records who would carry out criminal activities disguised as militants to create public opinion against the militants, brand them as perpetrators of crime, and to create among villagers a section of people to make them unsympathetic and hostile toward militants. These

---

[81] "Simranjit Singh Mann's Resignation Letter to the Speaker Rabi Ray, October 10, 1990," *The Tribune*, October 9, 1990; *Aj-Di-Awaaz*, October 10, 1990.

[82] *The Tribune*, December 17, 1992.

commandos indulged in looting and extortions. According to *The Tribune* report (August 13, 1991), in the Bathinda district, recent kidnappers, some belonging to the Hindu Suraksha Samiti, had written letters in the name of the Dasmesh Regiment demanding ransom from the members of the minority community.

*Frontline* reported (May 14–27, 1988) that "in Punjab, the general population has an accepted view that the government has unleashed the death squads." This was the comment of a freelance journalist reporting on RAW actions. They found that RAW justified the use of imported AK-47s and antitank rocket-propelled grenades launchers through the Fifty-Ninth Constitutional Amendment by which the government can impose an emergency on the state and suspend the right to life.

*Economic and Political Weekly*, in a news report of the sixteenth day of April 1988, had asked, "Are the killings in Punjab, the handiwork of the extremists?" The report observed that strategic killings by officially planned agent provocateurs might help the government to precipitate further authoritarian control by assuming more military powers.[83]

Such activities added an ominous new dimension to the tragic scenario and led to an atmosphere of terror and insecurity. Chandan Mitra observed that "the undercover police operations have added to the confusion over genuine and fake militancy."[84] The *Washington Post* reported that the Indian security forces conducted a highly realistic mock hijacking of an airliner that fooled many people into thinking that it was a real terrorist action by Sikh militants. The purported hijackers issued several demands in the name of a Sikh extremist group. The exercise ended peacefully at an airport in West Central India but not without spreading alarm throughout the country.[85] Such obnoxious tactics were used to blame and defame the Sikh community, stroke up communal fires, and bring about reprisals to divert attention from real issues.

---

[83] Joyce Pettigrew, *Sikhs of the Punjab* (London, 1995), 133.
[84] *Hindustan Times*, February 4, 1992.
[85] Tavleen Singh, "Terrorist in the Temple," *The Punjab Story* (New Delhi, 1985), 48–49.

## The Killing of Innocent Civilians: The Brainchild of the Indian Government

The bombing of the Air India Flight 182 on June 23, 1985, killing 329 off the coast of Ireland, was the brainchild and handiwork of Indian consulate officials in Toronto. Some Indian officials had canceled their reservations on this flight in the nick of time. India's consul general Surinder Malik canceled seats for his wife and daughter on Flight 182. He claimed later that his daughter unexpectedly had to write some school examinations, so the trip to India was delayed.[86]

Another cancelation came from Siddhartha Singh, head of North American Affairs for External Relations in New Delhi. He had taken a trip to Canada to meet with his counterparts in the federal government in Ottawa. He visited Malik one week earlier before the crash. He was booked to return to India aboard the doomed Flight 182. Another cancelation on Flight 182 included the owner of a Toronto car dealership, who was a friend of Malik's.[87]

## Extrajudicial Killing of Jaswant Singh Khalra, a Human Rights Activist

Jaswant Singh Khalra was investigating four major cases at one time and continued to collect evidence and witnesses. These cases included the custodial killing of Behla, a human-shield case concerning the death of seven civilians, the cremation of thousands of unidentified bodies in Punjab, and that police had killed about 2,000 of their own policemen not collaborating in counterterror operations. CBI concluded that police had unlawfully cremated 2,097 people in the Tarn Taran district alone.

As per the CBI investigation records, quoted by the SC division bench in their judgment on the Khalra custodial death case, he was

---

[86] Zuhair Kashmeri and Brian McAndrew, *Soft Target: How Indian Intelligence Service Penetrated Canada* (1989), 87.

[87] Ibid.

a human rights activist working on the abduction, elimination, and cremation of unclaimed human bodies during the disturbed period. The court observed that the police had been eliminating young persons under the pretext of being militants and disposing of their bodies without record.

While searching for some colleagues who went missing, Jaswant Singh Khalra discovered files from the municipal corporation of Amritsar, which contained the names, ages, and addresses of those who had been killed and, later, burnt by the police. Further research revealed cases in three other districts in Punjab, increasing the list by thousands.[88]

The National Human Rights Commission released a list of some of the identified bodies cremated in the police districts of Amritsar, Majitha, and Tarn Taran between June 1984–December 1994. The supreme court of India and the National Human Rights Commission of India have certified this data's validity.

Khalra asserted there could have been over twenty-five thousand Sikhs killed and cremated by the state. There are still many Sikh families waiting to hear news of what happened to their missing loved ones, many wondering if they might still be alive. *Tribune India* had published a list of names.

On September 6, 1995, while washing his car in front of his house, Khalra was allegedly abducted by personnel of Punjab Police and taken to Jhabal Police Station. Although witnesses gave statements implicating the police and named former police chief Kanwar Pal Singh Gill as a conspirator,[89] police have denied ever arresting or detaining him and have claimed not to know his whereabouts.

In 1996, the Central Bureau of Investigation (CBI) found evidence that he was held at a police station in Tarn Taran and recommended the prosecution of nine Punjab police officials for murder and kidnapping. Those accused of his murder were not charged for

---

[88] Ram Kumar, Amrik Singh, Ashok Agrwall, Jaskaran, *Reduced to Ashes: The Insurgency and Human Rights in Punjab*, (Kathmandu: South Asian Forum for Human Rights, 2003).

[89] "K. P. S. Gill Visited Khalra in Jail, Says Witness," *The Tribune*, February 17, 2005, https://www.tribuneindia.com/2005/20050217/punjab1.htm.

ten years, though one of the suspects committed suicide in 1997. On November 18, 2005, six Punjab police officials were convicted and sentenced to seven years imprisonment for Khalra's abduction and murder.[90]

On October 16, 2007, a division bench of Punjab and Haryana High Court, chaired by Justices Mehtab Singh Gill and A. N. Jindal, extended the sentence to life imprisonment for four accused: Satnam Singh, Surinder Pal Singh, Jasbir Singh (all former subinspectors), and Prithipal Singh (former head constable). [91] On April 11, 2011, the supreme court of India dismissed the appeal filed against the sentence to life imprisonment for the four accused, scathingly criticizing the atrocities committed by Punjab Police during the disturbance period.[92]

Indian Army was given unprecedented powers to detain and arrest civilians by the enactment of the Armed Forces (Punjab and Chandigarh) Act 1983. The act empowered any commissioned or noncommissioned officer of the army if they were "of the opinion that it is necessary to do so for the maintenance of public order, after giving such due warning as he may consider necessary, fire upon or otherwise use force, even to causing of death." The act allowed such an officer to "arrest, without a warrant, any person who has committed a cognizable offense or against whom a reasonable suspicion exists that he has committed or is about to commit a cognizable offense."

Even Punjab chief of police K. P. S. Gill (named butcher of Sikhs) describes the actions as "suffering from all the classical defects of army intervention in civil strife" and stated that the Indian Army had acted "blindly."

This chapter has highlighted some of the examples of fake encounters and extrajudicial killing by law enforcement agencies with the connivance and the complicity of the central and state governments in Punjab. However, these are just the tip of the iceberg of

---

[90] https://ensaaf.org/jaswant-singh-khalra/.
[91] "Khalra Murder Case: HC Grants Life Imprisonment to 4 Cops," *The Times of India*, October 16, 2007.
[92] "Activist Khalra Custodial Death: SC Upholds Life in Jail for Punjab Cops."

the grave and gross violations of human rights. These are the crimes against humanity at the highest level of the government of India, with no end in sight. India, which claims to be the world's largest democracy, has repeatedly denied the visa to the members of the United Commission on Religious Freedom to hide its torture, massacres, and genocide of its minorities.

# Existential Threat to the Sikhs in India

India's crimes of 1984 began with its assault on, and the massacres at the Golden Temple and dozens of other Gurudwaras across India in the first week of June 1984, and continued with the nationwide government-sponsored pogroms of November 1984. In many ways, the crimes continue, not just in the cover-up and the sheltering of the criminals, but in actual outrages by the government and its minions to date. (Professor Cynthia Keppley Mahmood, University of Notre Dame)

The [Indian] army went into Darbar Sahib [Sikh Golden Temple] not to eliminate a political figure or a political movement but to suppress the culture of a people, to attack their heart, to strike a blow at their spirit and self-confidence. (Joyce Pettigrew, journalist and anthropologist)

From the time of Guru Nanak (1469–1539), Sikhs have been dedicated to the protection and propagation of fundamental human rights of equality, freedom, and justice for all. They have been under perpetual attacks from the hostile forces surrounding them, starting with the Mughals and then the British. Currently they are under existential threat from Hindutva (Hindu nationalism). These attacks

100

are aimed at their religion, identity, and language. The attacks are being carried out overtly in the form of the Sikh genocide and attacks on their religious institution. Covertly there is a long-drawn-out systematic plan of making them dependent upon the state for their mere survival. By killing them physically by genocide, economically by econocide and forced suicides, politically by treating Punjab as India's colony, and psychologically by the attack on their religion, language, and identity, India is not leaving any stone unturned to accomplish this goal.

India's different governments and national political parties have been consistent in their approach on how to deal with the state of Punjab and its people. Their objective is to keep Punjab occupied as a colony, drain its natural resources, keep its masses uneducated, and in abject poverty. A part of the plan is to keep feeding the narrative of Hindus versus Sikhs. Denial of Sikh religion, Sikh religious identity, Punjabi language, and attacks on Sikh religious institutions are frequent occurrences. Attacks on Sikh houses of worship (gurdwaras) in Punjab and the rest of India are going on unabated. The blocking of their access to Darbar Sahib (the holiest Sikh shrine) on the anniversaries of attacks on this holy site by Indian forces, denial of their entry to Sikh historical gurdwaras in Pakistan, searching Sikhs seeking entrance to these gurdwaras are not infrequent.

However, the Sikhs are fighting back vigorously. This is their DNA. Their success has been limited by their fracture into factions. This may have occurred naturally as a result of the protective mechanism because of the high degree of Indian intelligence penetration into Sikh circles. It is contemplated that someday, they would come together as a cohesive force to accomplish their shared common goal of sovereignty. They would need to be vigilant and guard against the diverting processes like flattery that they are brave, honest, and good people and, hence, need not worry about their own freedom.

The process of reducing Punjab into an ineffective state and Sikhs into powerless slaves began in 1948, with carving out areas of Punjab and giving those areas to adjoining states. The enacted Indian Constitution in 1950 denied the Sikh religious identity. The formation of the Punjab State was denied in 1956 by first denying the official status of the Punjabi language. On April 13, 1978, thirteen Sikhs were killed in cold blood, and none of the sixty-two persons charged were punished. Seventy-five percent of Punjab river waters has been diverted to adjoining states in violation of the riparian rights. The Indian Army invasion of Darbar Sahib in June 1984 and the November 1984 Sikh genocide has been described in other chapters of this book.

After having drained a rather big chunk of Punjab's natural resources, India has now moved on to the process of taking control and eventually ripping the farmers of ownership of their meager landholdings. The average farm size in Punjab is under five acres, most of them owning two to four acres of land. To accomplish this, India passed three farm laws in 2020 which has been discussed in another chapter. Farming is the backbone of Punjab's economy. Sikhs make up almost the entire population of Punjab farmers. Losing control of water and their land, the majority of Sikhs will be reduced to a powerless labor force. Sikhs have been fighting the foreign invaders stopping their entry to mainland India. This has been based on their being financially independent, physically strong, and deep faith in their religion. India is bent upon using Sikhs merely as weapons of war. The loss of financial independence and religious identity is a serious threat to their survival and faith. Political autonomy and sovereignty of Punjab is the only solution to the survival of Sikhs and the economic well-being of the people of Punjab.

### Escalation of Persecution of Sikhs in Modi's India

Immediately after the independence of India in 1947, the Sikhs started to realize that they were slaves in their country, for the freedom of which they had made an infinite number of sacrifices. They were forced into agitations to get their constitutional rights, which are ordinarily not denied to other Indians. There has been a systematic denial of their religion, identity, and language (Punjabi). There have been systematic attacks against their religious institutions and natural resources.

The fifth of June 2020 marked the thirty-sixth year of the Indian Army invasion of Golden Temple, the Vatican of Sikhism, and the escalation of violent suppression of Sikhs, a people of a minority faith in India. Three decades later, India's policy of suppressing Sikhs—through violence and other means and depriving the community of its separate religious identity and denying them political, human, and civil rights—continues.

With the coming to power of Narendra Modi, a known Hindu supremacist, the already-marginalized Sikh community is experiencing a sharp increase in all forms of state oppression. There have been continuing events of state violence against Sikhs that point at the historical pattern of oppression, which draws on the inherent flaws deeply entrenched against the community in the Indian legal and constitutional framework.

Numbering barely 1.8 percent of the population of India, the Sikh community has been at the receiving end of Indian governments' ruthlessness and terrorism for the past several decades. Whenever it has raised its voice for its political and religious rights, separate religious identity, and right to self-determination, Indian governments have answered with bullets, tortures, massacres, detentions under the black-draconian laws, like UAPA and TADA and the Sikh Genocide of 1984.

### Persecution of Punjab Independence Referendum Supporters

It is an irrefutable fact that Punjab, currently governed by India, was an independent and sovereign country, known as the Sikh Empire, till 1849, when the British took over. However, during decolonization in August 1947, instead of returning and restoring its sovereignty, Punjab was left under the governance of India. In August 2021, in an unofficial Punjab Independence Referendum being organized by the human rights group Sikhs for Justice (SFJ), Sikhs around the globe will be asked to vote for or against the secession of Punjab from India and reestablishment of the same as a sovereign country.

Firmly rooted in the international law of the right of self-determination of all peoples, SFJ's Punjab Independence Referendum campaign is a legitimate political movement employing a democratic modus operandi.

It is an indisputable fact that holding secessionist views and peacefully campaigning for independence is not a crime. A people's right to self-determination is a fundamental principle of international law, guaranteed under the UN Charter and the Bill of Rights.[93] Self-determination may be sought and exercised internally (within a parent state) or, in certain circumstances, externally through secession and independence. According to the International Court of Justice, a subgroup (in this case, Sikhs) may lawfully conduct an independence referendum and declare independence without the agreement of the parent state (in this case, India).[94]

Despite the peaceful democratic nature of the Punjab Independence Referendum, Indian authorities appear determined to crush the movement by unleashing a reign of terror through filing false charges, labeling the campaign as "terrorism" and its supporters as "terrorists" and detention and torture of Sikh activists supporting it. The Indian authorities are also exaggerating stories and fabricating evidence to implicate the referendum supporters in terrorism cases.[95] While there has been a repetitive and compulsive pattern of abuses, the following are the most recent and egregious cases of terror and intimidation against the referendum campaigners in Punjab, India:

- On the third and fourth November 2018, General Rawat,[96] chief of the Indian Army,[97] publicly alleged that SFJ's

---

[93] See article 1 of the UN Charter; article 1 of the International Covenant on Civil and Political Rights; and article 1 of the International Covenant on Economic, Social, and Cultural Rights. Peoples who have been denied self-determination within their parent state may, in exceptional circumstances, lawfully pursue external self-determination (via secession).

[94] See "Accordance with International Law of the Unilateral Declaration of Independence in Respect of Kosovo, Advisory Opinion," ICJ Reports 2010, July 22, 2010, 403.

[95] https://www.thestatesman.com/cities/punjab-police-bust-isi-backed-terror-module-sfj-link-1502703614.html.

[96] https://www.dailypioneer.com/2018/state-editions/indian-army-chief-reiterates-warning-on-revival-of-insurgency-in-punjab.html.

[97] https://economictimes.indiatimes.com/news/defence/stop-bid-to-revive-punjab-terror-now-or-itll-be-too-late-general-rawat/articleshow/66494478.cms.

Punjab Independence Referendum is the revival of insurgency in Punjab.

- On November 2, 2018, four Sikh referendum campaigners—Jaswinder Singh, Manjit Singh, Gurwinder Singh, and Harpreet Singh—were taken into custody for having Referendum 2020 posters and charged with sedition and were tortured.

- On November 1, 2018, Shabnamdeep Singh, a Patiala-based Sikh youth who was actively engaged in propagating the referendum on Facebook, was arrested and charged with the possession of a grenade, pistol, links with Pakistan's ISI, terrorism, and sedition (promoting the referendum). As per information received from the family members of Shabnamdeep Singh, the detainee is being continuously tortured.

- On October 19, 2018, Sukhraj Singh, Malkit Singh, Bikram Singh were arrested from Amritsar, Punjab, and have been charged with "propagating the Referendum campaign by affixing banners and posters in public places in Amritsar." [98]

- On October 10, 2018, three Kashmiri[99] Muslim students at an engineering college in Jalandhar, Punjab, were arrested with referendum material and falsely charged with possession of AK-47s.

- In June 2018,[100] Dharminder Singh and Kirpal Singh, who were campaigning for the referendum by printing and posting banners, were arrested, implicated in false, baseless, and fabricated terror charges and tortured in police custody.

---

[98] https://www.business-standard.com/article/pti-stories/two-members-of-khalistani-module-arrested-in-amritsar-118101900929_1.html.

[99] https://www.mynation.com/news/zakir-musa-punjab-2020-referendum-arrested-kashmiri-students-terrorist-pgogwb.

[100] https://leagueofindia.com/internal-challenges/punjab-police-arrest-two-khalistani-radicals-one-arms-supplier/.

- In April 2018,[101] four Sikh youths—Randhir Singh, Sukhwinder Singh, Manveer Singh, and Jaspreet Singh—who were planning to post the referendum banners during IPL Cricket Match in Mohali were arrested and charged with arson and terrorism.
- In July 2017, Gurpreet Singh and Harpunit Singh, who printed and affixed the referendum banners throughout Punjab, were arrested and charged with sedition and terrorism.[102].
- June 2017—Arrest of twenty-two Sikh political activists in Punjab for peacefully campaigning for the referendum in Punjab.

  Few days after the Sikh activists in Punjab—particularly those supporting the Independence Referendum—commemorated the thirty-third year of the Indian military's attack on the Sikh Golden Temple, twenty-two Sikh activists were arrested by the Indian security forces.

  The arrest of the twenty-two Sikh political activists was to suppress the support for a peaceful and democratic campaign to hold the referendum in the Indian-occupied Punjab on the basis that Punjab is the ancestral and historical homeland of Sikhs, and the will of the indigenous people of Punjab should be sought on the question of sovereignty.
- August 2016—Illegal detention and torture of Sikh activists and the referendum campaigners in Punjab.

On or about August 6–7, 2016, the Sikh referendum campaigners actively gathered signatures on an online White House petition, launched by SFJ, demanding the Obama administration's

---

[101] https://www.indiatoday.in/india/story/punjab-police-arrests-4-isi-trained-khalistani-terrorists-1205283-2018-04-05.

[102] https://www.indiatoday.in/india/story/pro-khalistan-sikhs-for-punjab-amarinder-singh-government-2020-referendum-1023168-2017-07-08.

support for the liberation of Indian-occupied Punjab.[103] These Sikh referendum campaigners were engaged in a peaceful and democratic activity. They have been detained without warrants and implicated in false and fabricated charges. Not only that the Sikhs' demand for referendum and right to self-determination is legal, but the campaign for the demand for a referendum is carried out only and only through democratic and peaceful means. In this case, the Indian Police itself declared that Sikh campaigners have been arrested for "distributing referendum-related material and T-Shirts." To justify its illegal actions, the police later imputed the false charges of "planning to carry out some terror activity" on the detained campaigners. The detention of the campaigners, in this case, is carried out to stop and suppress the Sikh referendum campaign (see http://www.tribuneindia.com/news/punjab/terrormodule-linked-to-nris-busted-in-punjab-before-i-day/278666.html).

Jaspreet Singh, Kuldeep Singh, Hardeep Singh, and Bikramjeet Singh, the four referendum campaigners were arrested while gathering signatures for an SFJ-sponsored White House petition relating to Sikh separatism.[104] Seemingly arrested for "distributing referendum-related material and T-Shirts," they were later charged with planning to carry out terror activity, a charge which observers claim to be false.[105] The India-based Lawyers for Human Rights International visited the four detainees in prison and found that they were not only illegally detained but also had been "brutally tortured."[106]

On February 7, 2019, three Sikhs—Arwinder Singh, twenty-nine; Surjit Singh, twenty-seven; and Ranjit Singh, twenty-nine—were awarded life imprisonment under the charge of waging a war

---

[103] Existential Threats to Sikhs in India, May–June 2019, https://petitions.whitehouse.gov/petition/august-15th-not-independence-day-sikhs-supportliberation-indian-occupied-punjab-create-khalistan.

[104] https://petitions.whitehouse.gov/petition/august-15th-not-independence-day-sikhs-support-liberation-indian-occupied-punjab-create-khalistan.

[105] See "Urgent Appeal to UN Special Rapportuer on Torture," filed by SFJ on August 30, 2016, annex 9

[106] See "Lawyers for Human Rights International," August 29, 2016, annex 10

against the state. Legal experts condemned this sentence as one of its kind as it was based on the recovery of some literature and not any ammunition or an act of violence. The accused were charged based on "books, literature, and pamphlets" in their possession for propagating the establishment of Khalistan.[107]

## November 2015, Sarbat Khalsa (Global Sikh Assembly) and Iron-Fisted Response of the State

In November 2015, the Sikh community announced to hold Sarbat Khalsa (translated as a Global Sikh Assembly), a historical Sikh institution that calls upon the community to gather and deliberate on the current-day issues faced by the Sikh community. The event holds unparalleled religious, social, and political sanctity for the Sikh community. Over half a million Sikhs from around the globe attended the 2015 Sarbat Khalsa, including delegations from the Sikh diaspora in the United States, Canada, and European Union.

This Sarbat Khalsa gathering was a peaceful and democratic process to discuss important issues related to the Sikh nation. The Indian government responded by employing all tools of oppression, including illegal detention and filing false charges against the Sikh political activists to outright violence against participants by the police. In many cases, sedition charges were filed against Sikhs solely for holding a peaceful political and religious gathering.

In October 2015, torn pages of the Holy Book of Sikhism, Sri Guru Granth Sahib (SGGS), were found in a village of India's Punjab, leading to widespread resentment among the followers of the faith. Sikhs in Punjab gathered in large numbers to hold peaceful protests against the desecration of the Holy Book. The state police reacted ruthlessly by crushing those peaceful demonstrations with uncalled-

---

[107] https://timesofindia.indiatimes.com/city/ludhiana/3-sikh-youths-get-life-term-for-waging-waragainst-state/articleshow/67876157.cms.

for shooting and baton charge. Police opened fire[108] on the unarmed and peaceful crowd of Sikhs, killing two men[109] in cold blood.

It was the determination of Justice Jora Singh Commission, appointed by the Punjab government, that the police firing, killing two people (Gurjeet Singh and Krishan Bhagwan Singh) and injuring six, was absolutely unwarranted. The victims were killed "in sitting position." "What impelled the police official(s) to fire at them, and that too, from a close range, is beyond comprehension. More so, when the victims were defenseless and unarmed," the report says, recommending action as per law against the erring officials who fired gunshots.[110] Several dozen protesters were injured in police baton charge and tear gas. There was no compelling reason for the police to unleash brutal force on demonstrators holding a peaceful sit-in over the desecration of their faith's supreme scriptures.

The protests over the defilement of Sri Guru Granth Sahib continued to grow. The state government's failure to take any action against the guilty, some of whom were the relatives of Punjab governor Amrinder Singh, resulted in more protests. However, the state's iron-fisted response to the legitimate and democratic demonstrations continued; the administration had to order paramilitary deployment in Punjab.[111] While more incidents of desecration of Sri Guru Granth Sahib continued to take place in Punjab, the government of India, instead of securing Sikhs' right to practice and defend their faith, deployed paramilitary forces ostensibly to further crush the protests and demonstration by the Sikh population.

---

[108] *Indian Express*, October 15, http://indianexpress.com/article/india/india-news-india/holy-book-desecrationbadals-battle-crisis-as-police-firing-kills-two/.

[109] *Times Report* on Sikhs Shot Dead by Police October 15. http://www.ibtimes.co.uk/kotkapura-clashes-two-deadsikh-protesters-clash-police-after-desecration-holy-book-1524099.

[110] https://www.hindustantimes.com/punjab/big-people-behind-bargari-sacrilege-police-firing-in-behbal-kalan-unwarranted-zora-panel/story-AEP2nf3Ubnj4x0qgMsdlSO.html.

[111] www.ksl.com/article/37023802.

## History of State Violence Against Sikhs in India

The civil society has documented the long history of human rights abuses committed by Indian authorities against pro-Khalistan Sikh activists during the 1980s–1990s, premised on false labeling, encouraged by politicians, and perpetrated by prosecutors and police. Unfortunately, the culture continues to this day.

Unlike the referendum campaign, the separatist movement of the 1980s and 1990s had a militant edge. However, the brutal counterinsurgency operations were, in the words of Human Rights Watch, "the most extreme example of a policy in which the end appeared to justify all means, including torture and murder." [112]

During the 1990s, India's state violence against Sikhs was accompanied by the misuse of the criminal justice system by prosecutors and police. The US Department of State described the Punjab Police practice of faked encounter killings in 1993. In the typical scenario, police take into custody a suspected militant or militant supporter without filing an arrest report. If the detainee dies during interrogation or is executed, officials deny he/she was ever in custody or claim that the detainee died during an armed encounter with police or security forces. Alternatively the police may claim to have been ambushed by militants while escorting a suspect. Although the detainee invariably dies in "cross fire," police casualties in these "incidents" are rare. [113]

Although the militancy associated with Sikh separatism evaporated in the 1990s, the Indian authorities still employ the illegal, violent, and abusive methods associated with that period.

---

[112] "Protecting the Killers: A Policy of Impunity In Punjab, India," Human Rights Watch 19, no. 14: 2, https://www.hrw.org/reports/2007/india1007/.

[113] US State Department, Bureau of Democracy, Human Rights, and Labor, "Country Reports on Human Rights Practices—1993: India," January 31, 1994.

# How the Sikh Campaigns for Fundamental Rights Are Being Crushed by Successive Indian Regimes

---

There are certain basic human rights from which the people should not be alienated. Among these are the right to life, liberty, and pursuit of happiness. United Nations Universal Declaration of Human Rights (UDHR) in 1948 delineated all these rights in detail. The First Amendment of the United States Constitution guarantees freedoms concerning religion, expression, assembly, and right to petition. It guarantees freedom of expression by prohibiting congress from restricting the press or the rights of individuals to speak freely.

India's constitution also provides the right to free speech and expression. However, it has several strings attached, which make it weak and vulnerable to the will of the ruling governments. This right is available to citizens of India and not to foreign nationals. However, under Article 19(1a), this right is not absolute, and it allows the government to frame reasonable restrictions in the interest of the sovereignty and integrity of India, security of the state, friendly relations with foreign states, public order, decency and morality and contempt of court, defamation and incitement of offense.[114] These clauses, which permit the restriction of expression and free speech, are subject to manipulation at the whim of the ruling party. Thus, though in theory, Indians have the right to free speech, practically it is too soft

---

[114] http://www.legalserviceindia.com/legal/article-572-constitution-of-india-freedom-of-speech-and-expression.html.

to be able to protect this fundamental right. Indian Constitution has failed several tests at different times to protect the right to free speech. A few examples are the Indian Police attack on peacefully demonstrating Sikhs on July 4, 1955, in the city of Amritsar, demanding the establishment of Punjab State, and more recently the Indian police attack of peacefully campaigning farmers protesting against the new farm laws enacted in 2020.

## July 4, 1955, Attack on Golden Temple and Peacefully Protesting Sikhs

On July 4, 1955, the Indian Police started the slow extermination of Sikhs by launching its first attack on Darbar Sahib. About two hundred Sikhs were killed by the Indian forces, three thousand were injured, and more than twelve thousand arrested during the attack.

Sikhs were carrying on their peaceful struggle to form a Punjabi-speaking state by peacefully offering arrests, shouting, "Punjabi Suba Zindabad," (long live Punjab State). During the Punjabi Suba Morcha (campaign), Sikh protesters continued to grow in numbers. All the jails in Punjab had been filled, and it had become increasingly difficult to contain the Sikh movement.

Finally India decided to crush the movement by all means necessary. Ashwani Kumar, DIG of Jalandhar (out of town from the adjoining district) Police, asked for permission to practice unlimited privileges and promised to destroy the movement within five days. Upon getting permission, he ordered the police to confiscate handguns, rifles, and other firearms belonging to the SGPC. Censorship was put on Sikh newspapers, disallowing them to highlight the truth and describe the real situation. The police stopped the printing of the newspapers and closed down the main buildings. Many Sikh journalists and news reporters were arrested, their printed materials confiscated, and burnt by the police. The printing press was stopped. It was all a part of the plan so that no one would know the extent of the police operation, and the public will stay uninformed.

## *Operation Blue Star, 1984 Media Blackout*

The Golden Temple in Amritsar was under siege during Operation Blue Star. Much of the operation was covered by the print media through selective information and photographs released by the government, intelligence, and army sources.

While most of the journalists were gathered in a hotel in Amritsar and hauled to the adjoining state of Haryana, Brahma Chellaney, a reporter for the Associated Press (AP) news agency, managed to stay inside the Golden Temple because he had arrived in Amritsar a day before the attack, and escaped detection. His story quoted post-mortem medical reports as saying "several" people inside the temple had been shot at close range with their hands bound—killed in cold blood—and that around 1,200 people had died in the blitz, around double the official figure. It was picked up by *London Times*. New Delhi charged Chellaney[115] with violating Punjab press censorship, two counts of fanning sectarian hatred and trouble, and later with sedition. In September 1985, eight months after impounding his passport, the government returned it and dropped all charges.[116] The government feared that the trial will bring out the truth about the Indian Army's invasion of the Golden Temple.

The *New York Times* editorial titled "Truth on Trial—in India" stated, "What is at issue here is not just censorship, but vindictiveness… Not since India's emergency' in 1975–1977 has anyone working for a foreign news organization there been threatened with jail for doing his job."[117]

For five days, Punjab has been cut off from the rest of the world. There was a twenty-four-hour curfew. All telephone and communication lines were cut. No foreigners were permitted to enter Punjab, and all Indian journalists were expelled. There were no newspapers,

---

[115] https://www.indiatoday.in/magazine/society-the-arts/media/story/19841115-ap-correspondent-brahma-chellaney-charged-with-violating-press-censorship-in-punjab-803449-1984-11-15.

[116] Rahul Singh, "The Strange Case of Brahma Chellaney," *Indian Express*, January 21, 1985.

[117] https://www.nytimes.com/1984/10/23/opinion/truth-on-trial-in-india.html.

no trains, no buses—not even a bullock cart could move. Orders to shoot on site were widely carried out. The whole of Punjab, with its thousands of villages and major cities, was turned into a concentration camp.

### How the Indian News Media Vanished During the November 1984 Sikh Genocide in Delhi

In another crushing blow to the Sikhs' fundamental rights, India's constitution ceased to exist during the mass massacres of the Sikhs in November 1984. During the 1984 Sikh Genocide in November 1984, after the assassination of the then-Prime Minister Indira Gandhi, India's democracy had died, and India's Constitution was burning. The police, prominent politicians, and the parliamentarians were busy planning, executing, supplying materials, financial support, and incendiary materials to burn the Sikhs alive. India's consciousness had also died. The police not only did not stop the bloodthirsty mobs, but they also participated in the killing and provided logistics and all sorts of support to the attackers. The news media had vanished.

In a conversation for social media broadcast, Jarnail Singh recounted why he chose to become a journalist. "While in college, I went to the Delhi Public Library. It housed the newspaper record of 40 years," the former reporter recalled. "I looked for reportage in 1984. I was stunned to discover that there was none of it from the first three days (of November 1984) when thousands of people were burnt alive on the streets of Delhi."[118]

Singh protested by throwing his shoe at the then-home minister P Chidambaram during a news conference in 2009 that resulted from the Congress Party issuing Lok Sabha election tickets to the notorious suspects of the Sikh pogrom, on the ground that they were "exonerated" by the country's law enforcement mechanism. He was eleven when the Sikh Genocide of 1984 took place in Delhi. The dis-

---

[118] https://www.dailyo.in/politics/sajjan-kumar-jarnail-singh-1984-riots-verdict-sikhs-indira-gandhi-media-congress/story/1/28454.html.

play of the anger he carried inside him led to his protest resulting in the ruling party's withdrawal of the candidates who were responsible for the mass killings of Sikhs.

Rahul Bedi, who covered 1984 for *The Indian Express*, wrote how the police had magically disappeared from the scene during the Sikh Genocide in November 1984. Thirty-four years later, Delhi High Court declared this a crime against humanity. And the handful of visible police officers present at the scenes were unwilling or under orders not to open fire upon cowardly mobs, wrote Bedi.[119]

## Black Cats—Undercover Police Let Loose to Kill Sikhs

Human Rights Watch and Physicians for Human Rights (PHR), while conducting investigations of human rights abuses, discovered that police employed undercover agents, known as Black Cats, to eliminate suspected militants. They interviewed a lady whose husband worked undercover as a Black Cat for police. She stated that her husband was given four AK-47 guns that were captured from the militants. He and his coworkers traveled dressed in plain clothes and often had full beards to make them look like Sikh militants. They carried their police identification with them just in case they were accidentally picked up by regular police. Once they got information on militants, they would get verbal orders from SSP to abduct them if possible and bring them to the police station for interrogation or torture. If they were unable to abduct someone, they had the orders to shoot and kill. The Black Cats hit squads operated in the state of Punjab clandestinely and were responsible for murdering and pillaging.[120]

During the armed struggle of the 1980s and 1990s, many Hindus were also killed by Indian police in staged encounters to

---

[119] https://indianexpress.com/article/opinion/columns/anti-sikh-riots-1984-sajjan-kumar-delhi-indira-gandhi-assassination-thirty-four-years-later-5499496/.

[120] "Simranjit Singh's Mann Resignation Letter to Speaker Rabi Ray, October 10, 1990," *The Tribune*, October 9, 1990.

defame Sikh freedom fighters, and by the Sikh militants in revenge killings.

## Three Sikhs Imprisoned for Life for Carrying Literature on Khalistan

Three Sikhs—Arwinder Singh, Surjit Singh, and Ranjit Singh—were convicted in the court of additional sessions judge Randhir Verma. The three were handed life imprisonment for carrying some literature on Punjab Independence Referendum. Punjab and Haryana High Court advocate Rajwinder Singh Bains stated that it was a first of its kind case in which the three accused have been convicted for recovery of literature and without any recovery of any weapon or any act of violence.[121]

## Illegal Detention and Torture of Sikh Activists and the Referendum Campaigners in Punjab

On or about August 6–7, 2016, the Sikh Referendum campaigners actively gathered signatures on an online White House petition launched by SFJ, demanding the Obama administration's support for the liberation of Indian-occupied Punjab.[122] These Sikh Referendum campaigners were engaged in a peaceful and democratic activity. They have been detained without warrants and implicated in false and fabricated charges. Not only that the Sikhs' demand for referendum and right to self-determination is legal, but the campaign for the demand for a referendum is also carried out only and only through democratic and peaceful means. In this case, the Indian Police itself declared that Sikh campaigners have been arrested for distributing referendum-related material and T-shirts. To justify its illegal actions, the police later imputed the false charges of planning

---

[121] http://timesofindia.indiatimes.com/articleshow/67876157.cms?utm_source=contentofinterest&utm_medium=text&utm_campaign=cppst.

[122] https://petitions.obamawhitehouse.archives.gov/petition/august-15th-not-independence-day-sikhs-support-liberation-indian-occupied-punjab-create-khalistan.

to carry out some terror activity on the detained campaigners. The detention of the campaigners, in this case, is carried out to stop and suppress the Sikh referendum campaign.[123]

Jaspreet Singh, Kuldeep Singh, Hardeep Singh, and Bikramjeet Singh, the four referendum campaigners, were arrested while gathering signatures for an SFJ-sponsored White House petition relating to Sikh separatism.[124] Seemingly arrested for "distributing referendum-related material and T-Shirts," they were later charged with planning to carry out terror activity, a charge which observers claimed to be false.[125] The India-based Lawyers for Human Rights International visited the four detainees in prison and found that they were not only illegally detained but also had been "brutally tortured."[126]

## India's Crackdown on Peacefully Protesting Farmers

Hundreds of thousands of farmers protested on the outskirts of Delhi since November 2020, demanding that the Bharatiya Janata Party (BJP) led government withdraw three farm laws passed in September. The protests were peaceful until January 26, India's Republic Day, when protesters broke through police barricades to enter Delhi and clashed with the police.

The police in BJP-ruled Uttar Pradesh, Madhya Pradesh, Karnataka, and Haryana states have filed cases of sedition and promoting communal disharmony against six senior journalists and editors—Rajdeep Sardesai, Mrinal Pande, Zafar Agha, Paresh Nath, Anant Nath, Vinod K Jose, and a Congress Party politician, Shashi

---

[123] http://www.tribuneindia.com/news/punjab/terrormodule-linked-to-nris-busted-in-punjab-before-i-day/278666.html.

[124] https://petitions.whitehouse.gov/petition/august-15th-not-independence-day-sikhs-support-liberation-indian-occupied-punjab-create-khalistan.

[125] See "Urgent Appeal to UN Special Rapportuer on Torture filed by SFJ on August 30, 2016," annex 9.

[126] See "Lawyers for Human Rights International, August 29, 2016," annex 10.

Tharoor—for allegedly "misreporting" the facts around the death of a protester during the farmers' protests in Delhi in 2021.[127]

On January 30, Delhi Police also detained the journalists Dharmender Singh and Mandeep Punia, who were covering the protests, alleging that the two "misbehaved" with the police. Punia had been investigating a mob who threw stones at the farmers and vandalized their tents at the protest site on the Singhu border, between Delhi and Haryana, on January 29. While the police released Singh the next day, they sent Punia, a freelance journalist, to judicial custody for fourteen days for allegedly obstructing and assaulting a police officer. The Press Club of India, Press Association, the Indian Women's Press Corps, the Delhi Union of Journalists, and the Indian Journalists Union also demanded the withdrawal of cases and pressed for the repeal of the colonial-era sedition law used to silence dissent.

Sikhs for Justice, a human rights advocacy group based in New York, filed a complaint to the United Nations against India on March 30, 2021, related to the suppression of freedom of opinion and expression, freedom of assembly and association, executions, and torture. The perpetrators identified were Narendra Modi, prime minister of India; Amit Shah, Union home minister of India; Ajit Doval, National Security adviser of India; Yogesh Chander Modi, director general of National Investigations Agency of India; S. N. Shrivastava, commissioner of Delhi Police; and Arvid Kumar, director of Intelligence Bureau of India.

The January 26, 2021, farmers' rally was a part of their ongoing protests since November 2020, against the three Farm Bills passed in 2020. Several hundred thousand farmers have been protesting at the borders of the capital, Delhi, including Singhu, Tikhri, and Ghazibad. The three farms laws were designed to benefit the corporate allies of the ruling party, BJP, and PM Modi, while further plunging the struggling farmers of Punjab into debt and death spiral. Modi government has been using violence, intimidation, and sedition charges to suppress the farmers' protest.

---

[127] https://sikhsiyasat.net/india-8-journalists-covering-farmer-protests-charged-drop-cases-protect-media-freedom-human-rights-watch.

The following points have been highlighted in the complaint:

1. On January 26, 2021 (Republic Day of India), large-scale violence was committed by the Indian Police and other security forces against the farmers in Delhi, resulting in death and injuries to the protesting farmers.
2. Killing of protesting farmers at the hands of the Indian Police
3. Police brutality through baton charge, beatings, and use of water cannon of filthy cold water in November, December, January 2020–2021.
4. Intimidation of protesting farmers, their family members, and supporters
5. Filing of false criminal charges, including sedition against farmers, their family members, and supporters
6. Raids at the homes and workplaces by the security forces to interrogate and intimidate the protesting farmers and their supporters

These attacks have been targeted against persons belonging to a specific group, ethnic origin, language, political opinion, or religious belief.

Sikhs for Justice donated $10,000 for supporting human rights on March 1, 2021. A spokesperson of the United Nations High Commissioner for Human Rights confirmed the receipt of this donation. Answering the objection from the Indian government for accepting this donation, the spokesperson answered that they do not decline such donation unless these are from groups or individuals on the UN sanctions lists, or organizations or individuals engaged in activities contrary to the charter or the principles of the United Nation. India was referring to the designation of the Sikhs for Justice as a terrorist organization in July 2019, simply for propagating the right to self-determination of the people of Punjab. India has filed multiple charges of sedition and terrorism against Sikhs for Justice supporters without a single case of any terroristic activity to sub-stantiate such charges. Gurpatwant Singh Pannun has been threatened with violence and charged with sedition, under the Unlawful Activities Prevention Act (UAPA), for arranging peaceful demonstrations in front of the India Consulate offices in the United States, Canada, and the UK on December 10, 2020.

## *The ICJ Condemned the Unlawful Repression of Peaceful Protests*

Thousands of farmers from all over India, and most heavily from Punjab, Haryana, and Uttar Pradesh, have demanded the repeal of a new set of agricultural laws, fearing that these will eventually lead to the loss of ownership of their land and force them to become laborers. The Indian government has been suppressing the farmers' right to peaceful protest and assembly. Since early February 2021, police have used metal barricades, cement walls, and placing iron nail-embedded metal plates over the road surfaces to block the roads leading to Tikri, Singhu, Ghazipur, the three main borders where the farmers have assembled. They have done so to prevent any vehicles from entering Delhi. The barricades have also served to deny male and female farmers and their families, including children, consistent access to water and sanitation facilities. On February 11, 2021, the ICJ condemned the unlawful repression of peaceful protests and urged the Indian authorities to respect the right to freedom of assembly of Indian farmers who have been demonstrating in Delhi since November 26, 2020, against newly promulgated agricultural laws.[128]

## *India Cuts Internet Services at Singhu Border*

India blocked mobile Internet services in several areas around New Delhi on Saturday, January 30, 2021, as protesting farmers began a one-day hunger strike after a week of clashes with authorities that left one dead and hundreds injured.[129]

---

[128] https://sikhsiyasat.net/india-authorities-must-stop-suppressing-peaceful-protests-by-farmers-and-their-allies/.

[129] https://www.reuters.com/article/us-india-farms-protests/india-cuts-internet-near-delhi-as-hundreds-of-farmers-begin-hunger-strike-idUSKBN29Z08R.

### UN Calls for Protection of Rights to Peaceful Assembly

Amid the mobile Internet service ban at Delhi's borders, United Nations Human Rights Organization stated that peaceful assembly and expression should be protected both offline and online.[130] This was triggered when the Sikhs for Justice team discussed with the UN to protect the rights of the peacefully protesting farmers. In this message, the United Nations called on the authorities of India to exercise maximum restraint in the ongoing farmers' protest

### Overseas India Is Cracking Down on Sikhs' Right to Assembly and Free Speech

*India launches objections to Sikh social media posts*—Tom Blackwell reported in *National Post*, on September 15, 2020, that an Indian law enforcement agency asked Twitter to delete a post by a Canadian Sikh advocacy group, an unusual move by a foreign power that has sparked allegations of attempted international censorship. India claimed the tweet by the World Sikh Organization (WSO)—discussing what the group calls a "genocide" of Sikhs in 1984—violated that country's laws, the social media company said in an e-mail to the WSO. Twitter's legal department notified WSO that it was not taking any action at this time, but the organization may seek legal counsel or voluntarily delete the content.[131]

### India Tries to Stop London Declaration of Punjab Independence Referendum

When US-based human rights advocacy group Sikhs for Justice was preparing for the London Declaration of Punjab Independence Referendum 2020 in Trafalgar Square, London, on August 12, 2018,

---

[130] https://www.nationalheraldindia.com/international/rights-to-peaceful-assembly-and-expression-should-be-protected-un-human-rights-body-on-farmers-protests.

[131] India claimed the tweet by the World Sikh Organization—discussing what the group calls a "genocide" of Sikhs in 1984—violated that country's laws.

India launched a vigorous complaint to the UK government. Britain rejected India's demand stating that "In the UK, people have the right to gather together and to demonstrate their views, provided that they do so within the law."[132]

India's Ministry of External Affairs spokesperson, Raveesh Kumar, stated that they have issued a demarche to try to convince the UK government to disallow the London Declaration of Punjab Independence Referendum 2020 arranged by Sikhs for Justice, whose intention is to spread hate, and it may affect bilateral ties. UK answered, "In the United Kingdom, people have the right to gather and demonstrate views within the law," the statement said. "We will not tolerate groups who spread hate or raise community fears by bringing disorder to towns and cities. Police have powers to deal with such activities."[133]

## How India Spies on Sikhs Overseas

Two Indian citizens living in Germany have been found guilty of spying on Kashmiris and Sikhs for India's intelligence agency. The couple has been sentenced to suspended jail terms and large fines. A German court convicted an Indian married couple of spying on Kashmiri and Sikh groups in Germany on behalf of India's foreign intelligence service. The court in Frankfurt found Manmohan S., fifty, and his wife, Kanwal Jit K., fifty-one, guilty of handing information on such groups to India's Research and Analysis Wing (RAW). Their last names are not given under German privacy laws. Manmohan S. was handed a one-and-a-half-year suspended jail sentence for illegal espionage activities, while Kanwal Jit K. received a fine equivalent to 180 days of income for aiding and abetting such activities.[134]

---

[132] https://www.hindustantimes.com/world-news/theresa-may-govt-rejects-india-s-request-to-ban-sikh-separatist-event-in-london/story-qQvW2SY2C92M0maHSTBLFK.html.

[133] https://scroll.in/latest/886349/india-issues-demarche-notice-to-uk-against-a-campaign-for-referendum-on-khalistan.

[134] https://www.dw.com/en/germany-indian-couple-convicted-of-spying-for-delhi/a-51638156.

## How India Carries Out Disinformation Campaign Against Sikhs in Canada

India has been carrying out a disinformation propaganda war against the Sikhs in Canada and other countries starting before the 1984 Indian Army invasion of Darbar Sahib (GTA). India has deployed thousands of intelligence agents all over the world, monitoring and interfering in the Sikhs' activities involving religion and politics.

These activities involve the propagation of false information, fabrication of lies about Sikhs and their activities, targeting mainstream and Punjabi news media in the favor of India and against the Sikhs and their organizations. In 1986–1987, several Indian diplomats were asked by the Canadian authorities to leave Canada for their espionage activities against the Sikhs.

The World Sikh Organization of Canada has released a report shedding light on Indian disinformation campaigns targeting Sikhs in Canada. The report, entitled "Exposed: India's Disinformation Campaign Against Canada's Sikhs," was released on February 3, 2020.

This report looked at the history of Indian interference and disinformation in Canada, including after the recent resignation of MP Navdeep Bains from his role as minister of Innovation, Science, and Industry. WSO president Tejinder Singh stated that this report exposes Indian interference and disinformation campaigns targeting Sikhs in Canada. In the aftermath of the farmer protests in India, we are seeing escalated attempts by actors in India to push disinformation, particularly about Sikhs here in Canada. The report reveals that a standard methodology has been developed to push false narratives on Sikhs in Canada. There is also evidence to now suggest that India's intelligence agencies are active in Canada and actively target Canadian politicians and media.[135]

---

[135] https://sikhsiyasat.net/exposed-indias-disinformation-war-against-canadas-sikhs-new-report-by-wso/.

During his visit to India in 2012, Indian news media repeatedly asked Canadian prime minister, Stephen Harper, the question about the Sikhs' campaign for Khalistan and their activities in Canada.

> Stephen Harper is pushing back at suggestions that Ottawa needs to do more about Sikh separatist activity in Canada, saying his government already keeps a sharp lookout for terrorist threats and that merely advocating for a Khalistan homeland in the Punjab is not a crime. He said violence and terrorism cannot be confused with the right of Canadians to hold and promote their political views. Mr. Harper said he believes other political parties in Canada agree that merely advocating for a Khalistan homeland in the Punjab is not illegal. (*Globe & Mail*, November 8, 2012)

The Sikh people in Canada and many other Western countries have been subjected to defamation and manipulation by Indian intelligence agents, who have been persistently trying to interfere in the management committees of the Sikh gurdwaras and activities of different Sikh organizations. Maloy Krishna Dhar, a former joint director of the Indian Intelligence Bureau (based in Ottawa, Canada, on a diplomatic posting from 1983–1987), confirmed in his book *Open Secrets* that his mission was to infiltrate gurdwaras/Sikh organizations to malign the Khalistan movement and also to cultivate "a few friends amongst the Canadian Members of Parliament." With multiple Indian intelligence agency spies removed from Canada during the 1980s, Dhar's claims have proven true.

## Bahamut Group: An Elusive Hacker-for-Hire Platform for Generating Fake News

According to BlackBerry, Bahamut is an elusive hacker for hire, and it is plausible that it is a mercenary group for hire that sells its services to different clients and groups. Bahamut's activities have historically focused on the Middle East, in a large number of countries. Another nexus of activity was observed in South Asia, with India and Pakistan in particular, and a focus on Sikh rights advocates and Islamist groups active in the Kashmir region. The researchers identified a large number of fake websites tied to Bahamut that appeared to have no relation to one another and served a variety of interests, including exploit sales, fitness, travel, Sikh independence, and secession from India. Some of them were benign, but others were used for phishing purposes. In addition to the websites, a plethora of fake social media accounts promoted or directed people to these websites.[136]

## APT C-35 India Cyber Mercenary Group Targets Sikhs

APT C-35 is an Indian cyber mercenary group that targets Sikhs who support Punjab Independence Referendum 2020. APT C-35 Indian mercenaries have launched several phishing websites and mobile apps relating to Referendum 2020 as bait to target pro-Khalistan Sikhs in India. It also targets Sikhs with religious inclinations.[137]

Qihoo 360 Technology, a Beijing-based major software company, released a cybersecurity report asserting that in India, Sikhs

---

[136] https://www.csoonline.com/article/3585137/elusive-hacker-for-hire-group-bahamut-linked-to-historical-att https://zeenews.india.com/technology/chinese-security-firm-releases-cyber-terrorism-against-sikhs-in-india-report-2348617.ack-campaigns.html.

[137] https://zeenews.india.com/technology/chinese-security-firm-releases-cyber-terrorism-against-sikhs-in-india-report-2348617.

with the religious and political inclination and Khalistan Referendum 2020 websites and mobile apps are under attack from Indian cyber mercenary group known as APT C-35.[138]

---

[138] https://na01.safelinks.protection.outlook.com/?url=https%3A%2F%2F zeenews.india.com%2Ftechnology%2Fchinese-security-firm-releases-cyber terrorism-against-sikhs-in-india-report-2348617.html&data=04%7C 01%7C%7C66cc9ddd26bb440fc8f808d8eb9430ad%7C84df9e7fe9 f640afb435aaaaaaaaaaaa%7C1%7C0%7C637518368985237163%7C Unknown%7CTWFpbGZsb3d8eyJWIjoiMC4wLjAwMDAiLCJQIjoiV2lu MzIiLCJBTiI6Ik1haWwiLCJXVCI6Mn0%3D%7C1000&sdata=Sh0 FbkDaRX2u3m0miz1jBFoY2p89Jlhmn1Cv1ZrFG1o%3D&reserved=0.

# Punjab: 1947 Onward

## *Post-Independence Punjab*

> I ask You (Sikhs) to accept my word and the
> Resolution of the Congress that it will not betray
> a single individual, much less a community. Let
> God be the witness of the bond that binds me
> and the Congress to you. I venture to suggest that
> Congress' non-violent creed is the surest guaran-
> tee of good faith, and our Sikh friends have no
> reason to fear that it would betray them. For,
> the moment it does so, the Congress would not
> only thereby seal its own doom but that of the
> country too. Moreover, Sikhs are brave people.
> They know how to safeguard their rights by the
> exercise of arms if it should ever come to that.
> (Mohandas Karamchand Gandhi, *Young India*,
> March 19, 1931)

This was the assurance Mahatma Gandhi gave to the Sikhs, repeatedly reiterating that their rights will be protected. It went as far as
stating that Sikhs can exercise arms should it ever come to that.
While it is hard to ascertain the truth and commitment behind these
statements, what happened after 1947 in the Republic of India has
been downright opposite of what was promised. Not only the Sikhs
were denied religious freedom, they have been also treated as unequal
citizens of India. The Sikhs certainly miscalculated that they would
use the force of the sword to get their rights if these were denied.

This is how the Congress Party trapped Sikhs into their web of lies and deception. It cannot be considered inappropriate if one would conclude that the Hindu-dominated Congress Party had its clandestine plan to subjugate Sikhs and draw from the natural resources of Punjab and use Sikhs merely as the weapons of war.

Mahatma Gandhi was assassinated on January 30, 1948, at the age of seventy-eight, by Nathu Ram Godse, a Hindu nationalist and member of Rashtriya Swayamsevak Sangh (RSS), a Hindu nationalist volunteer organization. RSS is an Indian right wing, Hindu nationalist, paramilitary organization. RSS is also the parent organization of Modi's political party, Bhartiya Janta Party. Had Mahatma Gandhi lived longer, what influence he would have had on the Congress Party's policies is anybody's guess.

Then there was Jawaharlal Nehru, the first prime minister of India, who blatantly stated that the Sikhs had missed the freedom train and that he could not entertain any idea of giving power in the hands of enemies, referring to the Sikhs. At that time, Sikhs were simply demanding the formation of Punjabi Suba (Punjab State), which was denied when other states were reorganized.

### The Self-Governing Sikh State Was Occupied and Subjugated

Between 1799 and 1849, the Sikh Empire enjoyed all the vestiges of sovereign statehood over the Punjab and surrounding territories. It was, for all intents and purposes, a Sikh state. British colonial dominion brought Sikh sovereignty to an end but largely retained the territorial integrity of the defunct Sikh Empire, along with traditional Punjabi power structures. Partition[139] split Punjab between India and Pakistan and resulted in unimaginable pain and suffering for millions of Sikhs, Hindus, and Muslims caught on the wrong side of the border. Despite paying a disproportionately high price in the struggle for independence, and notwithstanding clear promises of self-governance by leaders of the Indian Congress Party, Sikh inter-

---

[139] The term *partition* hereinafter refers to the division of British India into two independent dominions of India and Pakistan in 1947.

ests were ignored at the point of (and after) independence. Following independence, the government of India reneged on its promises to grant Sikhs their political, religious, and cultural autonomy. Punjab's territory was carved up in a series of constitutional reforms. Sikhs are denied the constitutional recognition of their religion and subjected to other forms of discrimination, as well as sectarian and economic violence. Sikh national identity appears to hold no place in independent India.

## A Tale of Betrayal of the Sikh Nation and Relentless Communal Violence

Following the assassination of Michael O'Dwyer in 1940, in London, by Udham Singh, the British realized that they had to leave India. Michael O'Dwyer was lieutenant governor of Punjab, who ordered General Reginal Dyer to carry out the massacre of Punjabis on April 13, 1919, at Jallianwala Bagh, Amritsar, by first trapping them in a large open space by deception. Reginal Dyer died of multiple strokes and brain hemorrhage a few years later.

Extensive negotiations among three groups—Hindus, Sikhs, and Muslims—failed to produce an agreement among these three parties. Each of the three groups wanted a country of their own. While the Muslims realized that their ultimate best option was a separate Pakistan, Sikhs had a more difficult decision.

They had three choices: First, to reestablish Punjab's sovereignty as it was in 1849 when Punjab fell to the British after about eight battles. This was their best choice. However, Sikh leadership was represented by religious leaders not well versed in world politics. They lacked the expertise in the art and psychology required for tough negotiations. On political matters, they consulted the Hindu-dominated Congress Party, thus putting their faith in the hands of their worst enemies. They failed to heed the warning from Muhammed Ali Jinnah, who told them that they had seen Hindus as coslaves but not when they would be the masters, and you (the Sikhs) their slaves.

Video link to Jinnah's speech:

https://www.bing.com/videos/search?q=jin
nah%27s+speech+video+for+Sikhs&&view=-
detail&mid=815201448959A48F83AC815201
448959A48F83AC&&FORM=VDRVRV

The second choice was to go with Pakistan. Here they realized that they would be a minority in Pakistan and possibly subject to religious repression. Sikhs had fought innumerable battles against the Muslims, starting from the Guru Arjan (the fifth Sikh guru), and had suffered extreme tortures under the Mughal rulers. They had vivid memories of the attacks on Harmandar Sahib by these rulers. There are fundamental differences between Sikhism and Islam, even though they share the concept of a common brotherhood. Thus this was not a good choice for Sikhs.

The third was to go with Hindu India. Sikhs had serious doubts about the assurances made by Nehru and Gandhi, but somehow, they succumbed to the false promises made to them by the cunning and deceitful Congress Party. They were well aware of the Brahmanical philosophy to assume Sikhism in its folds and vast interior. They had fought the mahants (chief priest, referring to a non-Sikh priest controlling a Sikh gurdwara) to take control of their gurdwaras and Darbar Sahib. They were cognizant of the fact that the Hindu hill kings had attacked Guru Gobind several times. These Hindu kings who had endured persecution under the Mughal rulers and considered them their worst enemies did not deliver on the promise of coming to the support of Banda Singh Bahadur's battle against the Mughals.

The brave Sikhs of Punjab are entitled to special considerations. I see nothing wrong in an area set up in the North of India wherein Sikhs also can experience the glow of freedom. (Jawahar Lal Nehru, *Lahore Bulletin*, January 9, 1930)

In the light of the above background, Sikhs had a sort of unofficial referendum to go with India under these conditions. Starting in 1947, India has reneged from all of the above assurances. Additionally Sikhs have been subjected to repression, persecution, and genocidal violence. There have been systematic attacks on their religion, language, and natural resources. There has been a systematic denial of their identity, right to free speech, language, and association. However, to their dismay, shortly after 1947, Sikhs discovered that they had missed the train of freedom for which they had paid a heavy price in the form of lives and blood. They had lost highly fertile land, their Sikh institutions, including Nankana Sahib Gurdwara (the birthplace of Guru Nanak, founder of Sikh religion) that were left in Pakistan Punjab. Thus it appears reasonable for them to seek independence by secession through the exercise of their right to self-determination under the United Nations Charter.

### Denial of Sikh Religious Identity

When India's Constitution was being drawn up in 1950, Sikh representatives Bhupinder Singh Mann and Hukum Singh refused to append their signatures to this document.[140] The Indian Constitution denied religious freedom to Sikhs. Despite the historically unchallenged status of Sikhism, after the partition, India's Constitution was drafted and promulgated in the face of Sikh members of the constitution assembly with provisions that dealt a fatal blow to the separate religious identity of Sikhs. Hukum Singh quoted B R Ambedkar, the main architect of the Indian Constitution: "*Democracy in India is only a top-dressing on Indian Soil, which is essentially undemocratic.*" He warned about emergency provisions, "*The mere Proclamation of Emergency ought not to have been allowed to abrogate civil liberties.*"[141] Hukum Singh stood vindicated when an emergency was imposed by PM Indira Gandhi in June 1975.

---

[140] https://asiasamachar.com/2020/09/21/33862/.
[141] Ibid.

Drawing the authority from Article 25 (b), the constitution labels "Sikhs as Hindus," the minority Sikh community is being denied many legal and religious rights, including the freedom to follow its family law, and by forcing the Sikh community to follow Hindu Personal Law. The legislation promulgated in India for the last several decades has clubbed Sikhs with Hindus so that Hindu Personal Law applies to Sikhs.

The Hindu Indian government exerts its dominance over Sikhs through such unjustifiable constitutional clauses. How would a Sikh accept that he/she is married by Hindu customs? A Sikh marriage ceremony is *Anand Karj*, also called *lavaan* (blissful union). A Sikh couple gets married by circumambulating around the Holy Scripture, Sri Guru Granth Sahib. At the same time, the *gyani* (priest) recites special hymns specifically marked for this purpose, authored by the fourth Sikh guru, Guru Ram Das. This is mind-boggling that successive Indian governments have not made any attempt to correct this monumental error in its constitution despite the protests. It is equivalent to stating that the Christians are Jews, Muslims are Christian, and Buddhists are Hindus. People are proud of their heritage. Denying them their religion or heritage is a violation of their dignity, downright dangerous, and playing with fire. It is the most insulting to a Sikh if someone calls him/her a Hindu.

Sikhs have a serious grievance that in India, Hindu law is applied to them when they are not Hindus. Such wrong labeling and classification violate fundamental principles of religious freedom and solidifies the denials of the separate religious identity of Sikhs. It is unjust on the part of the state, claiming itself secular, to compel a minority community to accept a label that challenges its independence and distinct nature and identity. For whatever reason, not even Manmohan Singh, Sikh prime minister of India from 2004–2014, could reverse this gross racial and hateful clause of the constitution.

### Denial of Statehood to Punjab

The *States Reorganization Act, 1956* was a major reform of the boundaries of India's states and territories, organizing them along linguistic lines. Although additional changes to India's state boundaries have been made since 1956, the States Reorganization Act of 1956 remains the single most extensive change in state boundaries since India's independence in 1947.

While the country's map was redrawn based on language, the Indian government remained resolutely opposed to the demand of a Punjabi-speaking state due to communal bias against Sikhs. Despite the secular and democratic principles of Sikhism, the religion and the religious prejudices remained the most dominating and dictating elements in the Congress Party's policy toward Punjab. The natural status for the Punjabi-speaking state based on the principle of equality was not only denied in the first place, but it was also vehemently opposed despite concentrated peaceful efforts by Sikh organizations.

When Master Tara Singh broached the subject of a linguistic Punjabi State with Sardar Patel, India's then-home minister, his reaction was very curt and astonishing. He said, "I am ready to concede it. However, you will have only so much land as falls to your proportion of the population. So, the Punjab area would be halved. And you will have to take back all Sikhs from the rest of India. Now you form 17% of the army.[142] They will have to be dismissed." Master Tara Singh felt aghast. This meant that while the commitment of the Congress for linguistic states was valid for other parts of the country, it was heretical for Sikhs to demand a Punjab State.

Dr. Ambedkar also raised the issue of Dalitstan with Mahatma Gandhi. Ambedkar was given an answer he was stunned to hear. Mahatma Gandhi told him that he will be risking the massacre of hundreds of thousands of Dalits in doing so. Ambedkar quietly backed off.[143]

Following this, Sikh leaders held several conferences, peaceful agitations, and tried to establish a Punjabi-speaking state, but all the efforts and demonstrations went unheeded. The impression gained

---

[142] *The Illustrated Weekly of India*, June 10–16, 1984.
[143] Gurdarshan S. Dhillon, "Struggle for Punjabi Speaking State," *Truth About Punjab: SGPC White Paper* (1996), 51.

traction among Sikhs that the discriminatory policies of the government were aimed at reducing them to a subpolitical status.

## Rejection and Criminalization of Peaceful Demand for Statehood of Punjab

Sikh leadership realized that the Congress leadership left them no voice but to start a campaign for a unilingual Punjabi-speaking state. Sikhs started peaceful agitations to bring the Congress government to the negotiation table to create the Punjabi-speaking state. However, the Sikhs peacefully demanding the creation of the state of Punjab were labeled as terrorists, separatist, and unpatriotic. In 1955, Indian Police entered the Darbar Sahib complex and arrested several Akali leaders. At this time, Sikhs were carrying out peaceful agitation for establishing Punjab State and not secession.

During the Punjabi Suba Morcha (campaign), Sikh protesters continued to grow in numbers. All the jails in Punjab had been filled, and it had become increasingly difficult to contain the Sikh movement. The movement was started by Shiromani Gurdwara Parbandhak Committee (the elected Sikh body to manage the gurdwaras) at Darbar Sahib. It was considered the headquarters of all the operations, and the government took strict measures to prevent Sikhs from going there. The police surrounded Darbar Sahib in large numbers. No one was allowed to enter the premises without permission and having been searched by the police. Many Sikhs were arrested just on the basis that they were going to Darbar Sahib. It was naturally assumed that they were going to join the protestors. Even tourists were insulted and arrested. This brutal action of the police was more than enough to awaken the Sikh nation. They marched toward Darbar Sahib in large numbers and forced police to retreat and leave the vicinity of Darbar Sahib.

Finally the Indian government decided to crush the movement by any means necessary. Ashwani Kumar, DIG of Jalandhar Police, asked for permission to practice unlimited privileges and promised to destroy the movement within five days. Upon getting permission, he ordered the police to confiscate handguns, rifles, and all other firearms kept by SGPC, Sikh leaders, and Akali Dal members. Censorship was put on Sikh newspapers, disallowing them to highlight the truth and educate the public of the real situation. The police stopped the printing of the newspapers and closed down the main buildings. Many Sikh journalists and news reporters were arrested. The police confiscated and burnt all of the printed materials. It was all part of the plan so that no one would know the extent of the police operation, and the public masses will stay uninformed.[144]

After disarming Sikh leadership, the police started its operation. First, Darbar Sahib was surrounded by thousands of police officers, and the public was stopped from going in and out of the complex. Then the rest houses were searched, and everyone found was arrested. All of the political members and leaders within the vicinity of Darbar Sahib were arrested and taken to jail. Everything was searched in the SGPC office. Then the police moved to Manji Sahib. When Sikhs protested, they were met with heavy sticks and tear gas.

By this time, the police had fortified every building standing outside of the main complex and started to throw tear and poisonous gas at Sikhs. Then the police entered the main complex and fired upon Sikhs gathered there to protest peacefully. Many bullets were fired at the main building and Akal Takht Sahib. All the religious activities such as *kirtan* and *Akhand Paath* were stopped, and every Sikh—including women—were verbally abused, beaten, and then arrested. This was all done to immobilize the Sikh movement for the statehood of Punjab. The police kept full control of Darbar Sahib for four days. More than three thousand Sikhs were arrested, including many of the leaders and employees of SGPC. Several thousands, including women and children, were injured.[145] Gurdwara Manji Sahib was also attacked; about two hundred Sikhs were massacred there.

---

[144] https://khalsaforce.in/4-july-1955%E2%80%AC-indian-police-entered-temple-precincts-used-tear-gas-disperse-assembled-volunteers/.
[145] https://khalsaforce.in/4-july-1955%E2%80%AC-indian-police-entered-temple-precincts-used-tear-gas-disperse-assembled-volunteers/.

Several peaceful agitations and demonstrations took place in Amritsar. The vehemence with which the Punjabi Hindus opposed Punjabi Suba invoked an equally strong support of Sikh masses in favor of it. However, the government remained unmoved. The negotiations between Sikh leadership and the government failed to bring about any resolution.

With the Chinese invasion of India in 1962, Akali Dal decided to suspend the demand for Punjabi Suba (state) and asked Sikhs to join the country's defense. *It is noteworthy that the Punjabi contribution in men and materials equaled the rest of the states put together.* Punjab contributed more than 20 million rupees to the National Defense fund, besides gold weighing twice the weight of Jawaharlal Nehru. Sant Fateh Singh presented a check of Rs. 50,000 to Jawahar Lal Nehru on behalf of the SGPC and called upon Sikhs to spare no effort to drive out the Chinese.

However, Jawahar Lal Nehru remained adamantly opposed to the creation of Punjabi Suba until his death in May 1964. His successor, Lal Bahadur Shatri, followed his footprints. He made it amply clear that Sikhs are not to be trusted. Sant Fateh Singh, Sikh religious and political leader, a key figure in the Punjabi Suba movement, declared on August 16, 1965, that he would go on fast-until-death on September 15, to highlight Sikhs' demand for Punjabi Suba. However, because of the Indo-Pak War, he decided on September 9, to postpone his fast. This gesture was highly appreciated by the then-president, Dr. S. Radhakrishnan.

The people of Punjab provided unparalleled support to Indian troops during the Indo-Pak War in 1965. Sikhs in the army fought gallantly. Sikh civilians showed unparalleled support for the country and the military till the cease-fire was declared on September 26, 1965. The governor of Punjab proudly stated that the people in Punjab—cultivators, traders, workmen, and even women everywhere—exhibited rare qualities of resourcefulness, forbearance, and fortitude. They gave valuable assistance to the army and the police in many ways and the public service of all categories played their role magnificently. The people of Punjab supported the Indian Armed Forces with enthusiasm and daring spirit. Ordinary people offered and provided whatever resources they possessed. Truck drivers drove their vehicles into the war zone to keep the supply lines open to the military forces.[146]

Impressed by the Punjab people's contribution, the country felt unable to resist the demand for a Punjab-speaking state anymore. Accordingly the decision to reorganize the state of Punjab on a linguistic basis was taken at the meeting of the Congress Working Committee, which passed this resolution—"Out of the existing state of Punjab, a state with Punjabi as State language be formed. The government is requested to take necessary steps for this purpose."[147]

Home Minister Nanda's response to Indira Gandhi was that he had suggested Hukum Singh's name for the chairman of the committee under the mistaken impression that he was opposed to Punjabi Suba demand. At that time, it was too late to mend matters. Hukum Singh later wrote, "The intention of the government then was to use me against my community, secure an adverse report, and then reject the demand for Punjabi Suba."[148]

Gulzari Lal Nanda (then India's home minister) continued to oppose the Punjabi Suba and put obstacles at every step and tried to make the demarcation on a communal basis and not a linguistic basis. He refused to accept the linguistic boundaries, unambiguously demarcated and for long accepted by all concerned. Nanda took multiple steps to oppose the formation of the Punjabi Suba. First, he appointed Boundary Commission, which was not necessary at all. Second, he made the 1961 census, which was officially known to be communally oriented and frivolous, to be the basis for demarcation. This was the proof that the demarcation had to be on a communal basis and not a linguistic basis. Third, in the framing of the Punjab Reorganization Act (1966), he introduced provisions (78–80), which made Punjabi Suba permanently an ineffective substate.[149]

---

[146] Mark Tully and Satish Jacob, *Amritsar: Mrs. Gandhi's Last Battle* (New Delhi, 1985), 42.

[147] *The Statesman*, March 10, 1966.

[148] *Indian Express*, April 4, 1983.

[149] Gurdarshan Singh Dhillon, *Truth About Punjab: SGPC, Amritsar, White Paper* (1996), 60.

Punjab Reorganization Act 1966 resulted in handing over the control, administration, maintenance, distribution, and development of the waters and hydel power of Punjab rivers to the central government. This act violated the Indian Constitution because (a) it made legislation about the river waters and hydel powers of Punjab rivers, though these subjects were in the exclusive jurisdiction of the states; and (b) it was discriminatory because it honored the riparian principle to Yamuna waters by letting it remain as a subject for the exclusive jurisdiction of the Haryana government, while at the same time, it provided central control for the maintenance, distribution, and development of the water and the hydel power of Punjab rivers.

After great hardship, a large number of peaceful demonstrations, loss of lives of hundreds of Sikhs, when Punjabi Suba was finally created in 1966, it was much smaller and about one-tenth of the original state of Punjab before 1947. This too happened only when the Indian government was under so much pressure and was left with no choice but to accede to the demand of Sikhs. It is important to note that the Punjabi-Hindu leadership opposed Punjabi Suba to the end. The state that was finally created was crippled and turned into a permanently ineffective substate under the virtual control of the Indian government. The powers kept by the Indian government had a far-reaching effect in ruining the economic well-being and future of the people of Punjab. It was this permanent reduction of Punjab to a virtual central government "colony" that became the basis of the Akali struggle during the subsequent years.

## India's News Media's Bias Against Sikhs

Sikh-Hindu relationship was quite amicable until 1947. However, since then, it started to deteriorate when the Punjabi Hindus did not support the Punjabi Suba movement. They denied Punjabi as their language under the influence of the central government and the government-controlled Indian news media. This led to the Punjab State being smaller than it could have been had the Punjabi Hindus declared the language they spoke. The relationship got further strained when the active association of Arya Samaj leaders, many of whom were influential in the Congress Party, openly favored the Nirankaris. The Arya Samaj leadership and their influence were a major factor in the deterioration of the Sikh-Hindu relationship. It is also evident in the report "Hindu-Sikh Conflict in Punjab: Causes and Cure" by S. M. Sathananthan (London), K. T. Lalwani (London), S. Raghunath Iyenger (Lagos), Prof. G. P. Mansukhani (Bombay), and Asha Bhatnagar (Jaipur) et al. They came to Punjab from faraway places and studied the situation. They moved from place to place and met many people and concluded that the Sikhs are denied their basic rights for which they have to launch agitations. These same rights are freely available to the majority community of India. Their conclusion was based on the fact that the people of Punjab were denied their state when other states were created, and the capital city of Chandigarh was not given to Punjab. The majority of the Hindu population of Punjab opposed Punjabi Suba, and Sikhs alone had to struggle for Punjab statehood.

The report stated:

> If you were to trace the background of a reporter or an editor behind a particular anti-Sikh report, you would probably find him to be an Arya-Samaji. Late Lala Jagat Narain's persistent role in anti-Sikh activities (including those of his support to the Nirankaris) and his staunch communal tendencies were reflected in his popular daily newspaper in Punjab.[150]

### Unconstitutional Denial of Rights of Sikhs

Lala Jagat Narain, the founder of Hind Samachar Media Group, was critical of Sant Bhindranwale's increasing influence and demands for justice and equal treatment for Sikhs. Narain carried out propaganda of blasphemy against Guru Gobind Singh, tenth Sikh guru, the founder of Khalsa. Guru Gobind Singh had sacrificed his entire

---

[150] Sathananthan et al., *Hindu Sikh Conflict in Punjab—Causes and Cure* (1983).

family, including his four sons, wife, father, Guru Tegh Bahadur, and his mother, Mata Gujri. No Sikh will ever tolerate any blasphemy against Guru Gobind Singh. It was unfortunate that the more reckless the criticism by the Arya Samaj press, led by Lala Jagat Narayan, the greater the bitterness and injury among Sikhs at all levels. During this charged atmosphere, Lala Jagat Narain was murdered on September 9, 1981.[151] The next day, a mob of Hindus attacked Sikh shops and burnt the Akali Patrika premises in Jalandhar. Some passerby Sikhs also fell victim to the mob's fury.[152] This incident created a sensation, and many Hindus started blaming Sant Bhindranwale. The Punjab Police, under pressure from the Hindu press, came to a hasty conclusion of finding a link between the public speeches of Sant Bhindranwale and the murder of Jagat Narain. However, the police could not find any clear evidence of the direct or indirect involvement of Sant Bhindranwale.

At the time of the murder, Sant Bhindranwale was on a preaching mission at Chando Kalan, a small town in the Hassar district of Haryana State. When Police arrived at Chando Kalan with warrants of his arrest, Bhindranwale had already left. After this, a contingent of five hundred police officers of Punjab and Haryana surrounded the village of Chando Kalan on the night of September 12, 1981 and behaved disgracefully with the innocent Sikh inhabitants, including women, elderly men, and children. Every Sikh house was searched, and their valuables were reported to have been looted. The policemen set on fire two of the Taksal's buses containing several copies of Sri Guru Granth Sahib (SGGS). This sacrilegious act committed by the police made the government's position indefensible in the eyes of Sikhs. There were protests all over the state against this act of sacrilege of SGGS. On September 16, 1981, police lathi-charged (beaten by sticks) the students of Khalsa College, Amritsar, peacefully demonstrating against the incident of Chando Kala. The police

---

[151] G. S. Dhillon, *India Commits Suicide* (Chandigarh: Singh and Singh Publishers, 1992), 148.

[152] *The Ajit*, September 11, 12, 1981.

entered the campus of the college and beat the students studying in their hostels.[153]

Meanwhile, when Sant Bhindranwale reached his headquarters at Gurdwara Gurdarshan Prakash at Chowk Mehta, it was surrounded by the police and paramilitary forces. On the other hand, several thousand Sikhs from all over the state gathered outside and inside the gurdwara to protect Sant Bhindranwale. After ascertaining that he was wanted by the police, he informed the authorities that he will offer himself for arrest on September 20, 1981, at the appointed time. Before his arrest, Sant Bhinderanwalle advised his supporters not to turn violent under any circumstances when police took him away.

The mayhem following his arrest climaxed with police gunfire resulting in the death of eighteen innocent Sikhs and is said to have been staged by the government intelligence agencies.[154] When Sant Jarnail Singh Bhindranwale was being taken away, despite his advice and the entreaties by his staff for everyone to stay calm and peaceful, some people became emotional. According to one account,[155] someone tried to grapple with the senior superintendent of police on duty. There are reports that this too was orchestrated to give police an excuse to open fire. Birdal Nath, the then-director general of police, had regarded Lala Jagat Narain's murder as his loss, and other members of the Punjab bureaucracy wanted a good slaughter of Sikhs at Chowk Mehta. He planned to storm the Chowk and had a commando unit trained for capturing Bhindranwale. Joginder Singh Anand, deputy inspector general, later committed suicide presumably[156] because of remorse associated with this massacre. The sant's arrest and the massacre led to a violent reaction in several places,

---

[153] Anil Saari, "Mehta Chowk: Could the Clash Have Been Avoided?" *Sunday Edition*, October 4, 1981, p.15.

[154] https://www.sikhiwiki.org/index.php/Misrepresentation_and_vilification_of_Sant_Bhindranwale_%3D%3D, part 3.

[155] Personal conversation with a member of the family of the police officer involved.

[156] Letter from Simranjit S. Mann to chief secretary to government, Punjab, dated January 22, 1984.

followed by more oppression. It was much later, after continued demands by Sikh leadership, that the inquiry was instituted.

According to Sant Jarnail Singh Bhindranwale:[157]

> There was an inquiry into the Mehta affair. Amrik Singh and others were working in connection with that. They were arrested and put in jail. The inquiry was completed, but it was not made public. This is because, according to its findings, many big leaders will have to be punished. They are sitting on it.

## Denial of Bodies of Sikhs Murdered by Police to Their Families

The authorities routinely refused to release the bodies of Sikhs killed by police gunfire in faked encounters to the families of the victims. Sant Bhindranwale repeatedly mentioned that the bodies of the victims of the September 20, 1981 police gunfire at Chowk Mehta were not returned to the families, nor were their post-mortem examination reports made public. The police regularly followed the policy of disposing of the bodies of Sikhs as unclaimed,[158] denying the families the simple solace of a funeral. Many Sikhs were simply kidnaped and disappeared. In 1995, Jaswant Singh Khalra, a human rights activist, was abducted, tortured, and murdered by police.[159] His body was disposed of by the police and never given to his family. This chapter is continued as the Rise of Sant Jarnail Singh Bhindranwale.

---

[157] Sant Jarnail Singh Bhindranwale's speech on July 19, 1983.
[158] Ram Narayan Kumar and Lorenz Skerjanz, *Disappearances in Punjab* (1995).
[159] "Activist Khalra Custodial Death: SC Upholds Life in Jail for Punjab Cops."

# Rise of Sant Jarnail Singh Khalsa Bhindranwale

*Sant Jarnail Singh Khalsa Bhindranwale*, leader of the Sikh organization Damdami Taksal, was born on June 2, 1947, in Punjab, in village Rode in the Faridkot district. From his childhood, he had a strong religious inclination. He joined the Taksal as a student in 1965. He was a brilliant student, gifted with unusual memory, who grew up to be an effective preacher of Sikhism. At thirty years of age, on August 25, 1977, he succeeded Sant Kartar Singh as head of Taksal.

From July 1977–July 1982, he toured cities and Punjab villages extensively to preach the Sikh faith. His message was to quit drugs, take *amrit* (the baptismal process in Sikhism), and become a *gursikh* (good Sikh). His teachings were based on love. He said, "If we speak to someone with hatred and try to assert our superiority, it will create hatred in the mind of everyone. So long we have the spirit of love, so long as we have the support of Satguru[160] Hargobind Sahib, the Master of Miri and Piri,[161] is there any power that can subdue us?"[162]

Sant Jarnail Singh Bhindranwale had a compelling personality and spoke simple village idioms. Those who listened to him were impressed by his simple living, personal charm, and clear thinking.

---

[160] *Satguru* means "the true guru;" used for any of Sikh gurus and Sri Guru Granth Sahib.

[161] *Miri* is temporal power, and *piri* is spiritual authority. Sri Hargobind Sahib wore two swords representing miri and piri. He is often referred to as the master of miri and piri.

[162] Ranbir Singh Sandhu, *Struggle for Justice: Speeches and Conversations of Sant Jarnail Singh Khalsa Bhindranwale* (1999), i.

Joyce Pettigrew, who met him in 1980, wrote,[163] "There was a very close association between the Sant and the people, as I witnessed, on a visit to meet Sant Bhindranwale in Guru Nanak Niwas."

He became popular because of his sharp and clear thinking about the Indian government's discrimination against Sikhs and the undermining of Sikh identity. When he raised his voice against the injustice and persecution of Sikhs, he was labeled as a separatist and terrorist. The police would capture his men and subject them to unspeakable tortures without arresting them or filing any charges against them. His popularity increased when he objected to the killing of thirteen unarmed Sikhs who were peacefully objecting to the desecration of Sikhism by Nirankari Sikhs. In the ensuing court case, all the sixty-two accused were set free; none were punished. This enraged Sikhs, and Bhindranwale was the only Sikh leader to object to this gross injustice.

He jolted Sikhs to the realization that they are slaves in India, the country that they call their own, and the country for which they made infinite sacrifices. Sant Jarnail Singh Bhindranwale and the other martyrs who suffered harassment, religious discrimination, and persecution peacefully exposed and resisted state oppression; and finally, when attacked in their place of worship by the Indian Army, gave their lives in defense of their faith and freedom.

## A Sampling of Sant Jarnail Singh Bhindranwale's Views

Sant Bhindranwale clearly defined his mission by stating that his goal was to administer amrit (formal initiation into Sikh faith), to explain the meaning of *Gurbani* (contents of the Sikh Holy Scripture), and to teach Gurbani to those around him. He emphasized that a Hindu should be a true Hindu, a Muslim a true Muslim, and a Sikh a true Sikh.

Sant Bhindranwale promoted respect for all faiths. He never demanded Khalistan. He further clarified that we (Sikhs) are not in

---

[163] Joyce Pettigrew, *Sikhs of the Punjab: Unheard Voices of State and Guerrilla Violence* (London: Zed Books Ltd., 1995), 35.

favor of Khalistan nor are we against it. He did state that an Indian Army attack on Darbar Sahib will lay down the foundation of Khalistan (independent Punjab). He wanted the police to protect the public, rather than rob the people by extortion and bribery.

On possession of weapons:

> With reference to weapons, I shall only say that you should bear arms. If armed, there is no greater sin for a Sikh than attacking an unarmed person, killing an innocent person, looting a shop, harming the innocent, or wishing to insult anyone's daughter or sister. Also, being armed, there is no sin greater than not seeking justice. (Speech, October 20, 1983)

On defending Darbar Sahib:

> Do not commit any excesses, do not be unfair to anyone, but just as for a Muslim there is nothing but wilderness beyond Mecca, for a Sikh of the Guru, there is nothing but wilderness beyond Darbar Sahib. We do not go to anyone's home, we do not loot anyone's shop, nor do we lay siege to any place. However, if someone intoxicated by his power as a ruler attacks our home, we are not sitting here wearing bangles that we shall continue to suffer as eunuchs and as lifeless people. (Speech, May 18, 1983)[164]

Sant Bhindranwale was a religious leader who, early on, understood the open and the clandestine Indian plan to weaken Punjab and engulf Sikhism into Hindu folds. When in 1956, under the State

---

[164] Ranbir Singh Sandhu, *Struggle for Justice: Speeches and Conversations of Sant Jarnail Singh Bhindranwale* (Dublin: Sikh Educational and Religious Foundation, 1999), vi.

Reorganization Act, the state of Punjab was not created by denying the official status to the Punjabi language, the Sikhs came to
realize the deeper anti-Sikh and anti-Punjab sentiment of the Indian
government. When they carried out peaceful protests for the creation of Punjab (state), they were attacked, arrested, killed, tortured,
and humiliated.[165] Bhindranwale brought the awakening in the Sikh
masses to make them realize and understand how their rights were
crushed by labeling them as terrorists, separatists, and unpatriotic.
The state-supported Indian news media portrayed Bhindranwale as
a religious fanatic, anti-Hindu, and anti-India who wanted to break
up the country. However, until the last day of his life, Bhindranwale
did not demand Khalistan, contrary to the Indian government's propaganda. He, however, did state that an Indian government attack on
Darbar Sahib will lay down the foundation stone of an independent
Punjab (Khalistan).

Tully and Jacob state that "Despite the Government's propaganda, for many people, Bhindranwale remained a saint, or holy
man, not a terrorist."[166] The religious revival led by Sant Jarnail
Singh Bhindranwale resulted in a large number of Sikhs, especially
the youth, receiving initiation into the Sikh faith. According to
Khushwant Singh:

> Bhindranwale's Amrit Prachar (imparting
> education to take Amrit—a process for initia-
> tion into the order of Khalsa) was a resounding
> success. Adults in the thousands who took oaths
> in public to abjure liquor, tobacco, and drugs,
> were baptized. Videocassettes showing blue
> films and cinema houses lost out to the village
> Gurdwaras. Men not only saved money they had
> earlier squandered in self-indulgence but now

---

[165] https://khalsaforce.in/4-july-1955%E2%80%AC-indian-police-entered-
temple-precincts-used-tear-gas-disperse-assembled-volunteers/.
[166] Mark Tully and Satish Jacob, *Amritsar: Mrs. Gandhi's Last Battle* (New Delhi:
Rupa, 1985), 205–206.

worked longer hours on their lands and raised better crops. They had much to be grateful for to Bhindranwale, who came to be revered by them as Baba Sant Jarnail Singhji Bhindranwale. [167]

When Sant Bhindranwale stayed at Darbar Sahib complex during 1982 and 1983, four to five hundred persons were administered amrit each Wednesday and Sunday. On April 13,[168] 1983, over ten thousand were initiated, and during the month, ending on April 13, 1984 (as per Sikh calendar), forty-five thousand Sikhs received amrit. This revival was extremely significant, and the Sant Bhindranwale was emerging as the leading figure in the Sikh faith and a role model for the youth.

People sought his advice and intercession for personal problems and conflict resolution. Khushwant Singh reports:[169]

> One day a young girl came to see Bhindranwale,... She clutched his feet and sobbed out her story of how she was maltreated by her husband's family for failing to extract money from her parents and her husband's unwillingness to take her side. Bhindranwale asked her name and where she lived. "So, you are a daughter of the Hindus," he asked. "Are you willing to become the daughter of a Sikh?" She nodded yes. Bhindranwale sent a couple of his armed guards to fetch the girl's family. An hour later, a very frightened trio consisting of the girl's

---

[167] Khushwant Singh, *A History of Sikhs*, Volume 2: 1839–1988, Second Edition, (Delhi: Oxford University Press, 1991), 329.

[168] April 13, is a special holiday for Sikhs. It is the first day of the month of *Vaisakh* in Bikrami calendar. On this day in 1699, Guru Gobing Singh Sahib introduced a new process for formal initiation into Sikh faith. It is called receiving amrit (Amrit Chhakna) or *Khande dee Pahul*.

[169] Kuldip Nayar and Khushwant Singh, *Tragedy of Punjab* (New Delhi: Vision Books, 1984), 23.

husband and his parents were brought to his presence. "Is this girl a daughter of your household?" he demanded. They admitted that she was. "She tells me that you want money from her father. I am her father." He placed a tray full of currency notes before them and told them, "Take whatever you want." The three fell at his feet and craved forgiveness.

## Sant Jarnail Singh Bhindranwale Highlighted the Following Facts

*India versus Punjab*—When the rest of India was organized into linguistic status, Jawaharlal Nehru adamantly refused to agree to the creation of a Punjabi-speaking state. He feared that the creation of such a state would solidify Sikh identity with the homeland and a language with the resulting potential for secession. This attitude amounts to tyranny by the majority and effectively eliminates the safeguards provided in the constitution.

When speaking before the United Nations Human Rights Commission, Mr. G. Ramaswamy, India's attorney general, admitted that while it is his dream to bring about a Uniform Civil Code in India, most members of Parliament belonged to a majority religion, making it difficult to enact laws affecting religious minorities. However, this is an easy excuse to soften the criticism of India by the United Nations. First of all, India need not enact any new laws to protect minorities; laws to protect them already exist on the books. Second, India has been persistently violating the Universal Declaration of Human Rights. India has not ratified the UNCAT, United Nations Convention Against Torture and Other Cruel, Inhuman or Degrading Treatment or Punishment.

Arbitrary and hostile misinterpretation of Sikh prayer Raj Karega Khalsa—the Khalsa shall rule was one of the devices used to declare that this minority faith in India as inherently antinational and to eliminate those who chose to adhere to its beliefs, principles, and values. Some of the Indian press sections have consistently criticized religious minorities and made highly provocative and derogatory pronouncements about them. There has been no attempt by the government to check on this. Whenever the minorities have tried to protest these actions, they have been physically assaulted, fired upon, falsely imprisoned, tortured, raped, and massacred.[170]

Sant Bhindranwale believed that the Indian government had treated Sikhs and the state of Punjab as unworthy of equal rights and equal treatment under the law because they were suspected of secession. *However, this discriminatory behavior of the successive Indian governments compelled Sikhs to ask for secession.* Had the Indian governments paid attention to the genuine demands—which were already promised and agreed upon but later denied—Sikhs would not have been pursuing the independent Sikh state. Sant Bhindranwale wanted justice and equal treatment, which was not only denied but also strongly opposed. This was and still is the bone of contention between India and Sikhs.

### Equating Linguistic Identity with Political Separation

Since India's freedom from British rule, Sikhs demanded the creation of Punjab as a linguistic state. The militants among the Punjabi Hindus who opposed the formation of Punjab state presented the following reasoning to the parliamentary committee,[171] "The real motive underlying this demand is to have an area in which Sikhs are the majority and which can ultimately be carved out as an independent state and a sort of buffer state between India and Pakistan." This is a direct contradiction of the fact that Punjabi Hindus outnumbered Sikhs two to one in 1951. Besides, this was the right granted to all other major linguistic groups in India, which was deliberately denied to Punjab.

---

[170] Ranbir Singh Sandhu, *Struggle for Justice: Speeches and Conservations of Sant Jarnail Singh Bhindranwale* (1999), viii.

[171] Sanyukt Punajb Sanrakshan Samiti, *Memorandum Presented to the Parliamentary Committee on Punjabi Suba of Sarvadeshik Arya Pratinidhi Sahba* (New Delhi), 18.

## Initiation of Violence Against Sikhs

Sant Jarnail Singh Bhindranwale repeatedly declared[172] that he would never initiate a dispute or a confrontation. Tavleen Singh[173] reports:

> Contrary to the popular belief that he took the offensive, senior police sources in Punjab admit that the provocation came in fact from a Nirankari official who started harassing Bhindranwale and his men. There were two or three Nirankaris in key positions in Punjab in those days, and they were powerful enough to create a lot of trouble. The Nirankaris also received patronage from Delhi that made Sikh organizations like Bhindranwale's and the Akhand Kirtani Jatha, headed then by Bibi Amarjit Kaur's husband Fauja Singh, hate them even more.

According to Khushwant Singh, "Terrorist activity proceeded the Morcha[174] by more than six months and was born out of encounters faked by the Punjab Police, and the armed conflict between the Nirankaris and Sant Jarnail Singh Bhindranwale beginning April 13, 1978."

Harry Reasoner of CBS News[175] met Sant Jarnail Singh Bhindranwale in May 1984. About his conversation with the Sant, he reported,[176] "A Sikh is never an oppressor but only defends himself and his people. He said that I have never initiated any attack with my

---

[172] For example: Sant Jarnail Singh Bhindranwale's speech on May 18, 1983 and Harry Reasoner's report on CBS News *60 Minutes.*

[173] Tavleen Singh, "Terrorist in the Temple," *The Tribune Story*, ed. by Amarjit Kaur et al. (New Delhi: Roli Books, 1984), 32.

[174] *Morcha* is an organized struggle, movement, or campaign; here it refers to the peaceful protest movement started on August 4, 1982, by Shromani Akali Dal.

[175] Ranbir Singh Sandhu, *Struggle for Justice: Speeches and Conservations of Sant Jarnail Singh Khalsa Bhindranwale* (1999), l.

[176] Harry Reasoner, *60 Minutes*, CBS News, June 10, 1984.

tongue or my pen or with my sword. I only answer back or retaliate, he said, to actions initiated by the enemies of Sikhs."

When mobs, led by extremist Hindu organizations, repeatedly set upon and massacred Sikhs in various cities in Punjab and neighboring states, no protection or support was given by the law-enforcement agencies to the victims of this violence. Often, it was the victims of violence who were arrested. The attackers' actions were justified as an "understandable" reaction to Sant Bhindranwale's inflammatory speeches regarding human rights violations. For example, Tully and Jacob report,[177] "Satish Jacob saw police looking on as Hindu mobs burnt down the Gurdwara in Panipat... Sikhs pulled off buses and forcibly shaved. Eight were clubbed to death."

Any demonstrations or other protests organized by Sikhs against these atrocities were met with extreme police violence. In his speeches, Sant Bhindranwale emphasized[178] that at no time in history had any Sikh set fire to Hindu scriptures or a Sikh mob set upon any Hindus or their temples.

## Staged Crimes

To brand devout Sikhs as criminals, the government stage-managed numerous crimes. The police would orchestrate a crime and then ascribe it to Sant Bhindranwale. Following this, the law enforcement agencies would round up devout Sikhs, harass, rape, torture, and often eliminate them. Some heads of dead cows were discovered in the Hindu temple in Amritsar. The government and the Hindu press immediately placed the blame on Bhindranwale. The crime was staged. According to the report:[179]

Surinder Kapoor MLA created a sensation, when in a meeting of the Congress (Indira)

---

[177] Mark Tully and Satish Jacob, *Amritsar: Mrs. Gandhi's Last Battle* (New Delhi: Rupa, 1985), 117.

[178] https://www.youtube.com/watch?v=gX21Pvr0kok.

[179] *Delhi Recorder*, May 1983.

151

Legislative Party, Punjab, held March 6, 1983, he accused the then government of Punjab of hatching a conspiracy at Mohali of cutting a few heads of the dead cows and actually conveying them to Amritsar and throwing them stealthily in some Hindu temple and thus lit the first communal fire in the State.

Sant Bhindranwale and the All India Sikh Student Federation had nothing to do with this. They denied any involvement and denounced this activity but were blamed by the same government that showed no interest in persecuting a person caught red-handed throwing tobacco in the Darbar Sahib premises.[180] Bhindranwale explained, "No Sikh is in favor of placing cows' heads in the temple. We are also not in favor of killing the cow."[181]

Expressing his views on Khalistan, contrary to the Indian propaganda, Sant Jarnail Singh Bhindranwale did not advocate an independent Sikh state. His purpose in going to Darbar Sahib in July 1982, was to obtain, through peaceful protest, the release of Bhai Amrik Singh and other associates who, he believed, had been wrongfully arrested. When specifically questioned on the issue of Khalistan, he answered why the Sikh nation would want to break up the country for which it had made extreme sacrifices. "However, if the Indian government gives it to us, we will not decline the offer." He also stated that an Indian Army attack on Darbar Sahib would lay down the foundation of independent Punjab Khalistan.

### Sant Bhindranwale's Statement to the News Media About the Persecution of Sikhs

Most of the violence that took place in Punjab was falsely attributed to Bhindranwale. In an interview with a *Sunday* corre-

---

[180] Sant Jarnail Singh Bhindranwale interview in January 1983. Injuring a cow is offensive to Hindus; so is exposure to tobacco for Sikhs.
[181] Sant Jarnail Singh Bhindranwale's speech in February 1983.

spondent, he stated that the targets of his attacks were the "guilty" policemen who unleashed repression on the innocent Sikhs. He elaborated his argument by furnishing the following facts:

> A Sikh girl was stripped naked, and her father was forced to rape her... This happened in village Kahlkhurd, Moga Tehsil. The name of the father was Jagmir Singh; he was a scheduled caste. Write on...he told the journalist. A Sikh girl was stripped naked and paraded around Daoke village by policemen... They caught a Hindu policeman smoking biris (cigarettes), who spat in his mouth of Sikh Granthi (priest), and put tobacco into it. The name of Sikh was Jasbir Singh, village Chukpiti, Tehsil Moga. They caught another Sikh, and without finding anything on him, they (police) cut his thigh, tore the flesh out, and poured salt into the cuts. His name is Jagir Singh, village Ittanwali, he lives in Moga. Is this not wrong? There are no restrictions on the Hindu religious symbol; why is there a restriction on our (Sikh) religious symbol? Is this not discrimination? Then, where is it written that the police can get permission from the judge for a medical examination, and then instead of doing that, they take hot iron bars, shove them into the stomach, burn their foreheads, and "bhunno" (roast) them with bullets while they are still in their custody? Which law gives the government the right to do this? Kulwant Singh Nagoke (a Sikh freedom-fighter) was killed in police custody.[182] Jaswant Singh and Sukhdev Singh of Issathan had their stomachs burst open, and the flesh pulled from their bodies with sticks and

---

[182] https://www.1984tribute.com/shaheed-bhai-kulwant-singh-nagoke/.

their eyes taken out before being shot. Will they tell us what they found on them? What proof do they have against them?[183]

## Denial of Justice to Sikhs (Nirankari Massacre of Sikhs on April 13, 1978)

Nirankari (Punjabi word for "followers of the Formless One," i.e., God) is a religious reform movement within Sikhism. Nirankaris believe that God is formless, or Nirankar (hence the name Nirankari). They accept the authority of a living spiritual guide (Sikhs do not believe in a living guru, except SGGS being the virtual living guru). Its members differ from other Sikhs in their disapproval of the militant brotherhood of the Khalsa.

The Nirankaris held this convention in Amritsar on April 13, 1978. One day before the convention, on April 12, 1978, the Nirankaris took out a procession, during which their chief allegedly made some derogatory remarks against the Sikh religion. These provocative remarks led to much resentment among Sikh circles.

The next day, the followers of Sant Jarnail Singh Bhindranwale and those of Akhand Kirtani Jatha went unarmed to dissuade the Nirankari chief from denigrating the Sikh religion and its gurus.[184] The Nirankaris, who were well equipped with rifles and stun guns, fired at the approaching Sikhs, resulting in the death of thirteen of them. The tragedy was not circumstantial. Sikhs have been objecting to the way the Nirankaris have been violating and denunciating Sikh tenets. However, the Nirankaris had become more vocal with the clandestine support from the government.

A case was registered against sixty-two Nirankaris, including the Nirankari chief Gurbachan Singh and Niranjan Singh, an Indian administrative services officer, for being allegedly involved in the murders. The case was moved to Karnal from Amritsar, under the impression that a fair trial may be difficult because of the high profile

---

[183] G. S. Dhillon, *India Commits Suicide* (1992), 163.
[184] *The Tribune*, April 14, 1978.

of the case and the behavior of the press. However, in reality, the real cause was the predetermined outcome of the case and the expected high degree of public response and outcry from Sikhs if the trial were to be held in Amritsar. Sikhs also realized the pro-Nirankari attitude of the government because of the nonarrest of Baba Gurbachan Singh in pursuit of the warrants issued against him in the murder case and the transfer of the case out of Punjab.

The sessions court in Karnal acquitted all the sixty-two Nirankaris, including their chief, in the killings of the thirteen Sikhs in Amritsar on April 13, 1978. All Sikh organizations, including Akhand Kirtani Jatha and the Damdami Taksal, led by Sant Jarnail Singh Bhindranwale, raised many hues and an outcry against the decision since thirteen Sikhs were killed, and no one was punished.[185] The Akali government filed an appeal in high court against the verdict of the sessions judge, but surprisingly it was withdrawn when Punjab came under the president's rule.

## Exposing the Truth About Punjab

What transpired in India from 1947 onward can be summed up concisely as follows:

First, they came for your state and trifurcated it.

Then, they came for your religion and called you Hindus.

Then, they came for your language and denied it.

Then, they came for your state capital and made it a union territory.

Then, they came for your river waters and took—70% away.

---

[185] *The Indian Express*, January 5, 1980.

Then, they came for your religious institutions, invaded Darbar Sahib, and razed Akal-Takhat to the ground.

Then, they came with black-draconian laws, UAPA and TADA, and locked you up.

Then, they came for your women and violently gang-raped them.

Then, they carried out your genocide, and keep coming back for more.

Then, they came for your youth, and extra-judicially killed them.

Then, when you ask for justice, they call you terrorists, separatists, and anti-nationals.

Now India is coming for your land. Even though the farm laws enacted in 2020 were annulled in November 2021, the threat of land grab in Punjab persists as it has been on India's radar for decades.

Thus, the Sikhs are now at a crossroads. They need to decide their options. The question for them is: Do they want to maintain the status quo and continue to endure repression, persecution, econocide, and genocide? Or, do they want to reestablish the sovereignty of Punjab to protect their rights and thwart the looming existential threat in India?[186]

## Last Days of Sant Jarnail Singh Bhindranwale

Sant Bhindranwale had no political ambitions. He wanted to administer Amrit and teach Sikhi to the Sikh masses. He clearly understood human inequality and discrimination against Sikhs at every level in Punjab and India. As he advocated for justice, the

---

[186] Dr. Bakhshish Singh Sandhu MD, For Sikhs, "Independent Punjab-Khalistan Is the Only Option," November 1, 2020.

government labeled him a terrorist and separatist. The government used this as an excuse to repress further and persecute Sikhs to win the Hindu vote. India's government has never addressed the Punjab issue as political, denied Sikhs and Punjabis of their rights, which are ordinarily given to other Indians without asking. This has led to further alienation of Sikhs who have realized that they would never get justice and equal rights while India rules Punjab. Indian Army invaded Darbar Sahib (GTA) in June 1984, leading to the killing of about ten thousand Sikhs, which could have been easily avoided. The attack was preplanned and rehearsed for about two years, not to capture a political figure but to break Sikhs morally, physically, and economically.

Sant Jarnail Singh Khalsa Bhindranwale merged with his creator on the night between June 5 and 6, 1984, during the Indian Army invasion of Darbar Sahib.

# Indian Police Attack on Darbar Sahib 1955

Sikhs were carrying on their peaceful struggle to form a Punjabi-speaking state by peacefully offering arrests, shouting, "Punjabi Suba Zindabad" (long live Punjab State). On July 4, 1955, the government of India ordered police to enter Akal Takht and the Golden Temple complex. Achchar Singh, Jathedar Akal Takht, along with many others, were arrested. Police used tear gas and fired on the premises. About two hundred Sikhs were killed by the Indian forces, three thousand were injured, and more than twelve thousand arrested during the attack. Instances of government high-handedness and interference continued increasing. The backlash was immediate. So severe were its effects that the Punjab chief minister, Bhim Sen Sachar, presented himself before the Akal Takht to apologize for the attack.

During the Punjabi Suba Morcha (campaign), Sikh protesters continued to grow in numbers. All the jails in Punjab had been filled, and it had become increasingly difficult to contain the Sikh movement. Since the movement was started at Darbar Sahib, it was considered headquarters of all the operations, and the government took strict measures to prevent Sikhs from going to Darbar Sahib. The police surrounded Darbar Sahib. No one was allowed to enter the premises without permission and having been searched by the police. Many Sikhs were arrested just on the basis that they were going to Darbar Sahib. It was naturally assumed that they were going to join the protestors. Even tourists were insulted and arrested. This brutal action of the police was more than enough to awaken the Sikh nation. They marched toward Darbar Sahib in large numbers and forced police to retreat and leave the vicinity of Darbar Sahib.

Finally, the Indian government decided to crush the movement by all means necessary. Ashwani Kumar, DIG of Jalandhar (out of town from the adjoining district) Police, asked for permission to practice unlimited privileges and promised to destroy the movement within five days. Upon getting permission, he ordered the police to confiscate handguns, rifles, and other firearms belonging to the SGPC. Censorship was put on Sikh newspapers, disallowing them to highlight the truth and describe the real situation. The police stopped the printing of the newspapers and closed down the main buildings. Many Sikh journalists and news reporters were arrested, their printed materials confiscated and burnt by the police. It was all a part of the plan so that no one would know the extent of the police operation, and the public will stay uninformed.

After disarming Sikh leadership, the police started its operation. First, Darbar Sahib was surrounded by thousands of police officers, and the public was stopped from going in and out of the Darbar Sahib complex. Then all the rest houses were searched, and everyone found was arrested. All of the political members and leaders within the vicinity of Darbar Sahib were arrested and taken to jail. Everything was searched in the SGPC office. Then the police moved to Manji Sahib. When Sikhs protested, they were met with heavy sticks and tear gas.

By this time, the police had fortified every building standing outside of the main complex and started to throw tear and poisonous gas at Sikhs. Then the police entered the main complex with shoes and fired upon Sikhs who had gathered there to protest peacefully. Many bullets were fired at the main building and Akal Takht Sahib. All the religious activities, such as kirtan (singing of hymns) and Akhand Paath (continuous recitation of the Sri Guru Granth Sahib), were stopped. Every Sikh, including women, was insulted, beaten, and then arrested. This was all done to immobilize the Sikh movement. The police kept full control of Darbar Sahib for four days.

# Operation Blue Star, June 1984

Operation Blue Star was a preplanned and well-organized ghastly invasion of the holiest Sikh shrine, Darbar Sahib (Golden Temple Amritsar), by the Indian Army in June 1984, resulting in the death of more than ten thousand Sikh men, women, and children—mostly pilgrims. Before the attack, Punjab came to a standstill; all news media, transportation, and telecommunication were cut off. More than seventy thousand army personnel were brought in and spread all over Punjab. Sikh regiments were moved away from Punjab. The border with Pakistan was sealed. The details of this horrific attack and the events leading to it are discussed below.

## The Events Leading to Operation Blue Star

Soon after 1947, Sikhs realized that they had been betrayed, and the commitments made to them by the Indian National Congress before Indian independence in 1947 were a mere hoax. The Indian government steadfastly denied Sikhs every right as being its citizens. Indian Constitution did not recognize Sikhism as a separate religion. Hindu personal law started to apply to Sikhs. As a result, there were many peaceful morchas (nonviolent agitations) by the political parties of Sikhs, mainly the Shiromani Akali Dal. As a matter of historical records, over three hundred thousand Sikhs were jailed in these morchas, more than six times the number who were court arrested during the Quit India Movement of 1942. Besides incarcerations for varying periods, many Sikhs lost their lives during these morchas. It is important to make a special mention of *Darshan*

*Singh Pheruman*,[187] who died on October 27, 1969, at the age of eighty-four, after seventy-four days of fast unto death for the return of Chandigarh and left out Punjabi-speaking areas to Punjab, that were deliberately given to Haryana and Himachal Pradesh to deprive Punjab of the areas that genuinely belonged to it.

The Indian government of Indira Gandhi wanted to break Sikhs physically, mentally, and economically in line with the thoughts of her father, Jawahar Lal Nehru. His father, Moti Lal Nehru, had told him that by administering Amrit and creating Khalsa in 1699, Guru Gobind Singh had set the ground for furthering human equality and ending the caste system as preached by Guru Nanak. Human equality in Sikhism cuts the life thread of Brahminism. Brahmanism is the mastermind behind human inequality and perpetuation of the caste system, leading to millions of Indians' misery for thousands of years. At the time of the formation of states based on language, Punjab State was intentionally left out to weaken Sikhs politically and economically. This made Sikhs realize that their basic rights were being denied, prompting them to launch peaceful agitations.

When Sikhs asked for their statehood, they were labeled as separatists and antinational. India's government staged hate crimes to blame Sikhs to justify their torture and repression. The repression and persecution of Sikhs continued leading to the Indian Army invasion of Darbar Sahib in June 1984. The Indian news media played at the hands of the Indian government to poison the Hindu-Sikh relationship.

### Advance Planning and Preparations for Invasion of Darbar Sahib

To accomplish this goal, Indira Gandhi meticulously planned the Indian Army invasion of Darbar Sahib for about two years by making its replica for training the troops for the invasion. Negotiations

---

[187] https://indianexpress.com/article/india/india-news-india/darshan-singh-pheruman-forgotten-activist-for-unfinished-agenda-of-punjabi-suba-3099553/.

between Sant Bhindranwale and Indira Gandhi broke down on several occasions when Gandhi reneged at the last moment before the settlement's planned announcement. She did not want to risk Hindu votes in Punjab, Haryana, and Rajasthan. Srinivas Kumar Sinha, the vice chief of army staff, who was asked by Indira Gandhi to plan the attack at the Golden Temple, had reservations over the proposal. He sought premature retirement in 1983 on being superseded by Lt. Gen. Arunkumar Sridhar Vaidya for the post of army chief.

General Vaidya, the thirteenth army chief, who supervised the operation, was shot dead in Pune after his retirement by Bhai Sukhjinder Singh "Sukha" and Bhai Harjinder Singh "Jinda" in August 1986.

Third of June 1984, the Martyrdom Day of Guru Arjan Dev Ji, was when the army chose to surround Guru Arjan's temple. The onslaught started two days later on the night of June 5, around 7:00 p.m.

Mary Ann Weaver, a British correspondent in her report to *Sunday Times London*, June 17, 1984, wrote, "Not since independence has the Indian Army been used in such numbers-about 15,000 troops took part in the assault."[188] The rest of Punjab was flooded with soldiers to put down the internal rebellion. Tanks and armed personnel carriers supported the especially picked and trained soldiers. Yet it took them more than seventy-two hours of continuous warlike attack to gain control of the shrine defended by some 500 followers of Sant Jarnail Singh Bhindranwale and 150 men of Babbar Khalsa.

Not satisfied with the progress and slow action of the intelligence agencies like RAW (Research and Analysis Wing), Indira Gandhi established another intelligence agency exclusively under her control, The Third Agency.[189]

---

[188] Inderjit Singh Jaijee, *Politics of Genocide: Punjab 1984–1994* (1995), 27.

[189] Lt. Col. Partap Singh, *Khalistan: The Only Solution; The Bleeding Punjab*, US ed. (1991), 88.

## The Third Agency

Two years before Operation Blue Star, Indira Gandhi had organized a superintelligence agency code-named The Third Agency. This agency was charged with the crucial role of the escalation of the Punjab crisis. Its total loyalty was to the prime minister. It had, at its disposal, unlimited resources.

Its mandate in Punjab was to aid and abet the murders and killings in Punjab. It kept the supply of lethal weapons flowing into the Golden Temple.

The launching of army actions Operation Blue Star and Operation Woodrose were scripted, enacted, and closed by the intelligence agencies under the direction of Prime Minister Indira Gandhi. It was The Third Agency that had planned and executed the operation with the following objectives:

1. To clinch Hindu vote in the rest of India by punching the Sikh community in the nose
2. To take the wind out of the opposition's sail by doing exactly what they have been saying the government should do—attack the Golden Temple
3. To test the efficacy of The Third Agency, camouflaged by the RAW's blundering and an inefficient investigation bureau

One of the Indian government's methods to malign Sikhs and poison the Hindu mind was to constantly harp on the theme that Sant Jarnail Singh Bhindranwale was terrorizing Hindus. Home Minister P. C. Sethi informed the Parliament in February 1984, that out of 220 persons killed in Punjab between January 1, 1982–January 31, 1984, 190 were Sikhs and only thirty were Hindus. It is only where the government failed to do justice, and instead of punishing the criminals, started harassing and torturing the innocent Sikhs, Sant Bhindranwale advocated action against such people. The fact is that whatever killings took place selectively on the buses and in Gurdaspur and Amritsar district after killings of Sikhs in Haryana were done by

The Third Agency's secret agents with the political motive of creating fear in the minds of Hindus to win their votes in the ensuing elections. On June 1, 1984, Indira Gandhi ordered the army to launch Operation Blue Star. A variety of army units and paramilitary forces surrounded the temple complex on June 3, 1984, the Martyrdom Day of Guru Arjun. The onslaught started two days later on June 5.

Operation Blue Star was well thought out and planned long before the actual assault on Darbar Sahib with several objectives in view. The first was to swiftly capture Golden Temple for which a reserve division (nine infantry division) was deployed from Meerut. This was a balanced force of twenty thousand personnel. The second was to be prepared for an uprising in the countryside. The third was to attack thirty-seven other historic gurdwaras all over Punjab simultaneously. The last one was to seal the border with Pakistan. The bulk of the Indian Army, which was not committed to the Himalayan border facing China, was deployed in this tiny state. It would be safe to guess that more than half of the world's fourth-largest army's combatant troops were deployed ostensibly to kill Sant Jarnail Singh Bhindranwale and a few hundred of his associates, this being equivalent of using a sledgehammer to crack a nut.

## The Invasion Started at 7:00 p.m., on June 5, 1984

The attack on Darbar Sahib started at 7:00 p.m., on June 5, when the tanks of the Sixteenth Cavalry Regiment of the Indian Army started moving toward the Golden Temple complex. On the way, they passed the Jallianwala Bagh, where Gen. Reginald Dyer had massacred more than nine hundred people and injured about two thousand on April 13, 1919. That massacre dealt a mortal blow to Britain's hope of ruling India and was one of the most powerful inspirations of the freedom movement.

The selection of this day to attack was to achieve maximum kill and inflict maximum injuries. This was the day of commemoration of the Martyrdom Day of Guru Arjan (the fifth Sikh guru). A rather large number of Sikhs from all over Punjab come to Darbar Sahib on this day to celebrate and commemorate this historical event of great significance for Sikhs. Despite the Indian Army's claim that the troops were instructed to use minimal force and not attack Sanctum Sanctorum, they did the opposite and destroyed Akal Takhat. If it were the Indian government's focused goal to capture Sant Bhindranwale, another day could have been chosen. However, the real goal of Indira Gandhi was to break Sikhs physically, mentally, and psychologically. The idea behind the attack was to teach Sikhs a lesson that they were slaves in India.

Maj. Gen. Brar, his superior officer, Lt. Gen. Krishnaswamy Sunderji, and Lt. Gen. Ranjit Singh Dayal coordinated the attack. These three generals were successful in achieving only one of their objectives. The Golden Temple complex was cleared, but to say that Sant Jarnail Singh Bhindranwale was flushed out would be a gross overstatement. He was blasted out of the Akal Takhat. The shrine which, according to the original orders, was to suffer minimal damage was reduced to rubble. The evacuation of the hostel complex was accomplished, not without heavy civilian casualties.

Not making much headway after having suffered significant casualties, Brigadier A. K. Dewan asked Brar permission to use tanks to bombard Akal Takhat. Realizing that the infantry was in danger of being massacred, he asked his superior Sunderji to take in a tank. According to a junior officer, who did not want his name disclosed, he stated that Lieutenant Sunderji was enjoying his drink (Johnnie Walker Black Label), had stated that the three generals could not make up their mind as to what further action they should take. Sunderji lost his nerve and sought permission from the chief of army staff, Vaidya.

The two state ministers of Defense, Singh Deo and Arjun Singh, were present in the army headquarters operations room to whom Vaidya approached for decision. They, in turn, contacted Prime Minister Indira Gandhi for a decision. Reportedly her directions were, "I don't care if the Golden Temple and the whole city of Amritsar are destroyed. I want Bhindranwale dead."

It took only two hours for Sunderji to get permission to use tanks, and he immediately directed Brar to use as many tanks as were necessary. Vijayanta, the Indian Army's main battle tank, equipped with blowing up hard targets like armor and fortification, was brought in to attack Akal Takhat. Thus the whole of the front of Akal Takhat was destroyed. As many as seven tanks were brought in, which moved up and let loose a barrage of high explosives and squash head shells. All the overs fell in the thickly populated areas, causing extensive damage to the civilian population's life and property. *Darshni Deohri*, the area on top of the gateway to the causeway leading to Darbar Sahib, was destroyed, along with the priceless objects collected over the centuries, some sanctified by Sikh prophets themselves. While the Akal Takhat was pulverized into rubble, several buildings in the city were also destroyed by the shells that overshot their target.

It is understood that at this stage, Sant Jarnail Singh Bhindranwale permitted his followers to slip out of the complex, but only a few did so. Sant Jarnail Singh Bhindranwale, General Shabeg Singh, Bhai Amrik Singh, and Bhai Thahara Singh were murdered in compliance with Indira Gandhi's directions. An estimated 170 defenders of the shrine attained martyrdom in this battle, but only after they had killed or wounded over 2,000 of the attackers.

The government's white paper had grossly downplayed the causality figures on both sides, making this paper's information worth less than its own. The details of the misdeeds and the cruelties of the Indian Army are beyond description.

The invasion of the Indian Army was by no means a spontaneous reaction to the threat posed by protesting Punjabis. Rather the Indian military prepared and simulated this operation for several months before its execution. The army's assault included the deployment of tear gas, army tanks, and seventy thousand troops. Observers have widely speculated that the timing of the attack was also carefully selected to coincide with the first few days of June, a moment during which Sikhs around the globe commemorate the martyrdom of their fifth guru, Guru Arjan. Guru Arjan is celebrated for many reasons, including his martyrdom for the Sikh faith, his role as the architect of Darbar Sahib, and his compilation of Adi Granth (the first version of the Sikh Holy Scripture). The Sikhs flock to this site in Amritsar every June to honor his contributions.[190]

---

[190] https://www.huffpost.com/entry/remembering-the-massacre-of-sikhs-in-june-of-1984_b_3377276?utm_hp_ref=sikhism.

As a part of the planned strategy, almost all the battalions of the Sikh and Punjab regiments, and also the artillery and armored units, which had large numbers of Sikhs, were already moved out gradually from Punjab and the neighboring states to far-off states in central, southern, and north-eastern states. On the issue of the code word Operation "Blue Star," on May 27, 1984, the infantry, artillery, and armored formations of the Army Headquarters Reserves, and those of One Corps and Ten Corps stationed outside Punjab, were moved to Punjab by road and rail on May 28, 1984. Units of One, Two, Ten, and Eleven Corps were redeployed to the state of Punjab. Additional units of CRPF and BSF were also moved and placed under the command of the army. A total of thirteen tanks were deployed, and seven of these entered into the Parikrama (periphery around the holy water pool). One of these was destroyed by a young boy of age sixteen, who tied explosives around his body and jumped under the moving tank.

The so-called "brave" Indian Army, having suffered heavy losses, took its revenge on the unarmed innocent pilgrims and devotees. They killed an estimated six thousand pilgrims who had been trapped in the *sarai* (rest house). Seeing these brutal killings, hundreds of men, women, and children had locked themselves in the sarai rooms. Indian Army took out their wrath by throwing poisonous gas canisters and grenades inside the rooms, killing them mercilessly. If the trapped pilgrims tried to come out, they were shot dead or pierced with bayonets. Eyewitness accounts revealed that young girls and women were assaulted, raped, and disgracefully handled. Small babies and children were caught by their feet and thrown against the walls. Not satisfied with this revenge, they set on fire the rooms and buildings of Guru Ram Das Sarai, Guru Nanak Niwas, and Teja Singh Samundri Hall, burning alive hundreds of Sikh men, women, and children inside. To save themselves, some of them ran toward the bathrooms and the toilets, but the vindictive army killed them by throwing grenades and gas canisters in the closed bathrooms and the toilets. Many women were found in the rooms sitting dead, with their breastfeeding babies in their arms. Over a hundred young boys of ages eight to twelve were tied up and made to stand in line. They were beaten up with rifle butts and then asked if they still wanted

Khalistan. Their only answer was, *"Jo Bole So Nihal, Sat Sri Akal."* On hearing the Sikh war cry, the so-called "chivalrous" Indian Army officers were alarmed and shot every single child dead.

Even the *sevadars* (persons engaged in voluntary service-volunteers) looking after *langar* (free community kitchen) were not spared. Nearly twenty sevadars were caught; their hands and feet were tied with their turbans, they were beaten, dragged by their hair, and shot at point-blank range.

In one case, about sixty men were herded into a small room and kept there overnight. They were unarmed and repeatedly pleaded with the army to let them out as they were dying of suffocation and intense heat. The army ignored their every call. In the morning, when the door was opened, all but six had died.

The bloodthirsty Indian Army was not satisfied by merciless killing and molesting thousands of men and women. Children were not spared. Here is a statement of Ranbir Kaur, a schoolteacher. She, her husband, and twelve children were locked in room number 141 of Guru Dam Das Sarai:

> We were all huddled together. We did not know what was happening. The noise was terrifying. We had not been out of the room for more than 24 hours, and we had no food or water. It was an extremely hot summer night. I told the children that we must be ready to die. They kept on crying. Early on the morning of the 6th of June, the army came into Guru Ram Das Serai and ordered all those in the rooms to come out. We were taken into the courtyard. The men were separated from women. We were separated into older and younger women, and I was separated from the children, but I managed to get back to the older women. When we were sitting there, the army released 150 people from the basement. They were asked why they had not come out earlier. They answered that the door was locked

168

from the outside. They were asked to hold up their hands, and after fifteen minutes, they were shot dead. Other young men were told to untie their turbans. They were used to tie their hands behind their back, and the army hit their heads with rifle butts.[191]

The survivors were taken into interrogation camps. Mrs. Kamaladevi Chattopadhya, a famous social worker, petitioned the supreme court. Ranbir Kaur was released; she joined three of the twelve children who were also released. Nothing is known of the others.

To destroy the historical records of Sikhs, original documents, and manuscripts, the Sikh Research and Reference Library were deliberately set on fire two days after the cease-fire. Besides source materials, seven hundred copies of the Sikh Holy Scripture, Sri Guru Granth Sahib, were burnt.

The commanders of the Indian Army (Brar, Sunderji, and Dayal) got so flustered and enraged at being given a bloody nose by Shahbeg's boys that, in an instant, they forgot the principle of employment of minimal force when dealing with its people. They let loose everything they had—tanks and helicopters included—which destroyed the Akal Takht, symbolizing the concept of sovereignty—miri—and spiritual—piri—in the Sikh faith. Several other buildings surrounding the Darbar Sahib complex were also destroyed.

An officer of Kumaon Regiment,[192] who fought in the battle and was an eyewitness to the events of the night between June 5 and 6, gave the following statement, which was published in the August '84 issue of *Probe*:

> On the morning of June 6, The Golden Temple Complex was like a graveyard. Bodies lay all around in the buildings, on the **Parikarma**

---

[191] Partap Singh, *Khalistan: The Only Solution; The Bleeding Punjab* (1991), 96.
[192] *The Probe*, August 1984.

(periphery of Darbar Sahib's Sanctum Santorum)) and in the **Sarovar** (the Holy Pool surrounding the Sanctum Sanctorum). The sun was shining, and the stench from the bodies was becoming unbearable. Bodies of Jawans (soldiers) were identified and handed over to their respective regiments. I carried three soldiers on my shoulders. Each regiment carried out funeral rites of their own Jawans.

The army was instructed not to take any prisoners. Innocent Sikhs were shot point-blank with their hands tied in the back. The army played down the number of persons killed, the number of tanks deployed and the number of their own injured or killed. Naked dead bodies were lying over Parikarma of the Holy Pool. The Holy Pool water turned red with the blood flowing from Parikarma.

The civilians who had died, about 1500 of them, were piled up in the trollies and carried away. A lot of them were thrown into the rivers. The battle was a tragic one. I could not eat anything. Food made me sick. I used to drink a lot of rum and go to sleep. I am glad now to be relieved of my duty in Amritsar.

## Specific Task under Operation Blue Star

Operation Blue Star was carried out in three phases. Specific goals were established for each phase. A systematic approach to achieve those goals was defined. Nothing was left to chance. The Indian Army had been planning the attack for two years and carried out training exercises to accomplish the job in a few hours.

*Phase 1*: Killing as many Sikhs as possible, including men, women, and children, except the volunteers. The plan included destroying Akal Takhat and bombarding historical Sikh gurdwaras.

It was specifically planned to take no prisoners, provoke religious sentiments of the ardent and devout Sikhs by fiddling with their turbans and flowing beards, by removing their *kirpans*, and if they get provoked or show any resistance, to shoot them down on the spot. Cutting off Punjab from the rest of the world by suspending telephones, telegraph, and postal services so that no news circulates within Punjab, and no news reaches outside Punjab as to what is happening.

*Phase 2:* Combing and searching all the villages and towns of Punjab and shooting Sikhs without warning if any of them show even the slightest resistance. Cordoning villages and carrying out search operations to carry out a close personal search of all men, women, and young girls and children. Searching all houses and removing all weapons, even agricultural equipment and instruments that could be used as weapons. Monitoring all Sikhs traveling by buses, trains, cars, motorcycles, and carts from village to village and town to town in Punjab or traveling from outside the state or going outside of Punjab were to be searched thoroughly, and if anybody offered any type of resistance, he has to be shot as a suspect terrorist and beaten thoroughly and taken to the concentration camp.

*Phase 3:* After combing the villages was completed, the army was to continue operating checkpoints on roads and tracks and villages and towns to harass, humiliate, and search Sikhs to create a sense of fear in them. Full freedom and authority were given to the armed forces to harass and humiliate Sikhs to bring their morale down and encourage Hindus to raise their morale by giving them a sense of victory over Sikhs. Keep patrolling villages and towns to round up Sikhs within the age group of fifteen to thirty-five years with the intention of either killing them in fake encounters or evacuating them to concentration camps to kill them there, by torture.

The Martyrdom Day of Guru Arun was selected as the day for Operation Blue Star for the all-out war against Sikhs for conflicting maximum causalities. Statewide clamping of curfew a week before the attack and for many days after the "cease-fire," the killing of thousands of pilgrims in the Golden Temple complex and other gurdwaras will baffle anybody who does not know or has not analyzed the Indian government intentions. The government had deliberately thwarted all efforts for a negotiated settlement. The government clandestinely allowed the smuggling of truckloads of arms into the temple complex.[193] It was designed to win over public opinion to justify the unprecedented military offense, not only against the holiest Sikh shrine and other gurdwaras but also as a full-scale undeclared war against Sikhs.

The number of people who died in Operation Blue Star is variable depending upon whose figures one accepts. Prime Minister Rajiv Gandhi mentioned that seven hundred soldiers had lost their lives in Operation Blue Star (quoted in *The Tragedy of Punjab*, Kuldip Nayar and Khushwant Singh). The army attempted to conceal the exact number of its dead. The wounded were evacuated to hospitals all across India and usually shown as having been wounded in Ladakh.

In their book *Amritsar: Mrs. Gandhi's Last Battle*, Mark Tully and Satish Jacob[194] estimate that 950 pilgrims were inside the temple, along with 80 priests, sevadars (volunteers) and other temple servants, some 300 employees of the Shiromani Gurdwara Parbandhak Committee and their families who lived in the temple complex, and about 1,700 Akali supporters who had gone to participate in the Dharam Yudh. These people were quite apart from the supporters of Sant Jarnail Singh Bhindranwale and Babbar Khalsa. The total is about 3,680.

In their book *Sikh Struggle*, Ramnarain Kumar and George Sieberer wrote:

> The Army which had suffered a heavy toll in three days of battle went berserk and killed every Sikh who could be found inside the temple complex. They were hauled out of the rooms, brought to the corridors on the circumference of the temple, and with their hands tied behind their backs,

---

[193] Pav Singh, *1984: India's Guilty Secret* (Kashi House, 2017), 58.

[194] Mark Tully and Satish Jacob, *Amritsar: Mrs. Gandhi's Last Battle* (Rupa Publications India Pvt. Ltd, 1985), 185.

were shot in cold blood. Among the victims were many old men, women, and children.[195]

Brahma Chellany, the only foreign correspondent who managed to remain in Amritsar after the government had ordered all the journalists out of Punjab, reported doctors and police officials' statements that many of the Sikhs were killed in the attack had been shot at point-blank range with their hands tied behind their backs. Some of these bodies, with their hands tied behind their backs, were photographed. The testimonies of the survivors also bore this out.[196]

Indian Army simultaneously attacked thirty-seven other gurdwara of historical importance, killing hundreds of Sikhs. The numbers stated by the authorities were much less the numbers of cremated at the burial grounds. The dead bodies were hauled by army trucks and taken to unknown places for cremation.

When the villagers learned of the attack on Darbar Sahib, thousands of them began their journey toward Amritsar with whatever transportation they had, with their intentions of defending their holiest shrine. These marchers were subjected to aerial bombing, machine-gunning, and gunfire in a bid to stop them. At many points, unarmed Sikh Army deserters were intercepted and killed. According to Mr. Inderjit Singh Jaijee, the total number of killed during Operation Blue Star and simultaneous attack on other gurdwaras is about ten thousand.

The attack on Darbar Sahib and other gurdwaras was a strategy of breaking the Sikh spirit and inflicting maximum physical injury to reduce them to a status of slaves who would never again dare ask for their rights. What was started long before Operation Blue Star and culminated in the Sikh Genocide in November 1984, continues till today.

It is believed that in the aftermath of Operation Blue Star, several thousand video cassette copies were made of a documentary for overseas viewing. They were posted anonymously to individuals and

[195] Inderjit Singh Jaijee, *Politics of Genocide: Punjab 1984–1994* (1995), 28.
[196] Ibid., 29.

organizations in the Indian diaspora with a view of polarizing opinion and squash any sympathy harbored for the "terrorist" Sikhs of Punjab. The majority of the arsenal recovered from inside the shrine had been smuggled in under the supervision of the covert agency, created by RAW operatives and run by the director of the prime minister's secretariat. A week before the army action, the Punjab Police had intercepted two truckloads of weapons and ammunition entering Punjab from the Wagah border, about twenty miles north of Amritsar. Still they were allowed to go on their way to the Golden Temple at the behest of the covert agency.[197]

Operation Blue Star was planned over years. The Congress Party government kept on spreading misinformation about Sant Bhindranwale and his supporters to justify the invasion and misleading the people of Punjab and India. A replica of Darbar Sahib was prepared in the mountains two years in advance to practice the attack. A systematic plan was prepared. The border with Pakistan was sealed. Sikh regiments were moved away from Punjab. The army was deployed all over Punjab to prevent an uprising among the village folks. The attack was planned on one of the holiest days in Sikh history when a large number of pilgrims were gathered at the Darbar Sahib complex, leading to a maximum loss of human life and destruction of Akal Takhat. The invasion could have been easily prevented. Other simple methods to capture the political figure Sant Bhindranwale, like cutting off water and electric supply, were not deployed. A large number of other Sikh gurdwaras were attacked simultaneously.

Despite the massive use of the country's army and paramilitary forces and carrying out a mass killing of its people, Indira Gandhi failed to achieve her intended objective to deliver a devastating blow to Sikhs physically and psychologically. The successive Indian governments have been pursuing the strategy of econocide of the Punjab farmers, a vast majority of whom happen to be Sikhs.

---

[197] Pav Singh, *1984: India's Guilty Secret* (Kashi House, 2017), 58.

# The November 1984 Sikh Genocide

> Frenzied mobs of young Hindu thugs, thirsting for revenge, burned Sikh-owned stores to the ground, dragged Sikhs out of their homes, cars, and trains, then clubbed them to death or set them aflame before raging off in search of other victims.[198] (*Time Magazine*)

Sikhs for Justice (SFJ), a US-based human rights organization, and All India Sikh Students Federation (AISSF), a registered organization committed to working toward the betterment of the Sikh community, carried out a detailed investigation to determine the extent of the Sikh Genocide in 1984. Their determination revealed that the killing of Sikhs in Delhi, eighteen Indian states, and about one hundred Indian cities in 1984, after the assassination of Indira Gandhi by her Sikh bodyguards, was not a random act of violence but a well-planned genocide of the Sikhs, executed with the support of Congress (I) politicians, police, and several Hindu religious groups with the connivance of the Indian government.

Following the assassination of Prime Minister Indira Gandhi by her two Sikh bodyguards on October 31, 1984, the then-ruling party of India (the Indian National Congress), also known as Congress (I), organized and orchestrated attacks targeting Sikhs, a religious minority, throughout India. The personalized attacks were on the lives, homes, businesses, personal property, and places of worship of

---

[198] *Time*, November 19, 1984, http://content.time.com/time/magazine/article/0,9171,950203,00.html.

Sikhs in India. They were carried out with impunity and in a meticulous and malicious manner, resulting in the loss of thousands of lives. More than thirty thousand Sikhs were killed in this brief yet tragic period. Most of the victims were helpless and burnt alive in front of family members and neighbors. Hundreds of Sikh women were raped. Countless Sikh temples or places of worship, known as gurdwaras, were burnt to the ground. Sikh properties, homes, and businesses were looted, ransacked, and destroyed. Over three hundred thousand (300,000) Sikhs were uprooted and displaced during the melee.

The gravity, scale, and specifically the organized and intentional nature of these attacks were successfully concealed by the Indian government for three decades. The official story by the Indian government portrayed these events as the "November 1984 anti-Sikh riots of Delhi." These attacks were neither riots nor were they confined to the Delhi region. In actuality, from November 1–4, 1984, Sikhs had been targeted in at least eighteen additional states of India, including over one hundred cities throughout the nation. The ruthless attacks occurred in almost an identical manner to those that took place in Delhi. The hordes of marauders, fueled by ignorance, hatred, and prejudice, were relentless in their attacks. The attackers were motivated with a thirst for revenge, instigated by leaders of the ruling party of India, Congress I.

This report is supported by concrete facts and asserts that the November 1984 anti-Sikh riots were not riots. The attacks on Sikhs at this time were nothing short of genocide against a peace-loving population. The violence and mass murders that took place in November of 1984, as discussed at length herein, were tantamount to genocide should be declared as such under Article 2 of the UN Convention on Genocide.

## I. Highlights

On the morning of October 31, 1984, Prime Minister Indira Gandhi was assassinated by her two bodyguards. Ms. Gandhi's bodyguards happened to belong to the Sikh faith. Many believe that the assassination of the prime minister was in retaliation to her involvement in the military action code-named Operation Blue Star. In June 1984, Ms. Gandhi had ordered Operation Blue Star, a military attack, against the holiest Sikh shrine, Sri Darbar Sahib, located in Amritsar, Punjab. Under Prime Minister Gandhi's orders, the Indian Army entered the holy shrine with tanks, artillery, helicopters, armored vehicles, and chemical weapons. Operation Blue Star was to diminish the growing popularity of Sant Jarnail Singh Bhindranwale and his demand for justice and equal treatment under the law. Till the last day before his death, he did not advocate for an independent sovereign Sikh state. Indian intelligence agencies clandestinely created the demand for independent Punjab Khalistan to justify the repression and torture of Sikhs. This military action against the "Sikh Vatican," commonly known as the Golden Temple, resulted in the desecration of Sri Harminder Sahib and Sri Akal Takht Sahib ("the highest temporal seat of Sikhism"). This attack also resulted in the senseless killings of more than ten thousand Sikh pilgrims who had gathered at the Golden Temple on one of the holiest days of Sikhism. The demand for the right to self-determination was further crushed by the Indian government by launching military action against several dozen other Sikh gurdwaras (temples) across Punjab, simultaneously or immediately following Operation Blue Star.

During the months between Operation Blue Star and Ms. Gandhi's assassination, the Indian government went full force against Sikhs in terms of actions that resulted in public dehumanization. The effects of this demoralizing conduct were overwhelming to both the Sikh, and non-Sikh populations of India, who observed live beatings, burnings, and rapes committed during these so-called "riots." The nation of India and its leaders watched silently as the public burning of Sikh men, maiming of Sikh children, raping of Sikh women, and looting of Sikh properties occurred. Despite the lack of domestic public outrage at the killing of Sikhs in November 1984, the carnage and havoc speak for themselves. It is immense enough to be categorized as genocide under the UN Conventions, especially when such genocide was organized and orchestrated by the government itself, namely the ruling party of India, Indian National Congress, a.k.a. Congress (I).

Leaders of Congress (I) are largely responsible for the genocidal acts committed against Sikhs throughout India in November 1984. These leaders have not been prosecuted or otherwise brought to justice[199] despite ample evidence of their involvement[200] in organizing the attacks on Sikhs at that time. Evidence shows that during November 1984, death squads were led by Congress (I) leaders, including[201] Union Minister Kamal Nath, members of Parliament Sajjan Kumar,[202] Jagdish Tytler, Lalit Maiken, Dharam Das Shastri, HKL Bhagat, Arun Nehru, Arjun Singh, and even Bollywood movie star Amitabh Bachchan.

Ms. Gandhi's successor was none other than her son, Rajiv Gandhi, who condoned the mass killing of Sikhs in the aftermath of his mother's assassination, by declaring, "When a big tree falls, the earth around it shakes."[203]

To cover up the systematic nature of the massacre, successive Indian regimes have been misleading the worldwide community into believing that the 1984 killing of Sikhs was anti-Sikh riots, confined to Delhi alone,[204] despite ample evidence to the contrary. As an attempt to offset the demand for justice and accountability, succes-

---

[199] "India: Prosecute Those Responsible for 1984 Massacre of Sikhs," Human Rights Watch, hrw.org.

[200] Seema Mustafa, "1984 Sikh Massacres: Mother of All Cover-ups," *The Asian Age*, August 9, 2005.

[201] *Truth About Delhi Violence*, (Citizens for Democracy).

[202] See also, general sightings of Sajjan Kumar in Palam Colony, such as that by Kishandev Singh in law enforcing agency was inactive in '84 riots.

Verghese, *Outlook India*, January 17, 2002, http://www.outlookindia.com/pti_print.asp?id=34846.

[203] *Hindustan Times*, November 18, 2008, http://www.hindustantimes.com/india-news/1984-anti-sikh-riots-wrong-says-rahul-Gandhi/article1-352523.aspx.

[204] See People's Union, "Who Are the Guilty?"

Many Anne Weaver, "After Assassination, India turns to Rajiv," Christian Science Monitor, November 1, 1984.

1 (rioting broke out in at least six other states); "Assassination in India; Violence Ripples Through the Nation," *New York Times*, November 1, 1984.

sive Indian regimes have, over the past thirty-six (36) years, set up at least ten inquiry commissions and committees on November 1984, incidents. Even a cursory review of these workings, findings, reports, recommendations, and the government's action pursuant thereto reveal the hoax played through the facade of an investigation into the November 1984 killing of Sikhs.

These commissions did not have any judicial powers, and their scope of the inquiry was limited to the killings in Delhi alone. By doing this, the commissions were able to cover up the extent of the violence committed against Sikhs as well as belittle the attacks into a realm of utter deniability.

A recent article in the *Indian Express* newspaper spoke of the reactions of the Indian government and the government's blatant denial that the anti-Sikh Genocide of 1984 ever occurred. Directly quoted from the article:

> "[F]or some reason, the Rangnath Misra Commission rejected outright the majority of the affidavits filed by the victims as well as witnesses. The commission not only rejected Rahul Bedi's affidavit, and mine, but an officer of the commission called me informally to his chamber and dissuaded me from filing an affidavit arguing that I had not suffered in the anti-Sikh pogrom. The state prosecutor accused me of filing reports in The Indian Express at the behest of the management,"[205] said Joseph Maliakan.

The discovery of mass graves of Sikhs in the village of Hondh-Chillar, District Rewari, Haryana, in February 2011, as well evidence in several other states of India, including an additional nine gurdwara ruins in Delhi, mass cremation site in Pataudi and Gurgaon, state of Haryana, ruins of Sikh localities in West Bengal, Uttar Pradesh, and

---

[205] http://indianexpress.com/article/india/india-others/bodies-of-hundreds-of-sikhs-were-scattered-some-showed-signs-of-life/2/#sthash.zGnV82yq.dpuf.

Jammu and Kashmir are among recent discoveries which expose the extent of this attack. The recent discoveries also portray the organized schemes, the systematic planning, and the widespread nature of these attacks, as well as the successful concealment by the Indian governments during the last thirty years

The government of India has thwarted all attempts by victims to obtain justice,[206] including covering up abuse, destroying evidence,[207] affording impunity to Congress (I) leaders, as well as witness intimidation.[208] The wrongdoers have fought tooth and nail to avoid responsibility, especially in federal courts of the United States of America. The victims of the November 1984 anti-Sikh Genocide seek justice and have no other recourse but to approach the United Nations Human Rights Council.

Because the perpetrators of the 1984 anti-Sikh Genocide were never held accountable, it paved way for the Gujarat[209] massacre of 2002, where Muslims were also killed by the masses with the support, connivance, and cooperation of the Indian government. Furthermore, the absence of justice as precedent in India also enabled the 2008 killings of Christians in Orissa. Consequently the pattern of attacking religious minorities has not lost its allure in India. The Indian government has, does, and will perpetuate violence against minorities at the hand of the dominant Hindu religious leaders.

---

[206] See *Twenty Years of Impunity: The November 1984 Pogroms of Sikhs in India,* a report by ENSAAF 13.

[207] See April 30, 2013, report by US Commission on International Religious Freedom, stating "Resham Singh Resham Singh, a Sikh who was a taxi driver in 1984, alleges that he witnessed Congress Party leader Jagdish Tytler leading a mob."

[208] Harinder Baweja, "When a big tree falls, the earth shakes," *Tehlka,* 6, no. 16, (April 25, 2009).

Nidhi Bhardwaj, "1984 anti-Sikh riots: Eyewitness who could not testify before a court," CNN-IBN, April 11, 2013, http://ibnlive.in.com/news/1984-antisikh-riots-eyewitness-who-couldnt-testify-before-a-court/384460-37-64.html.

[209] Ghassem-Fachand and Parvis, *Pogrom in Gujarat: Hindu Nationalism, and Anti-Muslim Violence in India* (Princeton University Press, 2012), 1–2.

## II. Factual Backdrop

*A. Summary*—On the morning of October 31, 1984, Prime Minister Indira Gandhi was fatally shot by her two Sikh bodyguards. A few months earlier, in June 1984, Ms. Gandhi had ordered the military action code-named Operation Blue Star against the holiest Sikh shrine, Sri Harminder Sahib, in retaliation to the growing popularity of Sant Jarnail Singh Bhindranwale, his genuine demands for justice, and the growing popularity for the sovereign Sikh state. The military action against the Golden Temple not only resulted in the desecration of Sri Harminder Sahib and Sri Akal Takht Sahib ("the highest temporal seat of Sikhism") but also resulted in the killing of more than ten thousand Sikh pilgrims present in the Golden Temple at the time. The Demand for the right to self-determination by the Sikhs of Punjab was crushed by military action against several dozen other gurdwaras across Punjab concurrently, as well as immediately following the Operation Blue Star infiltration.

In the aftermath of Prime Minister Indira Gandhi's assassination by her two Sikh bodyguards, on October 31, 1984, the then-ruling party of India, the Indian National Congress, also known as Congress (I), organized and orchestrated personalized attacks targeting Sikhs, a religious minority, throughout India. The attacks on Sikh lives, their properties, and their places of worship were carried out in a meticulous and premeditated manner; the attacks resulted in more than thirty thousand Sikhs being killed—most of the deaths from being burnt alive. Additionally hundreds of Sikh women were raped, Sikh gurdwaras (temples) were lit on fire, Sikh properties were looted, and over three hundred thousand Sikhs being uprooted and displaced. The gravity, scale, and organizational nature of these attacks was concealed by the Indian government; they portrayed the genocide as "November 1984 anti-Sikh riots of Delhi." These attacks were neither riots nor were they confined to Delhi. In actuality, during the first four days of November 1984, Sikhs were attacked in eighteen states and over one hundred cities in India. The attacks occurred in an identical manner, and the attackers were being led by leaders of the ruling party of India, Congress (I).

Leading researcher and expert on relevant Sikh issues Cynthia K. Mehmood briefly summarizes what Sikhs have been subjected to in India as:

> India's crimes of 1984 began with its assault on, and the massacres at, the Golden Temple, and dozens of other Gurudwaras across India in the first week of June 1984, and continued with the nationwide government-sponsored pogroms of November 1984. In many ways, the crimes continue, not just in the cover-up, and the sheltering of the criminals, but in actual outrages by the government, and its minions to date.

> 1984 & I on the 25th Anniversary of the year a nation sank to a new low in dealing with a religious minority. (Cynthia K. Mahmood)

*B. Sikhs of India: a community lured, betrayed, and mistreated—* Sikhs are an identifiable religious community in India and across the globe. They have distinct religious traditions, a scripture, a linguistic script, and several social, political, and economic institutions. The Sikh religion was founded by Sri Guru Nanak (1469–1539) and shaped by his nine successors in the sixteenth and seventeenth centuries in Punjab. Over twenty-five million people worldwide identify themselves as Sikhs and adhere to the Sikh faith. This makes Sikhism the fifth largest religion in the world. Sikh doctrine teaches that all human beings—regardless of their religious identity or beliefs—have the potential to realize God through devotion, a truthful living, the pursuit of justice, and via the service of humankind.

During the Partition of India in 1947, Sikhs were brought into the fold of the Indian Union by treacherous and never-to-be-fulfilled promises of autonomy, independence, separate identity, and protection of rights by the leadership of the Indian National Congress, a.k.a. Congress (I). However, soon after the partition, the Indian government and the Congress (I) leadership went back on all promises made to the Sikh people of Punjab. One major setback to Sikh identity came in 1952 when, despite the unanimous opposition and strong objection of the Sikh community, Article 25 of the constitution of India was promulgated. Article 25 amalgamated Sikhism into the Hindu faith, thus dealing with a fatal and irreversible blow to the separate identity of Sikhs as a religious community and as an independent religion.

The obliteration of the idea of a separate Sikh identity through Explanation II to the Article 25(2b) of the Constitution of India, coupled with the economic exploitation of Sikhs in Punjab, gradually flourished into a powerful and meaningful movement in the early 1980s, calling for the creation of an independent Sikh nation state. Because the Sikhs were not rightfully granted the sovereignty they were promised, they resolved to take it through nonviolent and peaceful means. According to an editorial of *The New York Times*:

> There was a nonviolent Sikh protest movement, but it was eclipsed when the Prime Minister rebuffed its demands... Since Indian independence in 1947, Sikhs have pleaded for greater autonomy and specific recognition of their religion in the Constitution. (See *The New York Times*, June 8, 1984)

*C. June 1984: when the state launched an attack against a faith—* George Orwell's novel *1984* illustrated a future where the government controlled all aspects of life. The omnipresent government surveillance and public manipulation of which Orwell spoke would eventually become a reality for the Sikhs of Punjab when promises of independence were inconceivably denied, and the violence against them became a government-sponsored mechanism to prevent them from achieving their independence. To carry out the government of India's first mass crime against Sikhs, the June 1984 military operation (Operation Blue Star) and the massacre at the Golden Temple (the Sikh Vatican), the Indian government chose one of the holiest days of Sikhism. The choice of the June 1984 date was a tactic to maximize the loss of human life and to inflict a lasting and conclusive punishment to the collective Sikh psyche. As a result of the attack, Sri Akal Takht Sahib, the highest temporal seat of Sikhism, was reduced to rubble, and the Sikh Reference Library, an irreplaceable collection of books, manuscripts, and artifacts bearing on all aspects of Sikh history, burnt to ashes. Thousands of Sikh pilgrims were first caged and then shot at point-blank by the Indian Army during Operation Blue Star.

The Indian Government claimed[210] that Operation Blue Star was the "last resort" and was carried out to rid the Golden Temple of the followers of the Sikh separatist movement. The Sikh separatist movement was guided by the leadership of Sant Jarnail Singh Bhindranwale, head of Damdami Taksal. Ex-Indian military chief general Sinha's clear advice[211] against Operation Blue Star, along with the implementation of seventy thousand troops, gunship helicopters, tanks, and chemical gas, belies the Indian government's claims that Operation Blue Star was the last resort. The documented evidence shows that the actual purpose for the use of this degree of force against Sikhs during June 1984, was not to "flush out" a handful of separatists but to destroy the fulcrum of a mass movement launched by Sant Jarnail Singh Bhindranwale for the abolition of the Article 25 of the constitution of India, and the demand and for the right to self-determination by the Sikh people.

Anthropologist Joyce Pettigrew, explaining the purpose of Operation Blue Star, states that "the army went into Darbar Sahib not to eliminate a political figure or a political movement but to suppress the culture of a people, to attack their heart, to strike a blow at their spirit, and self-confidence."

---

[210] "Government of India master-minded disinformation campaign to create legitimacy for its actions. Its goal was to 'make out that the Golden Temple was the haven of criminals, a store of armory, and a citadel of the nation's dismemberment conspiracy" (Subramaniam Swami, "Creating a Martyr," July 1984, 7–8).

[211] "The Army Action was not the 'last resort' as Prime Minister Indira Gandhi would have us to believe..." Lt. Gen. SK Sinha (retired Indian Army general), Spokesman, July 16, 1984.

Days leading up to the Operation Blue Star, Indira Gandhi imposed strict press censorship[212] to suppress the civilian death toll and other related details, which would make the official reasons for military operation widely unacceptable and could expose the government's real motives behind the horrendous attack on the Golden Temple. Brahma Chellaney, a reporter for the Associated Press (AP), faced criminal charges[213] in connection with his reports on the military invasion of the Golden Temple. Chellaney reported that several Sikhs inside the Golden Temple complex were shot by Indian Army officers after having their hands tied behind their backs. While the government of India claims that only 493 civilians were killed in Operation Blue Star, BBC correspondent Mark Tully, who was present in Amritsar during the operation, estimated the civilian death toll to be well over 2,000. Anthropologist Joyce Pettigrew, the author of the book *The Sikhs of Punjab: Unheard Voices of State, and Guerrilla Violence*, places the number of civilian casualties to be over 5,000.

*D. November 1984: open license to kill the Sikhs*—On October 31, 1984, Prime Minister Indira Gandhi was assassinated by two of her bodyguards who happened to be Sikhs. Over the next five days, one of the worst genocidal massacres of modern times shook India. These events took place in Delhi (India's capital) as well as throughout one hundred cities and eighteen states across the country. During the gruesome attacks, Sikhs were sought out, specifically targeted, and deliberately attacked. Despite the attacks being dispersed throughout the country, the majority of the carnage occurred in identical manners. While the victims were both male and female Sikhs who encompassed all ages, the majority were men and young boys. The rationale for deliberately targeting males was an attempt to

---

[212] "Foreign journalists were barred from Amritsar after the assault, but Mr. Chellaney, an Indian national, was able to remain," ("The Truth on Trial—in India," *The New York Times,* October 23, 1984).

[213] "A warrant is out for the arrest of an Indian journalist who provoked displeasure by doing his job too well. Brahma Chellaney of The Associated Press was in the Punjab last June when Prime Minister Indira Gandhi ordered the attack on Sikh extremists occupying the Golden Temple in Amritsar," ("The Truth on Trial—in India," *The New York Times*, October 23, 1984).

hinder the further reproduction and procreation of an entire subset of the religious dichotomy of India. This genocidal element to the killings was pervasive, as almost 99 percent of those killed were Sikh males.

According to the Indian scholar Madhu Kishwar, the nature of the attacks confirms that there was a deliberate plan to kill as many Sikh men as possible, hence nothing was left to chance. That also explains why in almost all cases, after hitting or stabbing, the victims were doused with kerosene or petrol and burnt to leave no possibility of their surviving. Between October 31 and November 4, more than 2,500 men were murdered in different parts of Delhi, according to several careful unofficial estimates. There have been very few cases of women being killed, except when they got trapped in houses that were set on fire. Almost all the women interviewed described how men and young boys were special targets. They were dragged out of the houses, attacked with stones and rods, and set on fire. When women tried to protect the men of their families, they were given a few blows and forcibly separated from the men. Even when they clung to the men, trying to save them, they were hardly ever attacked the way men were. I have not yet heard of a case of a woman being assaulted and then burnt to death by the mob.[214]

A typical account of the atrocities was provided by a female witness whose "husband, and three sons...were all killed on 1 November." As investigators summarized her testimony:

> When a mob first came the Sikhs came out and repulsed them. Three such waves were repulsed, but each time the police came and told them to go home and stay there. The fourth time the mob came in increased strength and started attacking individual homes, driving people out, beating, and burning them, and setting fire to

---

[214] Singh Patwant, Malik Harji, *Punjab: The Fatal Miscalculation* (New Delhi, 1985), 171–78.

Kishwar, "Delhi: Gangster Rule," in Patwant Singh and Harji Malik.

their homes. The method of killing was invariably the same: a man was hit on the head, sometimes his skull broken, kerosene poured over him, and set on fire. Before being burnt, some had their eyes gouged out. Sometimes, when a burning man asked for water, a man urinates in his mouth. Several individuals, including her sister's son, tried to escape by cutting their hair. Most of them were also killed. Some had their hair forcibly cut but were nevertheless killed thereafter.[215]

The estimate of 2,500 dead offered by Kishwar (above) is almost certainly too low. The *New York Times*, in 1996, quoting a research study, stated that "piles of affidavits from victims' families prove that 5,015 Sikhs were killed, more than double the official figure." Whatever the exact death toll, it was "one of the darkest chapters in [India's] half-century of independence."[216] Throughout the massacre, Indian Police and security forces stood by or assisted in disarming Sikhs, rendering them defenseless. An Indian Supreme Court Judge, Justice V. M. Tarkunde, made a powerful statement in the aftermath of the massacre, "Two lessons can be drawn from the experience of the Delhi riots. One is about the extent of criminalization of our politics, and the other about the utter unreliability of our police force in a critical situation."[217]

In another article in the newspaper *India Today*, there are accounts of the mass killings that took place during the 1984 anti-Sikh Genocide that was recognized simply as riots by the Indian government. In "1984 Sikh Riot: They took their time to kill between

---

[215] See "Case 11" on Witness 84, http://www.witness84.com/human/ccsikri/histories/.

[216] John F. Burns, "Some Sikhs Get Justice Long After a Massacre," *The New York Times*, September 16, 1996.

[217] See Justice V. M. Tarkunde in "The Delhi Massacre: An Example of Malicious Government."

meals,"[218] the author focuses on the atrocities committed against the Sikh population at the time and the blatant disregard for the lives of people simply because of their religion, a violation of domestic, and international law, the law of nations, and the purest principles of morals and decency worshipped, and cherished by virtually every civilized country on earth. It is noteworthy that while the number of Sikh women killed was not nearly as high as the number of men, thousands of Sikh women were raped, often repeatedly, by rampaging attackers.

The attackers were directed by the leaders and workers of Congress (I). Many of the female survivors of this shameful massacre today live in Tilak Vihar, a locality of Delhi that has come to be known as the Widows' Colony. Since 1984, these women are languishing in the hope of justice, while those who raped them and killed their husbands, brothers, and sons roam freely. The official Indian attitude towards the widespread genocide reflects a belief that the "massacre was necessary to teach a lesson."[219]

*E. November 1984: evidence unearthed after twenty-six years*— Starting with the February 15, 2011, discovery of mass graves of Sikhs in the village Hondh-Chillar, District Rewari, Haryana, and subsequently, the evidence located in several states of India, including West Bengal, Uttar Pradesh, and Jammu and Kashmir, one can comprehend the gravity, and extent of the organization, and widespread nature of the namely identical attacks, which were successfully concealed by the Indian governments over the last twenty-six years. The discovery of this evidence reaffirms that the attacks were neither riots nor were they confined to the Delhi region. Instead, Sikhs were attacked in eighteen states and more than one hundred cities of India in an identical manner.

---

[218] http://indiatoday.intoday.in/story/1984-sikh-riot-senior-journalists-rahul-bedi-joseph-malliakan/1/158167.html.

[219] John F. Burns, "Some Sikhs Get Justice Long After a Massacre," quoting a Delhi magistrate Shiv Narain Dinghra.

The newly discovered evidence consists of:

a) Discovery of mass graves of sixty-five Sikhs in Delhi, killed in November 1984, discovered after twenty-six years.

b) Discovery of additional nine gurdwaras in Delhi that were attacked and destroyed and ruined in November 1984.

c) Official Records of Government of India showing that a total of thirty-five thousand (35,000) claims of deaths and serious injuries were filed by Sikhs who suffered during November 1984. Out of those more than twenty thousand (20,000), claims were from attacks that took place outside Delhi and in the states of Bihar, Chhattisgarh, Haryana, Himachal Pradesh, Jammu and Kashmir, Jharkhand, Madhya Pradesh, Maharashtra, Orissa, Uttarakhand, Uttar Pradesh, Tamil Nadu, and West Bengal.

d) Mass graves of Sikhs in the village Hondh-Chillar in the state of Haryana

e) Discovery of mass cremation site in Pataudi, state of Haryana

f) Discovery of ruined houses and buildings in Gurgaon, state of Haryana

g) Discovery of ruined Sikh houses and gurdwaras in the state of West Bengal

During November 1984, the localities and villages consisting of Sikh populations were attacked and wiped out identically throughout India. The remains of all such sites were either cleaned or rebuilt to purge traces of the genocidal attack on Sikhs carried out in November 1984, in attempts to continue efforts for the concealment of any traces of the November 1984 Sikh Genocide by the Indian government. The forlorn debris and human remains at recently discovered genocidal sites throughout India are irrefutable and convincing evidence that the widespread killing of Sikhs during November

1984 was, in fact, genocide. This new evidence justifies the need for a new investigation.

*F. Perpetrators, pattern, and modus operandi*—Contrary to what is commonly imparted, November 1984, was not the result of a spontaneous reaction of the public to the assassination of Prime Minister Indira Gandhi. Instead, it was an organized and politically engineered action by Congress (I) leaders. It was facilitated by the police and the administration and carried out by Congress (I)[220] recruits. These meetings were held by Congress (I) leaders throughout India on the night of October 31, and on the morning of November 1. The meetings consisted of inflammatory speeches against Sikhs, the distribution of voter lists, and ration cards identifying Sikh households, the supply of kerosene oil, and other weaponry used in attacking Sikhs. The police and the administration's cooperation was assured to the attackers. Rajiv Gandhi's justification of the anti-Sikh violence against Sikhs was quoted as follows, "When a big tree falls, the earth shakes."[221]

The inaction of the then-Home Minister Narasimha Rao proves that violence against Sikhs had the full approval of the highest officials in the Indian government. The entire anti-Sikh pogrom was nothing short of a conspiracy hatched by the Congress (I), the political regime in control of the most central and majority ruling states of India. Through a deeper analysis, the mass-scale nature of the violence in such a short period indicates that the attacks had been preplanned and contemplated possibly as early on as Operation Blue Star (Kothari 1985) and underlines the existence of an institutional structure (Brass 2006, pp. 63–105) readily available.

---

[220] *Truth About Delhi Violence,* (Citizens for Democracy).

"Congress (I) worker Hem Chander distributed iron rods, and lathis to assailants gathered in Inderpuri," (Citizens Justice Committee, Incidents in Inderpuri, New Delhi [Dec. 10, 1985]).

[221] https://www.dnaindia.com/india/report-when-a-big-tree-falls-the-earth-shakes-how-rajiv-gandhi-justified-1984-anti-sikh-riots-2697259.

The scale and nature of violence fundamentally changed between October 31, and November 1. During this night, several meetings of Congress (I) senior and local leaders were held including the one at Ten Akbar Road, the Congress (I) headquarters, to mobilize their local supporters. The Congress (I) leadership then took the task of actively organizing the attacks that were to continue unabated throughout India for several days to come and to simultaneously numb the sentiments of the general public toward their Sikh neighbors. This was done through highly inflammatory anti-Sikh statements, which were broadcasted day and night through government-controlled radio and television channels. Many of the Congress (I) leaders, i.e., Congress (I) member of Parliament (MP) Sajjan Kumar and Congress (I) trade union leader and metropolitan Councilor Lalit Maken, provided alcohol and money to attackers, luring them to perpetrate the killings. Attackers were also provided with free transportation from their localities to Sikh neighborhoods. Transportation included Delhi Transport Corporation (DTC) buses, as well as police vehicles. These modes of transportation were used extensively to move the attackers to those areas of the city where Sikhs were concentrated. Congress (I) leaders supplied attackers with lathis (bamboo sticks), uniform-sized iron bars, knives, *trishuls* (trident), clubs, and highly inflammable substances such as kerosene and phosphorous. Attackers were also supplied with the names and addresses of Sikhs available from electoral lists, ration cards, and school registration.

Between October 31, and November 4, 1984, using All India Radio and Door-Darshan (national television), the Congress (I) leaders delivered statements such as "blood for blood," "the bloodstains should reach the home of Sikhs," and "Sikhs are the traitors of the nation." These hateful statements were aired throughout India. Not only did Congress (I) leaders organize meetings to gather perpetrators, distribute weapons, and identify targets, but they also acted as direct leaders for the attackers. In addition to previously named culprits, the names of Congress (I) officials accused of leading attacks and inciting the killings of Sikhs that can be read in most of the affidavits filed by victims and survivors are the following: Dharam Dass

Shastri, Jagdish Tytler, H. K. L. Bhagat, Balwan Khokhar, Kamal Nath, Tek Ch, Rajinder Sharma, Dr. Ashok, and Shyam Singh.

In Delhi, the attacks started simultaneously in various parts of the city, between the hours of 8:00 a.m. and 10:00 a.m. on November 1. The first targets in the localities populated by Sikhs were the Sikh gurdwaras. The Shri Guru Granth Sahib was desecrated by attackers who urinated on it and then burnt down the gurdwaras. Sikh properties were targeted as well as symbols of the Sikh faith. Turbans, uncut hair, and beards were the next target, making this a direct and personal attack. The modus operandi of killings was meticulous, systematic, and reproduced everywhere. Assailants raided previously identified Sikh households, grabbed the men, and pulled them out. The attackers tore off their turbans, beat them with iron rods and/or knives, and ultimately necklaced them with a tire, which was set on fire. The Sikhs who were seen by the attackers in the streets were mercilessly chased and killed through the same technique. Killing, looting, and arson went on unabated the entire day and continued to escalate into November 2. The crowd stopped trains to pull out Sikh passengers to kill them. Women and children were generally spared, though some were also killed, and many of them gang-raped, often as their relatives were forced to watch.

The first resulting attack on a Sikh in India took place roughly twenty-four hours after the assassination of Ms. Indira Gandhi, thus negating the theory that the killing of Sikhs in November 1984, was a spontaneous outburst of the public. It was the Congress (I) party that unleashed a nightmare of organized violence against the Sikh community of India on November 1, 1984, which continued unabated for at least the next four days. Despite clear evidence of official government involvement, police connivance, and participation of Congress Party leaders and workers in attacking the Sikhs, successive Indian governments have successfully led the world to believe that the November 1984 massacre of Sikhs was a local, spontaneous, and sporadic outburst of public reaction to Ms. Indira Gandhi's assassination by her bodyguards, who happened to be Sikh. In reality, as per the surviving victims' recount, the anti-Sikh Genocide of November 1984 was the systematic and government-sanctioned attempted annihilation of the

Sikh people in response and to avenge the death of the Indian prime minister Indira Gandhi. A commission appointed by the government of India under the chairmanship of Justice G. T. Nanavati released a report in 2005. The report confirmed that "it received 2,557 affidavits naming Congress leaders for inciting, and leading mobs in Delhi during those days."[222]

*G. Congress (I), the Nazi party of India*—The evidence shows that Indian National Congress,[223] a.k.a. Congress (I), who was in control of the central government as well as the majority of the states in India, through its workers and with the active connivance and cooperation from the police and the administration organized, orchestrated attacks on the Sikh population of India with the intent to obliterate the Sikh community fully or partially. Even a cursory look at the states where Congress (I) was in control corroborates the claim that Sikhs were mostly killed in the Congress-controlled states. The chief ministers were the heads of states at the local level and exercised complete control over the state machinery and the local Congress (I) Party machine and acted under the authority of Congress (I). Despite the widespread killings and lawlessness, the martial law was never imposed, and the Indian Army was not called in until after November 4, 1984. In the state of Madhya Pradesh,[224] the chief minister was Arjun Singh of Congress (I). Between November 1 and 4, 1984 throughout the state of Madhya Pradesh, Sikhs were attacked, killed, tortured, and raped, their properties looted, and their temples (gurdwaras) burnt.

---

[222] See 2005 report of Nanavati Commission on November 1984.

[223] Lionel Baixas, "The Anti-Sikh Pogrom of October 31 to November 4, 1984," *Online Encyclopedia of Mass Violence*, accessed November 6, 2014, http://www.massviolence.org/The-1984-Anti-Sikhs-pogroms-in-New-Dehli, ISSN 1961-9898.

[224] Madhya Pradesh is the home state of Congress leader Kamal Nath. Nath is infamous for his involvement in leading the mob that attacked Gurudwara Rakab Ganj Delhi. Several Sikhs were killed in that attack. Nath has continuously been winning the election as member of Parliament (MP) from the state since 1984. MPs exert and enjoy a great deal of control and influence over the party workers and cadres in their home states.

In October–November 1984, the present state of Chhattisgarh was a region located within the state of Madhya Pradesh where Congress(I) officials, members, and workers directed and took part in attacks on Sikh people, properties, and temples, which resulted in at least thirteen deaths.

One of the modus operandi of the attacks on the Sikhs who were traveling on trains at that time took place in the city of Morena. A crowd of one thousand people, comprised mostly of Congress (I) workers and sympathizers, and led by Congress (I) leaders gathered at the railway station. They first stopped the Utkal Express Train going to New Delhi but found no Sikh passengers on it. Almost immediately, the Chahtisgarh Express Train from New Delhi pulled into the station and was brought to a halt by the crowd, which then proceeded to drag out two dozen Sikh men, women, and children from the train and slaughtered twelve, including a ticket taker.

In the state of Utter Pradesh (UP), the chief minister was Narayan Dutt (ND) Tiwari of Congress (I). According to the central government's official records, 260 Sikhs were killed across the state between November 1 and 4, 1984. These numbers are believed to be grossly understated. For example, in the city of Kanpur alone, approximately three thousand FIRs (first information reports of crime filed with the police under the Indian Criminal Law Procedure) were lodged with the police. Approximately 4,200 houses, shops, godowns, and factories were destroyed in the violence that went on for thirty-six hours, starting on November 1, 1984.

In October–November 1984, the present state of Uttarkhand, a region located in the state of Uttar Pradesh (UP), was controlled and governed by the state of Madhya Pradesh under Congress (I) chief minister Arjun Singh. In the areas comprising today's state of Uttarkhand, at least 201 attacks were directed and/or carried out against the Sikhs, their properties, and temples by Congress (I) leaders, workers, and sympathizers with the purposeful and substantial assistance of the local police and administrators.

In the state of Bihar, the chief minister was Chandrashekhar Singh of Congress (I). Throughout the state of Bihar, 160 attacks on Sikh lives and properties took place between November 1 and 4, 1984, led by Congress (I) officials, leaders, and workers where Sikhs were murdered, and many others tortured, and where Sikh properties were looted and destroyed. In October–November 1984, the present state of Jharkhand was part of the state of Bihar, which was governed and controlled by Congress (I) and Chief Minister Chandrashekhar Singh. In the areas comprising today's state of Jharkhand, at least 460 attacks were directed at the Sikhs, their properties, and temples by Congress (I) officials, leaders, and workers and the police and local administrators who either purposefully assisted the attackers and/or planned the attacks. At least eighty-four Sikhs lost their lives in those attacks, and several hundred were seriously injured.

In the state of Gujarat, the chief minister was Madhav Singh Solanki of Congress (I). Many attacks on Sikh lives and properties took place between November 1 and 4, 1984, across the state of Gujarat; however, no accurate account of the casualties has ever been released by the government.

In the state of Haryana,[225] the chief minister was Bhajan Lal of Congress (I). Throughout the state of Haryana, sixty-five attacks on Sikh lives and properties took place between November 1 and 4, 1984, led and/or directed by Congress (I) officials, leaders, and workers, and the police and local administrators who either purposefully assisted the attackers and/or planned the attacks. The attacks resulted in numerous deaths, serious injuries by torture, and damage to real and personal property.

In the state of Himachal Pradesh, the chief minister was Virbhadra Singh of Congress (I). Throughout the state of Himachal Pradesh, seventy-eight attacks on Sikh lives and properties took place between November 1 and 4, 1984, which were led and/or directed

---

[225] Haryana is the state where on February 15, 2011, a mass grave of Sikhs, killed on November 2, 1984, was discovered in the village Hondh-Chillar in District Rewari. The residents of the village were killed, women raped, Sikh temple burnt and desecrated by attackers, who according to eyewitnesses came in buses owned and operated by the government of Haryana. The attackers were led by Congress leaders, and they exclusively targeted Sikh population of the village.

by Congress (I) officials, leaders, and workers, and the police and local administrators who purposefully assisted the attackers and/or planned the attacks. The attacks resulted in numerous deaths, serious injuries by torture, and damage to real and personal property.

In the state of Maharashtra, the chief minister was the Vasantdada Patil of Congress (I). Numerous attacks on Sikh lives and properties took place between November 1 and 4, 1984, across the state of Maharashtra; however, no accurate account of the deaths and injuries suffered by Sikhs have ever been released.

In the state of Manipur, the chief minister was Rishang Keishing of Congress (I). Numerous attacks on Sikh lives and properties took place between November 1 and 4, 1984, across the state of Manipur; however, no accurate account of the deaths and injuries suffered by Sikhs have ever been released.

In the state of Kerala, the chief minister was K. Karunakaran of Congress (I). Numerous attacks on Sikh lives and properties took place between November 1 and 4, 1984, across the state of Kerela; however, no accurate account of the deaths and injuries suffered by Sikhs have ever been released.

In the state of Meghalaya, the chief minister was W. A. Sangma of Congress (I). Numerous attacks on Sikh lives and properties took place between November 1 and 4, 1984, across the state of Meghalaya; however, no accurate account of the deaths and injuries suffered by Sikhs have ever been released.

In the state of Mizoram, the chief minister was Pu Lalthanhawla of Congress (I). Numerous attacks on Sikh lives and properties took place between November 1 and 4, 1984, across the state of Mizoram; however, no accurate account of the deaths, injuries, and losses suffered by the Sikhs have ever been released.

In the state of Orissa, the chief minister was Janaki Ballabh Pattanaik of Congress (I). Throughout the state of Orissa, 143 attacks on Sikh lives and properties took place between November 1 and 4, 1984, which were led and/or directed by Congress (I) officials, leaders, and workers and the police and local administrators who purposefully and substantially assisted the attackers and/or planned the attacks. The attacks resulted in numerous deaths, serious injuries by torture, and damage to real and personal property.

In the state of Rajasthan, the chief minister was Shiv Charan Mathur of Congress (I). Numerous attacks on Sikh lives and properties took place between November 1 and 4, 1984; however, no accurate account of the deaths and injuries suffered by Sikhs have ever been released.

*H. A tale of ten commissions and committees*—As an eyewash to offset the demand for justice and accountability, the Indian government, over the past thirty years, has set up ten commissions and committees to inquire into the November 1984 occurrence. Even a cursory review of their workings, findings, reports, recommendations, and government actions pursuant thereto reveals the hoax executed through the facade of an investigation into the November 1984 killing of Sikhs. These commissions did not have any judicial powers, and their scope of the inquiry was limited to killings in Delhi alone, which in no way encompasses the entirety of the Sikh Genocide of 1984. This is merely another way to conceal and belittle the extent and scale of the rampaging violence committed against Sikhs during this time. Listed below is a brief overview of the inquiry commissions/committees set up during the past thirty years:

- November 1984, Marwah Commission: Set up to inquire into the role of the police in the carnage; was abruptly told by the central government to stop the probe. Its records were selectively passed on to the next commission.
- May 1985, Misra Commission: Set up to probe if the violence was organized. Its August 1986 report recommended the formation of three new committees: Ahooja, Kapur-Mittal, and Jain-Banerjee.
- November 1985, Dhillon Committee: Set up to recommend rehabilitation for victims. This committee asked that insurance claims of attacked business establishments be paid, but the government rejected all such claims.

- February 1987, Kapur-Mittal Committee: Inquired, again, into the role of the police. Seventy-two policemen were identified for connivance or gross negligence, thirty recommended for dismissal. No one was punished.
- February 1987, Jain-Banerjee Committee: Looked at cases against Jagdish Tytler and Sajjan Kumar and recommended cases be registered against both. Later, Delhi HC quashed the very appointment of the committee.
- February 1987, Ahooja Committee: Set up by Misra Commission to ascertain the number of people killed in the massacre in Delhi. In August 1987, Ahooja's report put the figure at 2,733 Sikhs killed.
- March 1990, Potti-Rosha Committee: Appointed as a successor to the Jain-Banerjee Committee. Potti-Rosha also recommended the registration of cases against Sajjan Kumar and Jagdish Tytler.
- December 1990, Jain-Aggarwal Committee: Appointed as a successor to Potti-Rosha and also recommended cases against HKL Bhagat, Tytler, and Kumar. No cases were registered, and the probe was stopped in 1993.
- December 1993, Narula Committee: In its report in January 1994, it was the third committee in nine years to repeat the recommendation to register cases against Bhagat, Tytler, and Sajjan Kumar.
- May 2000–2005, Nananvati Commission: One-man commission appointed by the BJP-led government. Found "credible evidence" against Tytler and Kumar. The CBI has been consistently trying to give a clean chit to Tytler. No other Congress leader named in the report has been indicted and charged.

## III. November 1984 Sikh Genocide,[226] Not Riots[227]

UN Convention on the Prevention and Punishment of the Crime of Genocide, 1948 defines the crime of genocide as:

Any of the following acts committed with intent to destroy, in whole or in part, a national, ethnical, racial or religious group, as such: (a)Killing members of the group; (b) Causing serious bodily or mental harm to members of the group; (c) Deliberately inflicting on the group conditions of life calculated to bring about its physical destruction in whole or in part.

The convention confirms that genocide, whether committed in time of peace or war, is a crime under international law, which parties to the convention undertake "to prevent and to punish" (Article 1 of the convention). The primary responsibility to prevent and stop genocide lies with the state in which this crime takes place.

The International Criminal Tribunal for the former Yugoslavia (ICTY) stressed the importance of maintaining the rigor of the definition of genocide:

The gravity of genocide is reflected in the stringent requirements which must be satisfied

---

[226] "Genocide means any of the following acts committed with intent to destroy, in whole or in part, a national, ethnical, racial or religious group, as such: (a) Killing members of the group; (b) Causing serious bodily or mental harm to members of the group; (c) Deliberately inflicting on the group conditions of life calculated to bring about its physical destruction in whole or in part; (d) Imposing measures intended to prevent births within the group; (e) Forcibly transferring children of the group to another group." (See Article 2 of the UN Convention on the Prevention and Punishment of Genocide, 18 USC § 1091(a)(c)(d)

[227] By the very definition, the word *riots* denotes a fight between two or more communities resulting in equal or proportionate loss of life and property to all the communities involved. Unlike any riots, November 1984, violence targeted only people belonging to Sikh faith and for being Sikhs. There have not been any reports of any Hindus being killed or attacked during anti-Sikh violence of November 1984. Sikhs were the sole and lone target of the violence, and thus the violence was not "riots."

before this conviction is imposed. These requirements guard against a danger that convictions for this crime will be imposed lightly. Where these requirements are satisfied, however, the law must not shy away from referring to the crime committed by its proper name. (*Prosecutor v. Radislav Krstic*, Case No. IT-98-33-A [April 19, 2004] 37)

In the past three decades, India has consistently labeled the massacre against Sikhs following Indira Gandhi's assassination as the anti-Sikh riots. *Riot* is defined as "a wild or turbulent disturbance created by a large number of people." Labeling November 1984, as riots not only mischaracterizes the massacre, but it also purposefully masks a brutal dimension—the fact that the attacks on the Sikh population of India during November 1984, were, in fact, genocidal in nature.

The following features of the November 1984 killing of Sikhs qualify it to be genocide rather than riots:

1) The targeting of a religious group for murder and extermination, as evidenced by: (a) slogans calling for the death of all Sikhs; (b) repeated attacks by gangs to ensure that all Sikhs were killed; (c) direct targeting of Sikh property; (d) destruction of symbols and structures of the Sikh faith; and (e) perpetration of other crimes such as rape and sexual assault, beatings, and physical attacks, looting and stealing, extortion, acts of humiliation such as stripping, and mutilation of corpses.

2) Participation of the police and administration in the instigation of the murders, as well as manipulation of records and destruction of evidence to evade criminal accountability.

3) Organized and systematic implementation of the carnage, as characterized by:
   a. A systematic and uniform method of killing;
   b. Meetings of Congress Party leaders and workers on the night of October 31, and the morning of November

1, before the initiation of the massacres. Leaders of the Congress Party distributed weapons and asked the attendees to kill Sikhs and promised rewards and assured impunity in return.

c.  Organized dissemination of rumors through state-run media.

d.  Use of government data and record, such as voter registration lists and ration cards to identify and locate Sikhs.

e.  Transportation of gangs of assailants in government vehicles.

f.  Supply and distribution of weapons and kerosene oil to the assailants by local Congress Party leaders.

g.  Supply and distribution of instantaneously combustible chemical powder by local Congress Party leaders.

In November 1984, the atrocious attacks against Sikhs were carried out throughout India to destroy the Sikh religious identity by a political party with the track record of openly detesting Sikhs. This conforms to the research published by the United Nations secretary general's special adviser on Genocide stating that "[genocidal] attacks do tend to take place in a country [like India which is] inhabited by diverse religious groups among whom conflicts, and differences are fomented by discrimination, hate speech inciting violence, and other violations of human rights."

The latest evidence that Sikhs throughout India were subjected to genocidal attacks is the recent discovery of mass graves of Sikhs in the village Hondh-Chillar, in the Indian state of Haryana. According to eyewitness reports, on November 2, 1984, the Sikh population of the village was attacked by a group of about five hundred people. These attackers were transported to the village in state-issued vehicles. The attackers were armed and led by leaders of Congress (I). The group was chanting the slogan, "Sikhs are traitors, and we will annihilate them." The attackers surrounded Sikh houses and started throwing petrol bombs into the houses. Men and children were beaten and thrown into the burning houses, and the women were first raped and then thrown into the fire to die. Eyewitnesses also account for the Sri Guru Granth Sahib being desecrated and a gurdwara set on fire.

How the Sikh population of the village Hondh-Chillar was exterminated coincides with the pattern of the contemporaneous attacks that took place throughout India. These statewide attacks have been documented in statements of survivors, witnesses, and reports of human rights groups. Therefore, what Sikhs, a religious minority, were subjected to during November 1984, was genocide because it was an organized, systematic, targeted, and intentional attack on a religious minority.

## IV. Justice for Sikhs—A Mirage

After thirty-seven years and the implementation of several inquiry commissions, justice for the victims of the November 1984 Sikh Genocide appears to be nothing more than a mirage.

An example of the denial of justice to victims of the November 1984 occurrence with the complicity of all the organs of the state and government of India is the treatment meted out to the writ petition filed by Manushi. In early 1985, an Indian-based (New Delhi) organization, Manushi, filed a petition in the supreme court of India demanding action against those leaders of the Congress (I) Party who were alleged to have masterminded the 1984 massacre of the Sikhs (Manushi No. 25, 1984). The said petition was filed against the Indian State, the home minister, and the home secretary; these are the officials who assume specific responsibility for the preservation of the safety of the life of Indian citizens. Also named as respondents in the suit were the Delhi Police through the police commissioner, the Congress (I) Party through its president, and the general secretaries, including the Congress (I) Lok Sabha (Parliament) members from Delhi.

The petition stated that by organizing a systematic massacre of the Sikhs, attacking their homes, businesses, and religious institutions, the Congress (I) leaders, with the active help and connivance of the city administration, including the police, had violated the fundamental rights of the entire Sikh population of India. These included the right to life (Article 21), the right to move freely throughout the country (19 [1d]), the right to practice any profession or carry out any occupation (19 [li]), the right to reside and settle in any part of the country (19 [le]), the right to freedom of conscience, and the right to freely profess and practice any religion. The previously mentioned rights, as well as all other fundamental rights of Sikhs, were violated by the state when they entered into an illegal conspiracy with organized gangs of hoodlums. The petition appealed to the court to:

a)  Order an independent inquiry into all the heinous crimes committed to uncover how the orders were given and by whom;

b)  Order an interim suspension from office of those who were leading the cover-up operations;

c)  Require that the inquiry result in the enunciation of basic principles that should govern the trials of these violators of constitutional rights;

d)  Pending the court's decision, freeze all assets of these organizations and individuals under inquiry;

e)  Offer institutional remedies to return the country to constitutional rule;

f)  Provide guidelines for the payment of punitive fines, reparations, and compensations from the frozen assets of the extragovernmental organizations and individuals who are convicted of having participated in the murderous attacks on the lives and constitutional rights of Indian citizens belonging to the Sikh minority.

Manushi's petition was unceremoniously dismissed by a bench of supreme court, presided over by Justice Ranganath Misra, without as much as a cursory hearing. The dismissal of Manushi's petition, without being heard by the supreme court of India, the highest judicial forum of the country, proves the complicity of all the state institutions of India in denying justice to the victims of November

1984. This pattern of denying justice is redundant, as it has been seen repeatedly, without fail, over the last thirty years.

Justice Misra was nominated to head the government-appointed inquiry committee known as the Misra Committee. Later Congress (I) government promoted and made Justice Misra chief justice of the country. After his retirement, Justice Misra became member Parliament (Rajayasabha) on the ticket of Congress (I), the same political party that Justice Mishra had exonerated in the 1984 violence cases during his career as a judge.

Although successive Indian governments set up several inquiry commissions/committees to investigate the November 1984 killing, a review of their scope, findings, and lack of government action on their recommendations reveals the hoax played through the facade of an investigation into the November 1984 killing of Sikhs. These commissions did not have any judicial powers, and their scope of the inquiry was limited to the violence in Delhi alone—another way to cover up the extent and scale of violence against Sikhs. These commissions and committees were used as eyewash to offset demands for justice and accountability for the November 1984 violence.

## V. Recognition of 1984 Anti-Sikh Violence as the Genocide

The following states, local governments, or individuals have recognized the genocide of the Sikhs by India:

### U.S. City of Harvey, Illinois, USA, Declares 1984 Anti-Sikh Violence as "Genocide" (November 10, 2014)

Resolution 2734 was a proposed motion in the City Council of Harvey Illinois. It was seconded and then unanimously approved. City councilman Joseph Whittington Jr. who presented the resolution followed its approval by addressing the Sikh community, "We would like to let you know that America is a great country. Harvey is a great place. We want to support you and I am glad to be a part, WE as a city council, are glad to be a part of '1984 Yes It Is Genocide.'"[228]

## Bakersfield California Passes Resolution Declaring the 1984 Systematic Killing of Sikhs in India as Genocide[229]

A RESOLUTION OF THE COUNCIL OF THE CITY OF BAKERSFIELD COMMEMORATING THE NOVEMBER 1984 VIOLENCE IN INDIA AS SIKH GENOCIDE (DECEMBER 12, 2015):

The City of Bakersfield, one of the largest cities in Southern California, issued a resolution recognizing the 1984 anti-Sikh violence in which thousands of Sikhs were systematically killed across India as genocide, and a violation of human rights.

The City Council also condemned any continuing human rights violations against religious minorities in India and expressed solidarity with the local Sikh population in remembrance of those who lost their lives in the November 1984 violence. The genocide resolution was passed in the presence of the Honorable Mayor Harvey Hall by council members Willie Rivera, council member, Ward 1, Terry Maxwell, council member, Ward 2, Ken Weir, council member, Ward 3, Bob Smith, council member, Ward 4, Harold Hanson, Vice Mayor and council member, Ward 5, Jacquie Sullivan, council member, Ward 6, Chris Parlier, council member, Ward 7

---

[228] https://www.sikhnet.com/news/us-city-declares-1984-anti-sikh-violence-genocide.

[229] https://sikhnews.net/301/bakersfield-california-passes-resolution-declaring-the-1984-systematic-killing-of-sikhs-in-india-as-genocide.

and recorded by the official City Clerk Roberta Gafford, CMC, and approved in form by Bakersfield City Attorney Virginia Gennaro, and Associate City Attorney Viridiana Gallardo-King.

## Ontario passes motion calling 1984 riots genocide (April 2017)

Liberal Party legislator Harinder Malhi who moved a motion in the Ontario Assembly termed the 1984 Sikh massacre as genocide. Ontario Assembly became the first legislature in Canada to carry a motion that described the 1984 anti-Sikh violence as genocide.

Harinder Malhi, a member of the Provincial Parliament of Ontario, belongs to Riding (as constituencies are called in Canada) of Brampton-Springdale, near Toronto.

The 1984 Sikh Genocide was triggered by the assassination of former Indian prime minister Indira Gandhi on October 31, 1984, by two of her Sikh bodyguards, in response to her actions leading to the Indian Army invasion of the Golden Temple Amritsar (Darbar Sahib) to eliminate Sikh freedom fighters.

## The City of Stockton California Passes Resolution Recognizing 1984 anti-Sikh Violence as Genocide (April 27, 2016)

The City of Stockton, California, the historic home of the first Gurdwara Sahib in the United States, and notable headquarters of the Ghadar Movement, for a second time officially recognized the 1984 Government perpetuated anti-Sikh violence in India as genocide.[230]

The honorable Mayor of Stockton, Anthony Silva, along with the City council members Christina Fugazi, Elbert Holman, Susan Lofthus, Michael Tubbs, Daniel Wright, and Michael Blower approved the resolution from the City of Stockton stating that the City of Stockton is in support of this resolution to recognize the intentional, deliberate and systematic killing of Sikhs in India during

---

[230] https://sikhnews.net/310/city-of-stockton-california-passes-resolution-recognizing-1984-anti-sikh-violence-as-genocide.

November 1984 as "Genocide" as defined under the laws of the United States and UN Convention.

## Kerman City, California, recognizes November 1984 systematic killing of Sikhs as genocide (November 4, 2015).

The city council of Kerman[231] recognized that the 1984 violence against Sikh lives, properties, and places of worship throughout India was carried out with the intent to destroy the Sikh community and was, thus, genocide, as defined under the law of the United States and the United Nations Genocide Convention 1948.

The city council also called upon Barack Obama, former president of the United States of America, and the congress to recognize the anti-Sikh violence of November 1984 as genocide.

Several other city governments in California and elsewhere have recognized the anti-Sikh violence as the Sikh Genocide.

## *VI. World Scholars on November 1984 Sikh Genocide*

[During November 1984] the mood in India "bore an ominous resemblance to that of the 1930's Germany, likening the orchestrated urban pogroms against Sikhs, and Muslims to so many Kristallnacht." (Paul Brass, professor of political science and international studies at the University of Washington, Seattle, *Cambridge History of India Series*)

The attacks on Sikhs in the early days of November 1984 killed at least as many people as the Chilean regime of Augusto Pinochet killed in more than 17 years. (Barbara Crossett, *New York Times* reporter)

Though some will find the analogy with Nazi Germany here too extreme, both the explicit

---

[231] https://www.fresnobee.com/news/local/article43072923.html.

targeting of Sikhs as traitors following Operation Blue-Star, and the clear earmarking of Sikh residence, and business in the post-assassination carnage speak to an incipient genocidal campaign. (Cynthia K. Mehmood, associate professor of anthropology, University of Notre Dame, Indiana, USA, and senior fellow at Joan B. Kroc Institute for International Peace Studies)

## VII. Conclusion

The actions of the Indian government in continuously denying Sikhs justice are evidence that the present and future of Sikhs in India is not secure. The facts and details reported in the preceding pages sufficiently establish that violence perpetrated against Sikh people in India during November 1984 was genocidal in nature, should thus be declared as such under Article 2 of the UN Convention on Genocide.[232]

---

[232] Sikhs for Justice (SFJ), New York, a USA-based human rights advocacy group; All India Sikh Students Federation (AISSF), a Punjab-based NGO.
    Edited by: Gurpatwant Singh Pannun, Esq. legal adviser, SFJ.
    Salman Yunus, director, research and litigation, SFJ.
    Jatinder Singh Grewal, director, international policy, SFJ.
    Harsahib Kaur, JD, Touro Law Center, NY BA-BS, Stony Brook University, New York.

# Operation Woodrose

*Operation Woodrose* was a military operation carried out by the Indira Gandhi-led Indian government in the months after Operation Blue Star to "prevent the outbreak of widespread public protest" in Punjab.[233] The government arrested all prominent members of the largest Sikh political party, the Akali Dal, and banned the All India Sikh Students Federation, a large students' union.

Simultaneously the Indian Army conducted operations in the countryside during which thousands of Sikhs, overwhelmingly young men, were detained for interrogation and subsequently tortured. Despite its purported success in controlling the armed insurgency in the Punjab region, the operation was criticized by human rights groups for the suspension of civil liberties and habeas corpus, resulting in the disappearances of thousands of Sikh men. After the operation, the central government was criticized for using draconian legislation to repress a minority community.

At the peak deployment, army personnel involved in curbing militancy ranged between two to three lakhs (two hundred thousand to three hundred thousand). They were drawn mainly from the corps based at Ambala, Bathinda, and Jalandhar.[234]

---

[233] Harnik Deol, *Religion and Nationalism in India: The Case of the Punjab* (Psychology Press, 2000), 108–109.

[234] Inderjit Singh Jaijee, *Politics of Genocide: Punjab, 1984–1994* (The University of Michigan, 1995), 216.

## *Deployment of Army in Punjab*

While Blue Star was unparalleled, dramatic, and destructive beyond words, the mopping-up operation, code-named Woodrose, was a nightmare for Sikhs living in Punjab villages. Woodrose was, in fact, an extension of Blue Star. In war, when the attacking forces capture an objective, it is followed through to mop up enemy troops, which may be hiding in the vicinity of the operation of the objective. In this case, the whole of Punjab State was brought under the process of mopping-up operations. The army, duly assisted by paramilitary forces and state police, indulged in the most inhuman treatment of Sikh inhabitants.[235]

Indian government deployed a massive amount of army and paramilitary force in Punjab and a sixty-thousand-strong Punjab Police to suppress the freedom movement in Punjab. The government finally decided to use the ultimate weapon in Punjab with the undeclared aim of putting down militancy, which amounts to introducing martial law from the backdoor. The civil authorities had never requisitioned army support; it operated unlawfully. All Sikh political parties and human rights organizations condemned this deployment. No modern civilized country has its armed forces deployed in such an unabashed manner against its people. Sikhs must understand that India does not consider them as its people. Sikhs have been denied their statehood, identity, religion, and language. They would be naive to think otherwise.

Declared or undeclared, Sikhs considered Operation Woodrose as the second war the Delhi government started against Punjab after Operation Blue Star. Sikhs decided to face it with bravado and self-confidence. It reflected on the Sikh tradition of never bowing to repression and injustice reminiscent of the tyrannical reign of the Mughal governor of Lahore Mir Mannu. Sikhs had then coined the phrase "the more they cut us, the more we grow."

---

[235] Lt. Col. Partap Singh, *Khalistan: The Only Option; The Bleeding Punjab*, US ed. (1991), 99.

The tiny state of Punjab covers barely 1.5 percent of India's landmass, and Sikhs comprise about 1.8 percent of the Indian population. However, it has the dubious honor of hosting more troops, paramilitary, and police than ever maintained by foreign rulers like Mughals and the British during peacetime. More Sikhs have been killed in free India than the freedom fighters killed during some two hundred years before August 14, 1947, comprising all communities. The army operated independently and in conjunction with other security forces, including Border Security Forces, Central Reserve Police Force, Rashtriya Rifles, commandos, ITBP (Indo-Tibetan Police Force), totaling 646 companies in June 1991. A major segment of the army was deployed in Punjab, comprising about 1.5 percent of India's land area. Together they committed brutalities with impunity unheard of in any civilized country.

Although the army was not deployed under a declared martial law or in aid to civil authority, it was in occupied territory. The two examples are the killing of innocent Sikh farmers in the village Nathu Ke Burj, some twenty-five kilometers from the Indo-Pak border, in a pure army ambush and Brigadier R. P. Sinha warning the village elders in Tehsil Ajnala in these words, "If there is any militant violence in your villages, all-male members will be killed, and your women will be taken to army camps to breed a new race."[236] The Indian State thus surpassed the Nazi regime; in his anti-Jewish drive, Hitler did not go as far as to breed a new race through cohabitation of military personnel with Jewish women.

Under these circumstances, successive Indian governments betrayed every promise of the partnership between Sikhs and the Congress Party of Nehru, Gandhi, and Patel. The latter has violated every term and condition of that partnership agreement, which no longer remains valid or functional and consequently stands dissolved.

---

[236] International Human Rights Organization, *Indo-US Shadow Over Punjab* (Ludhiana, 1992),82.

## *Violence Against Women*

It had become a sport with the police and paramilitary personnel to dishonor Sikh women. Two of the innumerable cases are described here. Surjit Kaur, a seventeen-year-old girl, was taken to Kathunangal Police Station and gang-raped by half a dozen cops over two days. When the bleeding did not stop, she was handed over to the guardians. No hospital would admit her. One private practitioner was prevailed upon to treat her. He did so but refused to give a written medical report as he was aware of the doctors' fate who had gotten on the wrong side of the police.

Another even more reprehensible episode involved two minor girls, ages thirteen (Satwinder Kaur, daughter of Joginder Singh, Granthi) and fourteen of the village Bham (Sarbjit Kaur, daughter of Makhan Singh of the same village), in Gurdaspur district. On the morning of June 11, 1989, Satwinder Kaur and Sarbjit Kaur went to the nearby canal to fetch clay. When they did not come back, the parents started to search for them but could not find them. On June 12, their fathers went to Sri Hargobindpur Police Station and reported the disappearance to R. L. Bagga, SHO (police), who did not register a complaint but told them to keep looking. They were picked by a police constable and a home guard. After satisfying their lust, they killed their victims and threw their naked bodies in a ditch. Despite the best efforts of their parents, village elders, social and human rights activists, and large-scale demonstrations at various levels, no case was registered by the authorities until a month later, when protests and agitations forced the governor of Punjab, S. S. Ray, to suspend the guilty. In India, it usually means that a departmental inquiry is held, and after months, the culprits are exonerated for "want of sufficient evidence."[237]

---

[237] Inderjit Singh Jaijee, *Politics of Genocide: Punjab 1984–1994* (1995), 126.

## The Danger and Threats from Indian Security

In Chandigarh alone, in June 1992, there were five reported cases of attacks on women. One evening, two CRPF men, posted near the Chandigarh-Punjab border, entered the hut of gardener Rampal and attempted to rape his wife. The gardener grabbed a length of pipe and killed both men. The next day, three CRPF and Chandigarh police constables attempted to rape a woman in the Burail labor colony. A minor girl was raped by a man in uniform in sector 31, and another minor girl was raped in sector 36. In another labor colony (number 4), a home guard attempted to rape a woman.[238]

State terrorism unleashed by police chief Ribeiro resulted in the liquidation of "identified" and "unidentified" militants in fake encounters and the families of militants and their sympathizers. Their houses were set on fire. Their womenfolk were taken into custody and molested. Brutal torture in Batala of two young women, Gurdev Kaur and Gurmeet Kaur, by S. S. P. Gobind Ram to force them to produce their husbands, missing for several years, led to much outcry against police. The two women were rendered incapacitated. PHRO revealed that state-sponsored vigilante groups, who often operated in militants' garb, were involved in several cases of molestation and rape of young Sikh girls and women.[239]

Such incidents tarnished the image of the police. Ribeiro ultimately realized that there could be no decisive battle against terrorism without a bold initiative to tackle the problem at the political level. He realized the futility of the policy of cold repression and the bullet-for-bullet strategy. He said, in unequivocal terms, "The police can only fight terrorism, not solve it."[240]

Such examples are too innumerable to enlist here. As many as twenty to thirty Sikhs were killed daily, in fake police encounters, by state-sponsored vigilante groups, and trigger-happy drunken cops.

---

[238] Ibid., 127.

[239] International Human Rights Organization, *Indo-US Shadow Over Punjab* (Ludhiana, 1992), 41.

[240] *India Today*, August 15, 1988.

Under Julio F. Ribeiro, director general of police, the police had no accountability. This was highlighted collectively by the senior-most civil servants, commissioners, and the administrative secretaries at a meeting with the chief secretary of Punjab, Tejinder Khanna. They described that there was total police rule and that they were virtually made irrelevant and humiliated. They were, however, too scared to have their statements recorded in the proceedings of the meeting. Reportedly Khanna personally wrote the following in the minutes of that meeting:

> Most of the police stations in Punjab, numbering around 250, have certain things in common. They have four unauthorized commodities: anyone between the ages of 10 to 30 illegally arrested young Sikh men. They are used for different purposes, such as staging fake encounters, extracting information, and extorting money from their parents and guardians. Second, unauthorized small arms and ammunition to place on the bodies of those killed in fake encounters. Third, instruments of tortures. Lastly, the garments of militants which the policemen used for masquerading as Sikh freedom fighters to raid homes of innocent people, extort money and indulge in other unlawful activities.

The fate of Sikhs in other states of India was even more pathetic. They are virtually treated as hostages and intimidated. There are numerous occasions when they have been massacred, their women are dishonored, properties looted and destroyed. The beating of Sikhs, pulling or cutting their beards or hair, are common occurrences.

Human rights organizations like Amnesty International, Asia Watch, and the UN Human Rights Committee have condemned human rights abuses in India, with particular reference to Punjab. Many other non-Sikh organizations in India, like Peoples Union for Democratic Rights (PUDR), Peoples Union for Civil Liberties

(PUCL), Committee for Information and Initiative on Punjab, have investigated and documented numerous cases involving extrajudicial killings, torture, and disappearances. The sole purpose of deploying the army in Punjab was to kill young Sikh males with hardly any Sikh youth remaining alive. This has been confirmed with the absence of marriage ceremonies in many villages of Punjab after 1984.

Joyce Pettigrew, a British anthropologist who made an impartial and in-depth study of the militancy in Punjab and several militant organizations, observed:

> All guerrillas mention that it was the security forces' behavior towards them and their families that finally drew them into the struggle. All mention that it was a matter of honor to resist. Operation Blue Star and Woodrose were attacks on the Sikh sense of honor. Particularly the attacks on amritdhari (baptized Sikhs), simply because they were amritdhari, caused outrage.[241]

The following statement is from a Hindu doctor working in rural areas of the Amritsar district:

> The police torture people very cruelly. Firstly, they begin by savagely beating them. Secondly, they bend their hands and arms backward and upward toward the ceiling and tie them there (Kachcha Fansi or half-baked hanging). Thirdly, they then administer an electric shock. In Tarn Taran, an electrically generated belt is used. Fourthly, they use wooden weapons on the body and crush the legs. I see fifty to one hundred per year in such like condition within a five to ten-kilometer radius. If a boy looks as though he is dying in the police station, they plan an

---

[241] Joyce Pettigrew, *Sikhs of the Punjab* (London, 1995), 139–40.

encounter some kilometers away, the day before.
It is very meticulously planned. Encounters are
always 100% bogus.[242]

The pattern in each village appears to be the same. During the early evening, the army cordons a village and announces over the loudspeakers that everyone must come out. All males between the ages of fifteen to thirty-five are trussed and blindfolded, then taken away. Thousands have disappeared in Punjab since the army operation began. The government has not provided any list of names; families do not know if sons and husbands are arrested, underground, or dead. [243]

---

[242] Joyce Pettigrew, *Sikhs of Punjab: Unheard Voices of State and Guerrilla Violence* (London: Zed Books Ltd., 1995), 69.

[243] Mary Ann Weaver, "India's Sikhs Are Bitter as Army Tries Weed Out 'Militants,'" Christian Science Monitor, October 15, 1984.

# Operations Black Thunder I and II

### Operation Black Thunder I

After the declaration of Khalistan on April 29, 1986, from Akal Takhat, the Indian government attacked Darbar Sahib on April 30, 1986. About three hundred National Security Guard commandos and seven hundred Border Security Force troops stormed into the Golden Temple complex and captured about three hundred Sikhs. This operation was approved by Surjit Singh Barnala, the then-chief minister of Punjab, and lasted eight hours.[244] A force of nearly two thousand paramilitary police completed a twelve-hour operation to regain control of the Golden Temple at Amritsar from several hundred Sikh radicals. The police stated that one civilian was killed and two escaped; almost all the major radical leaders managed to escape.[245]

### Operation Black Thunder II

Planning for Operation Black Thunder II was started in early 1988, in Manesar (Aravali hills), forty kilometers from Delhi, by National Security Guard (NSG) under patronage from the home minister rather than the Ministry of Internal Security. A large model of the Darbar Sahib complex was prepared. The practice was carried

---

[244] Steven R. Weishan, "Indian policemen raid Sikh temple," *New York Times*, retrieved July 5, 2018.

[245] https://www.nytimes.com/1986/05/02/world/india-police-in-control-of-sikh-temple.html.

out at a high school in Tauru and at a college in Nuh, Haryana. Both these schools had structures that resembled the *Parikarma* (perimeter) of Darbar Sahib. Regular visits to Darbar Sahib were carried out by the Special Action Group (SAG), who started growing beards to disguise their operation.

State-sponsored terrorist groups began massive murderous assaults from December 1987, liquidating families of militants and their sympathizers under Izhar Alam, senior superintendent of police, Amritsar. The police made regular announcements of recoveries of Russian-made rocket-propelled grenade launchers and Russian-made surface-to-air missiles from all over Punjab, which were imported earlier from Kabul by RAW (Indian external intelligence agency).

Threatening journalists suppressed free speech at Amritsar by Union Home Ministry. Kuldip Singh Arora, an Amritsar correspondent of United News of India, was picked up on April 13, 1988, under the ridiculous National Security Act for meeting militants inside the Golden Temple complex, a serious charge under the Terrorist and Disruptive Activities Act (TADA).

M. K. Dhar, former joint director of the intelligence bureau, in his book *Open Secrets*, described how the IB had quietly begun supplying AK-47s to the then Akal Takht, Jathedar Jasbir Singh Rode. Rhode is Jarnail Singh Bhindranwale's nephew. Rode, an IB operative who was anointed Jathedar of the supreme Sikh temporal seat, was tasked to create a Trojan horse comprising a fifteen-member squad to neutralize the terrorist gangs inside the temple. In all, three consignments of AK-47s were supplied to him before Operation Black Thunder II. However, this measure yielded only a limited result, with a total of three terrorists belonging to the Khalistan Commando Force being killed.[246]

Indian government deployed National Security Guard (NSG) commandos who took control of the complex and established a tight cordon. NSG sharpshooters, armed with sniper rifles and equipped with a night vision, shot at everything that moved, thus keeping

---

[246] https://www.tribuneindia.com/news/archive/comment/black-thunder-ii-operation-to-remember-233772.

all inside the temple complex pinned down. In the following days, NSG commandos quickly established control over all buildings in the outer areas of the temple complex.

At a policy level, it was decided to wear down the militants. Continuous sniping and heavy machine-gun fire brought on the *bungas* day and night and kept the militants pinned while increasing psychological pressure. The sound of gunfire was punctuated by periodic declarations of unilateral cease-fire, accompanied by calls for surrender, which resulted in flushing out of many of the militants, along with all the devotees caught inside. On May 18, a final batch of forty-six militants, who had taken refuge inside the Darbar Sahib three days earlier, walked out with their hands in the air, marking the end of the ten-day-long siege. Three NSG commandos were injured while conducting a flushing-out operation in the langar and Manji Sahib buildings. It is a different story that all the militants were subsequently acquitted for "lack of evidence" and that the Punjab Police had to resort to "other means" to keep them in jail. Despite provocations, there was no firing from inside the complex. To prepare the nation, the state-sponsored militants fired on Gadi Lohars, a nomad tribe celebrating marriage in Panipat, Haryana, on May 8, 1988, killing thirteen people.

Jasbir Singh Rode (Roday) who was at Punjab University, Patiala, rushed back to Amritsar to hear of the shooting incidents. On May 11, the local administration bluffed Rode to take him the following day, at 8:00 a.m., to enter Darbar Sahib from Santokhsar Gurdwara to restore the rituals. Precisely at this time, the security forces started firing. Rode, Savinder Singh, Jaswant Singh, Kashmira Singh, Bhai Mohkam Singh, and Gurdev Singh Kaunke (former acting Jathedar of Akal Takhat Sahib), along with twenty-four others were prevented from proceeding further. After protests, Rode decided to move ahead despite the firing. Kaunke told police, "You men are liars. It is you who are shooting, not the militants." He was struck with a CRPF rifle butt. Rode and his men were arrested for violating the curfew. The NSG was prepared and began Operation Black Thunder.

# Bounties for the Heads
# of Sikh Activists

Mughal emperors and British governors alike tried military solutions to the Sikh problem and succeeded only in adding to the roll of martyrs cherished by the proud and prickly people. Sikhs have long memories. They have never forgotten or forgiven the day in 1919 when General Dyer ordered his troops to open fire in the sacred city of Amritsar, and Mrs. Gandhi may well have cause to rue the day she did the same. (*Sunday Telegraph*, London, June 10, 1984)

It is common knowledge that the Indian government allocated, and the Punjab government distributed, large sums of money to the police in Punjab to torture and kill Sikhs who were suspected of having even the slightest involvement in the freedom movement. The police, many times, captured and killed innocent Sikhs and claimed bounties on their heads. It was even worse than the times when Mughals had put the prices on the heads of Sikhs. This time, the real difference was that the Indian government had convinced some Sikhs to kill their own. Sikh police officers killed militants and innocent Sikhs to claim bounties and promotions. The other difference being that the Mughals almost always returned the dead bodies to their families. In contrast, the Indian Police never returned the bodies to their heirs and were disposed of by throwing them in the rivers.

220

According to highly placed sources, the Union Government had made available a huge amount of Rs.—4,500 crores (4500,00,00,000)—to Surendra Nath, IPS, who held many prestigious posts from time to time, to prop up terrorism in Punjab and Kashmir in a bid to defame the Punjab and Kashmir militants. Both the union home minister Mr. S. B. Chavan and the Internal Security minister Mr. Rajesh Pilot were well aware that Mr. Nath had very successfully infiltrated "officials" of the Punjab and Kashmir government into various terrorist groups.[247, 248]

It was surprising for the people of Punjab that the Indian government, and especially the Home Ministry, pretended to be ignorant regarding the "seizures" made from Punjab Raj Bhawan after Mr. Nath's demise. The total "collection" amounts to rupees 800 crore,[249] including cash, jewelry, and other immovable property. According to sources, this body seems to be a part of the amount of Rs. 4,500 crore, which was placed at the disposal of Mr. Surendra Nath to root out terrorism.

Mr. Surendra Nath played an all-important role to give strength to the hitherto lesser-known CISF (Central Industrial Security Force). It is being alleged that some of its men were used to killing innocent persons, including the family members of the Punjab Police personnel, as well as teachers, doctors, engineers, media men, and political personalities.

A "suspended" police official, Bakhshish Singh, remained close to Mr. Surendra Nath. Mr. Singh was the security in charge of the all-time high-profile top Akali leader and the former Punjab finance minister Balwant Singh, who was gunned down by "terrorists" in broad daylight. Bakhsish Singh was immediately suspended after the ghastly murder of Mr. Balwant Singh. However, with the advent of Mr. Surendra Nath as the governor of Punjab, Bakhshish Singh, a Nath confidant, reappeared on the scene and enjoyed easy access to

---

[247] International Sikh Organization, *U.S. Congress on Sikh Struggle for Khalistan: Volume One, 1985–1998*, 263.

[248] Sukhbir Osan, "From The Hindutva," November 6, 1994, Surendra Nath Paid to Fan Militancy?

[249] A crore is ten million.

Mr. Surendra Nath, even at odd hours and was well informed of all the secret missions of the late governor.

Though the union home minister, Mr. S. B. Chavan, denied that currency has been seized from the Punjab Raj Bhavan, he further complicated the issue by saying that only Prime Minister Rao could say anything about the seizures made from the Raj Bhavan.

Though the veteran CPI leader and the former Punjab minister, Mr. Satyapal Dang, and the Khalistan protagonist Mr. Simranjit Singh Mann have asked for a CBI probe into the Punjab Raj Bhavan seizures, the government of India was maintaining a steady silence. Meanwhile, a human rights protagonist and an advocate of the Punjab and Haryana High Court filed a written petition in the supreme court for a CBI probe into the matter.

According to sources, the list of seizures prepared by intelligence agencies is exceptionally long. It consists of rupees 110 crore in cash, jewelry worth rupees 40 crore, immovable property worth rupees 650 crore, various political bungalows and farmhouses, and above all, his attempt to grab land near Kullu at a throwaway price of rupees 8 crore.

# India's Continuing Violence against Sikhs

India enacted black draconian laws like Unlawful Activities Prevention Act (UAPA) 1967, National Security Act, 1980, and its 1984 revision, the Punjab Disturbed Area Ordinance 1983, the Armed Forces (Punjab and Chandigarh) Special Powers Act 1983, the Terrorist Affected Areas (Special Courts) Act 1984, and the Terrorist and Disruptive Activities (Prevention) Act (TADA) 1985–1995. Under these acts, mere suspects could be arrested, detained for up to a year without any access to the law and or any charges filed against them. Their families were not informed about their whereabouts, condition, or status.

## Continuous Violation of UNCAT (February 4, 1985) By India

United Nations Convention against Torture and other Cruel, Inhuman or Degrading Treatment or Punishment is commonly referred to as UNCAT. While about 140 countries have ratified it, India has not. India openly commits unspeakable tortures of its citizens.

India has denied a visa to the delegation of the United States Commission on International Religious Freedom. "Our Commission has visited China, Russia, Saudi Arabia, and over 20 other countries. India, a close ally of the United States, has been unique among democracies in delaying and denying USCIRF's ability to visit," said commission chair Felice D. Gaer.[250] The question arises as to why India has denied a visa to the delegation of the United States Commission on International Religious Freedom. Obviously India is hiding massacres, rapes, tortures, and repression of minorities. The CIA (2018) has declared India's Vishva Hindu Prashad (VHP) and Bajrang Dal as militant organizations, and RSS a Hindu nationalist party.

According to the USCIRF 2020 report, the Trump administration has recommended imposing targeted sanctions on Indian government agencies and officials responsible for severe violations of religious freedom by freezing those individuals' assets and/or barring their entry into the United States under human rights-related financial and visa authorities, citing specific religious violations. It also recommended that the US administration designate India as a "country of special concern" (previously called Tier 1) for engaging in and tolerating systematic, ongoing, and egregious religious freedom violations as defined by the International Religious Freedom Act.[251]

In Punjab, the police and the military carried out torture, cruel and inhuman treatment of Sikhs with total impunity. Following Operation Blue Star, started Operation Woodrose, in which the police and the army were authorized to capture, torture, and kill Sikh youth from the villages. This was carried to such an extent that no marriages took place for about twenty years in many villages.

Terrorist and Disruptive Activities (Prevention) Act, commonly known as TADA, was an Indian antiterrorism law that went into force between 1985 and 1995, under the background of the Punjab insurgency and was applied to the whole of India. This act gave the police and the army widespread powers to arrest and detain without trial under vague provisions. Minimal legal safeguards for fair trial provided in the international human rights instruments did not apply to persons tried under TADA.

---

[250] https://www.hindustantimes.com/delhi/we-were-denied-visa-by-india/story-81zPa6TLEevRDmjxtrYkEL.html.

[251] https://indianexpress.com/article/india/religious-freedom-uscirf-report-downgrades-india-for-violations-6383796/.

## Violation of the Universal Declaration of Human Rights (UDHR), December 10, 1948

The *Universal Declaration of Human Rights* (UDHR)[252] is an international document adopted by the United Nations General Assembly that enshrines the rights and freedoms of all human beings. It was accepted by the general assembly as Resolution 217, at its third session on December 10, 1948, at the Palais de Chaillot in Paris, France.[253] Of the fifty-eight members of the United Nations at the time, forty-eight voted in favor, none against, eight abstained, and two did not vote.

Considered a foundational text in the history of human and civil rights, the declaration consists of thirty articles detailing an individual's "basic rights and fundamental freedoms" and affirming their universal character as inherent, inalienable, and applicable to all human beings. Adopted as a "common standard of achievement for all peoples and all nations," the UDHR commits nations to recognize all humans as being "born free and equal in dignity and rights," regardless of "nationality, place of residence, gender, national or ethnic origin, color, religion, language, or any other status."[254] The declaration is considered a "milestone document" for its "universalist language," which makes no reference to a particular culture, political system, or religion.[255] It directly inspired the development of international human rights law and was the first step in the formulation of the International Bill of Human Rights, which was completed in 1966 and came into force in 1976.

The Universal Declaration of Human Rights (UDHR) represents the first global codification of rights to which all human beings are inherently entitled. In 1947, the newly established United Nations, largely in response to World War II's atrocities, set up a dedicated Human Rights Commission chaired by Eleanor Roosevelt

---

[252] "Universal Declaration of Human Rights," The British Library, retrieved August 16, 2015.

[253] "Human Rights Law," www.un.org.

[254] UDHR booklet, article 2.

[255] "Universal Declaration of Human Rights," www.amnesty.org.

(1884–1962). After eighteen months of deliberation, the commission drafted the UDHR, which was adopted by the UN on December 10, 1948.

The declaration consists of the following:

- The preamble sets out the historical and social causes that led to the necessity of drafting the declaration.
- Articles 1–2 established the basic concepts of dignity, liberty, and equality.
- Articles 3–5 established other individual rights, such as the right to life and the prohibition of slavery and torture.
- Articles 6–11 referred to the fundamental legality of human rights with specific remedies cited for their defense when violated.
- Articles 12–17 established the rights of the individual toward the community, including freedom of movement.
- Articles 18–21 sanctioned the so-called "constitutional liberties" and spiritual, public, and political freedoms, such as freedom of thought, opinion, religion and conscience, word, and peaceful association of the individual.
- Articles 22–27 sanctioned an individual's economic, social, and cultural rights, including health care. It upholds an expansive right to a standard of living, provides for additional accommodations in case of physical debilitation or disability, and makes special mention of care given to those in motherhood or childhood.
- Articles 28–30 established the general means of exercising these rights, the areas in which the rights of the individual cannot be applied, the duty of the individual to society, and the prohibition of the use of rights in contravention of the purposes of the United Nations Organization.

Cassin compared the declaration to the portico of a Greek temple, with a foundation, steps, four columns, and a pediment. Articles 1 and 2—with their principles of dignity, liberty, equality, and brotherhood—served as the foundation blocks. The seven paragraphs of the preamble, setting out the reasons for the declaration, represent the steps leading up to the temple. The main body of the declaration forms the four columns. The first column (Articles 3–11) constitutes the rights of the individual, such as the right to life and the prohibition of slavery. The second column (Articles 12–17) constitutes the rights of the individual in civil and political society. The third column (Articles 18–21) is concerned with spiritual, public, and political freedoms, such as freedom of religion and freedom of association. The fourth column (Articles 22–27) sets out social, economic, and cultural rights. Finally the last three articles provide the pediment which binds the structure together, as they emphasize the mutual duties of every individual to one another and society.

People often have questions about the UDHR, like, *what are my rights?*

The rights as set out in the Human Rights Act, 1998, are as follows:

- the right to life
- freedom from torture and degrading treatment
- freedom from slavery and forced labor
- the right to liberty
- the right to a fair trial
- the right not to be punished for something that was not a crime when you did it
- the right to respect for private and family life
- freedom of thought, conscience, and religion
- freedom of expression
- freedom of assembly and association
- the right to marry or form a civil partnership and start a family
- the right not to be discriminated against in respect of these rights and freedoms
- the right to own property
- the right to an education
- the right to participate in free elections and cultural life
- the right to a nationality.

Having voted in favor of this declaration, India has violated each one of these rights.

- The right to life

  *The Frontline* reported (May 14–27, 1988) that "in Punjab, it is an accepted view that the government had unleashed at least some of the death squads." This was a comment on a story reported by a freelance journalist that RAW was using imported AK-47s and RPG-7 antitank rocket-propelled grenades in Punjab to justify the Fifty-Ninth Amendment to the constitution, by which government can impose an emergency on the state and suspend the right to life.

  *Economic and Political Weekly* in the news report of April 16, 1988, has asked, "Are all killings in Punjab the extremists' handiwork?" The report observed that "strategic" killings by officially planned agent provocateurs may help the government precipitate further authoritarian control by assuming more military powers.[256]

  The thinking behind such drastic actions was to intimidate people and create a feeling of hate toward those carrying out the struggle for freedom and justice. The intention was to create an atmosphere of violence so that out of frustration, people absolve the state of its direct use of violence and other means of repression. The state brutality concerning Punjab reached new heights with the Fifty-Ninth Constitution Amendment Act (1988). Under this amendment, the policeman or any other officer could shoot or kill, torture and detain, arrest, incarcerate, or otherwise inflict mayhem without any fear of challenge in the court or illegality of the action. It was a total disregard of the basic human rights of the people of Punjab. As far as Sikhs were concerned, the right to life remained suspended, even though it was not honored in any meaningful way in

---

[256] Joyce Pettigrew, *Sikhs of the Punjab* (London, 1995), 133.

the republic of India since its independence in 1947. It exposed the fake Indian democratic setup.

Much before the emergency, Indira Gandhi realized that the judiciary's independence would impede her authoritarian ways. She insisted that Parliament had an absolute power to tinker with the constitution. When the supreme court rejected this contention of her government, she retaliated by superseding three senior judges and appointing Justice Mr. A. N. Ray (who was then holding the fourth position, in order of seniority), chief justice of India. Calls were openly given for a committed judiciary—a euphemism for a judiciary, committed not to the constitution but the executive. Though her shameful contention that since the fundamental rights (including the right to life and personal liberty and the right to move to the higher courts for the protection of the fundamental rights) had been suspended, the people had no protection against the deprivation of their life or personal liberty upheld by the apex court. She superseded Justice Mr. H. R. Khanna, the only judge who had given a dissenting judgment. She transferred several judges of the high courts to teach them a lesson and create an example for the others.[257, 258]

- Freedom from torture and degrading treatment

As per the statement of a Hindu doctor working in rural areas of Amritsar district:

> The police torture people very frequently. Firstly, they begin by savagely beating them. Secondly, they bend their hands and arms backward and upwards and tie them there. Thirdly, they then administer an electric shock. Fourthly, they use wooden

---

[257] July 1, 2015, by Prof. Prabhakar Sinha, Tags: "Emergency."

[258] http://pucldemo.cusp.studio/writings/emergency-india-can-history-repeat-itself.

weapons on the body and crush the legs. If the boy looks as if he is dying in the police station, they then plan an encounter some kilometers or so away and state that he was killed in a police fight.

Thus, Indian government officials carried out unspeakable torture of Sikhs in police custody and then killed them in fake encounters.[259]

Only Death Stops the Pain: Death is deliverance for this Sikh youth who died due to excessive torture in police custody. The scalp has been torn off, fingers cut, and the body is a mass of bruises. Thousands of innocent Sikhs have died like him, and thousands now detained, await the same fate at the hands of the fascist Hindu government of India.[260]

- Freedom from slavery and forced labor
  Sikhs are slaves in India. Their demands for their rights are answered with bullets and tortures. When Sikhs made peaceful demonstrations for their rights under the constitution, they were attacked and ruthlessly killed.

  However, forced labor and sexual exploitation are happening all over India, particularly in the northeast section of the country.[261] In 2016, 18.3 million people were reported in slavery in India. The most current data from the National Crime Records Bureau indicate that there were 8,132 reported cases of human trafficking across

[259] Joyce Pettigrew, *Sikhs of the Punjab* (London, 1995), 69.
[260] *World Sikh News* 5, no. 44 (November 10, 1989).
[261] https://www.globalslaveryindex.org/2018/findings/country-studies/india/.

India in 2016. However, a large number of these cases go unreported, only a fraction being reported.

There is evidence pointing to an emerging trend in Northeast India where organized trafficking syndicates operate undetected along the open and unmanned international borders, duping or coercing young educated girls seeking employment outside their local area into forced sexual exploitation.[262] The recent survivor interviews in Kolkata and West Bengal indicate that the victims (most of whom knew their recruiters) were lured with the promise of good jobs and were forced into sex work. A conditioning period involves physical violence, threats, and debt bondage. Rape was also commonly used to limit a worker's ability to resist sex work.[263]

- The right to liberty

Even after having had multiple referendums of her own, India is vehemently opposing Sikhs for Justice's Punjab Independence Referendum. Referendums have happened in multiples countries and more than once in the same region, including the Quebec Referendum twice in 1980 and 1995, Scotland in 2014, Brexit Referendum in 2016, and others. Canada and the UK and other countries have allowed referendums. During these referendums, no one was tortured or sent to prison. However, in the case of the Punjab Independence Referendum, an unofficial referendum scheduled for November 2020, about two hundred Sikhs have been arrested, tortured, and sent to jail. Three of them (Ashwinder Singh of Nawanshahr, twenty-nine; Surjit Singh of Gurdaspur, twenty-seven; and Ranjit Singh of Kaithal in Haryana, twenty-nine)[264] have been sentenced to life imprisonment for merely distributing the literature

---

[262] http://euroasiapub.org/wp-content/uploads/2016/10/10ESSSept-4027-1.pdf.

[263] International Justice Mission, *Commercial Sexual Exploitation of children in Kolkata, India* (International Justice Mission, 2017), 93.

[264] https://timesofindia.indiatimes.com/city/ludhiana/3-sikh-youths-get-life-term-for-waging-war-against-state/articleshow/67876157.cms.

on the referendum.[265] This is in sharp contrast to no action being taken against the members of BJP, Modi's political party, who support the Hindutva (making India a Hindu country) agenda, and some of them have been awarded and honored.

- The right to a fair trial

    Army rule in Punjab[266] prevailed in Punjab for months before Operation Blue Star; it was an undeclared army rule in Punjab. That civil authorities had ceased to function will be clear from the following instance: An accused with eyes tightly bandaged was produced before the chief judicial magistrate, Shri Cheema. The court ordered the bandage to be removed. His orders were not obeyed; after hearing the case, the court ordered that the accused should be sent to jail and not returned to army custody. At once the junior commissioned officer in the army entered the courtroom and told the magistrate in Hindi, which everyone heard, "*Goli Khayega or remand dega*," meaning "you want to be shot or change the order." In the retiring room, the court's order sending the accused to jail was torn up and replaced by a remand order.

- The right not to be punished for something that was not a crime when you did it

    Sikhs and other minority community members are punished, persecuted, tortured, burnt alive by the majority community without any fear of reprisal. The police carry out tortures of detainees with the connivance of the Punjab government and enjoy impunity. Whatever the protection the Indian Constitution may have in its books, it is only for the academic exercises; it does not protect the minorities.

---

[265] https://www.tribuneindia.com/news/archive/bathinda/afdr-regrets-life-term-to-three-youths-727233.

[266] *Oppression in Punjab: Report to the Nation; Citizens for Democracy*, US ed. (A Sikh Religious and Educational Publication, 1986), 33.

The constitution then holds a value less than of the paper it is written upon if the government has no will or desire or the resolve to enforce it.

On March 20, 2020, more than seven years after a twenty-three-year-old medical student was gang-raped in a moving bus in Delhi, four men were convicted of murder. A total of six were charged. One of them hanged himself in prison. One was a minor, given a lighter sentence. The four men—Akshay Kumar Singh, Pawan Gupta, Vinay Sharma, and Mukesh Singh were hanged at Delhi's Tihar Jail, hours after the supreme court, in a midnight hearing, refused to grant them relief and stay their executions. The four were hanged simultaneously, a first in Tihar Jail's history. On December 16, 2012, the horrible crime took place when Nirbhaya (an assigned name to protect victim identity), a twenty-three-year-old medical student, was gang-raped; she died two weeks later.[267]

The Criminal Law Amendment Bill on Rape was adopted in April 2013. On April 2, 2013, India's president, Pranab Mukherjee, signed the antirape bill into law. The Criminal Law (Amendment) Bill, 2013, was approved by the country's upper house of Parliament, the Rajya Sabha (Council of States), on March 21. It was an amendment bill, retroactively applied to the above case in which the crime took place on December 16, 2012,[268] more than three months before the bill's passage. This horrible crime shook India's conscience. This law, made effective retroactively, violated the UDHR.

- The right to respect for private and family life

Sikhs are subject to search, detention, and extortion, and bribery under the everlasting threat from Punjab

---

[267] https://www.cnn.com/2013/09/13/world/asia/india-gang-rape-sentence/index.html.

[268] https://www.loc.gov/law/foreign-news/article/india-criminal-law-amendment-bill-on-rape-adopted/.

Police. Modus operandi of Indian governments can be best described as:

> Facilitate or stage[269] the events to kill and massacre minorities,[270] rape their women,[271] burn their houses,[272] order police and army[273] to assist in these processes,[274] award the police[275] for not protecting the victims and assisting the killers, or just turning the other way, burn the victims alive,[276] scoop the dead charred bodies into the oblivion, establish a commission to investigate, fire the commission[277] before its report is due, withhold the commission report,[278] not act on the report, and set up another commission,[279] hoping for a favorable report. After some time, state that it is not in the national best interest to release or act upon the report as it may open healed wounds... And repeat.

---

[269] Gurdarshan Singh Dhillon, *Truth About Punjab: SGPC, White Paper* (1996), 240.

[270] https://www.aljazeera.com/features/2019/12/6/witness-to-destruction-remembering-the-babri-mosque-demolition.

[271] https://khalsaforce.live/untold-story-november-1984-india-state-sponsored-massacre-sikhs/.

[272] https://www.indiatoday.in/india/story/babri-masjid-demolition-1992-ayodhya-shame-147819-2011-12-05.

[273] https://www.quora.com/What-was-operation-Woodrose.

[274] See Citizens for Democracy, Truth about Delhi.

[275] *U.S. Congress on Sikh Struggle for Khalistan: Volume One*, International Sikh Organization, 1985–1998), p. 263.

[276] https://indianexpress.com/article/india/india-others/bodies-of-hundreds-of-sikhs-were-scattered-some-showed-signs-of-life/.

[277] https://indianexpress.com/article/india/babri-masjid-demolition-mumbai-riots-1992-srikrishna-commission-report-and-action-taken-4970003/.

[278] https://www.milligazette.com/Archives/15092001/08.htm.

[279] http://www.carnage84.com/homepage/commissions_and_committees.htm.

Well-documented instances are attacks on Golden Temple Amritsar (1955, 1984, 1986, 1988); destruction of Akal Takhat in June 1984; Operation Woodrose, June to September 1984; the Sikh Genocide of November 1984; and burning dead bodies in a bonfire in Tarlokputi in Delhi in November 1984 to destroy the evidence. Ten commissions and committees were set up after the 1984 Sikh Genocide; most of their recommendations were not followed. Justice B. N. Srikrishna Commission (investigating the 1992–93 Muslim massacre in Bombay) was disbanded by the Shiv Sena-led government in January 1996; the recommendations of the Commission have neither been accepted nor acted upon by Maharashtra Government. The report of the Tiwari Commission on the Nellie massacre of Muslims in 1983 has never been released, to mention a few.

If there is uproar from the public, the guilty police are suspended to create a smokescreen, and investigations are promised or started with the eventual dismissal of the charges. The politicians are rarely charged if ever.

In most of the massacres and state-sponsored terrorism, the victims are not identified, their families are never notified, nor are the bodies of the dead persons given to their families.

- Freedom of thought, conscience, and religion

There has been a persistent denial of separate religious identity to Sikhs under the Indian Constitution. Founded in the late-fifteenth century by Guru Nanak, Sikhism is the world's fifth-largest religion, with over twenty-eight million followers, with distinct faith and principles, religious scripture (Sri Guru Granth Sahib), rituals, and practices. Sikhs in India comprise 1.8 percent of the total population, with the majority living in Indian-occupied Punjab. It is an undisputed historical fact that since its inception, Sikhism has been recognized as a separate religion in its standing except in post-colonial India, where Article 25 of the India Constitution labels Sikhs as Hindus. As a consequence of labeling Sikhs as Hindus in India's Constitution, Sikhs are subjected to Hindu personal law.

- Freedom of expression

   The right to free speech and expression is severely repressed by the Indian government prohibiting the distribution of literature and pamphlets on exercising the right to self-determination for the independence of Punjab-Khalistan by democratic and peaceful means.

- Freedom of assembly and association

   Systematic attacks on Sikhs' freedoms of speech, assembly, and association: Through concentrated attacks on Sikhs' right to free speech, assembly, and association, the government of India has demonstrated that it does not afford Sikhs the fundamental guarantees granted to all citizens by the Indian Constitution.[280] As set forth below, attempts to express the desire for self-determination by peaceful means and within the constitutional framework has been met with violence and suppression. Those arguing for self-determination have been labeled as terrorists, gagged, and jailed. The union government regularly imposes media blackouts and repressive censorship over the so-called sensitive issues such as the 1984 Sikh Genocide. In 2018, India came 138th (out of 180) in the World Press Freedom Index[281] and was labeled the fourth most dangerous country for journalists worldwide.[282] In the 1950s and 1960s, tens of thousands of Sikhs were detained on this basis. Detention and ill-treatment escalated in the 1980s and continues to the present day. According to Human Rights Watch:

   The Indian government has escalated pressure on civil society groups critical of its

---

[280] Constitution of India, Article 19.
[281] Reporters Without Borders, "India," https://rsf.org/en/india.
[282] International News Safety Institute, "Causalities Database: 2018," https://newssafety.org/casualities/2018/.

policies, using harassment, intimidation, and restriction on foreign funding. Free speech has come under attack from both the state and interest groups, and critics of the government often face charges of sedition and criminal defamation and are labeled "anti-national."

- The right to marry or form a civil partnership and start a family

  Brigadier R. P. Sinha of the armed forces warned the village elders in Tehsil Ajnala in these words, "If there is any militant violence in your villages, all-male members will be killed, and your women will be taken to army camps to breed a new race."[283] The Indian State thus surpassed the Nazi regime… In his anti-Jewish drive, even Hitler did not go as far as to breed a new race through cohabitation of military personnel with Jewish women. The interreligious relationships are almost always tense and have further deteriorated under Modi's regime. The Arya Samaj has been responsible for poisoning a once-amicable relationship between Hindus and Sikhs. https://www.sikhphilosophy.net/threads/hindu-sikh-conflict-in-punjab-causes-and-cure.31971/

- The right not to be discriminated against in respect of these rights and freedoms

  The Indian Constitution groups Sikhs, Buddhists, and Jains with Hinduism, and therefore, they are not legally recognized as distinct religions. Along with Muslims and Christians, Sikhs have been the target of communal violence. Relatively few Sikhs are represented within the high ranks of the governments and its civil services.[284]

---

[283] International Human Rights Organization, *Indo-US Shadow over Punjab* (Ludhiana, 1992), 82.

[284] https://minorityrights.org/minorities/sikhs/.

If there are 25 Anti-Terrorist statutes and blood-thirsty militia, if human rights are constitutionally murdered by the validation of Emergency, if a policeman may legally shoot an innocent and no court remedy exists, then that country is savage, not civilized... No law justifies spraying of police bullets except genocidal justice. And yet "police encounters" are invoked as if it were a defensive talisman. And unspeakable tortures in lockups are so common that they make no news and reports of such barbarity are shrugged off with a "can't help" sop... Portions of Punjab are currently out of bounds for human rights and social activists...three thousand Sikhs, men, women, and children incinerated or otherwise extinguished in the streets of Delhi did not rouse the Rajiv regime to register even a "First Information Report." (Justice Krishna Iyer)

- The right to own property

  There are several restrictions on buying property out of state for Indians and foreigners, which vary from state to state. Only an agriculturist can purchase agricultural land, and if a person holds such land anywhere else in India, he can still be deemed an agriculturist in another state like Maharashtra. The maximum limit for such land is fifty-four acres. A nonagriculturist cannot purchase agricultural lands.[285]

- The right to education

  A large proportion of India's population is illiterate. It fits the political parties well. The uneducated masses are poor and unaware of their rights and are living hand-to-mouth

---

[285] www.thehindu.com›Land-laws-across-India›article14414630.

on daily basis. This makes it easy to buy their votes for variable prices, ranging from Rs. 100 to thousands. India's per capita income was $1,720 in 2018 versus the USA, where the mean income per capita for 2018 was $50,413.

Disparities in India's education are huge; they stretch between the rich and the poor, women and men, rural and urban areas, and the backward classes and the privileged ones. Following independence, the Congress Party reduced the education budget, more adversely affecting the poor and the Dalits. It is important to note that many government school teachers send their children to private schools. On any given day, government school teachers simply do not show up, run their private businesses on the side. Consequently, many students drop out.

- The right to participate in free elections and cultural life

There is no such thing as free elections in India and specifically in Punjab. Votes are bought with bribery, distribution of free money, alcohol, and drugs. Then there is voting fraud by the manipulation of electronic voting machines. The political parties sell their ticket to the candidates for large sums of money, hoping they would recover multiples of the sums invested.

- The right to nationality

Sikhs for Justice is leading the campaign for Punjab Khalistan's independence by Punjab Independence Referendum. This unofficial referendum is legal, peaceful, and democratic. Despite having had several referendums of its own, India is vehemently opposing this campaign by falsely linking it to acts of terrorism by Sikhs for Justice and foreign agencies like ISI of Pakistan. India has demanded a *"restricted interpretation"* of the right to self-determination. *India's attempt to restrict this right is invalid.* India has been a party to the ICCPR and ICESCR since 1979. However, India registered the following reservation concerning Article 1 of both covenants:

Concerning article 1 of the International Covenant on Economic, Social and Cultural Rights and article 1 of the International Covenant on Civil and Political Rights, the Government of the Republic of India declares that the words 'the right of self-determination' appearing in [this article] apply only to the peoples under foreign domination and that these words do not apply to sovereign independent States or to a section of a people or nation—which is the essence of national integrity.[286]

Undoubtedly concerned with secessionist movements (notably Khalistan and Kashmir), India demanded a restricted interpretation of self-determination. In other words, when it came to peoples within its territory, India sought to limit the right of self-determination to internal (rather than external) self-determination, no matter what the circumstances.

However, the Indian reservation to Article(s)1 would likely be considered invalid under international law. As mentioned above, the right to self-determination has attained the status of jus cogens. This means that (i) the right to self-determination exists above and beyond

---

[286] "International Covenant on Economic, Social and Cultural Rights: 'Reservations, India,'" last accessed July 24, 2018, https://treaties.un.org/Pages/ViewDetails. aspx?src=TREATY&mtdsg_no=IV-3&chapter=4&clang=_en#EndDec.

the ICCPR and ICESCR, and (ii) any attempted derogation (either via ICCPR or ICESCR reservations or otherwise) is invalid.[287]

Furthermore, the ICJ has ruled that a reservation to a treaty contrary to its object and purpose is not permitted.[288] In March 1984, when guiding the ICCPR and ICESCR, the UN Human Rights Committee observed that "states set forth the right of self-determination to provide positive law in both Covenants and placed this provision as Article 1 apart from and before all other rights in the two Covenants."[289]

The UN Human Rights Committee described the right as inalienable. It noted that the "corresponding obligations concerning its implementation are interrelated with other provisions of the Covenant and rules of international law."[290]

In other words, the right of self-determination should be considered fundamental to the object and purpose of the ICCPR and ICESCR. Accordingly any state committed to these conventions must also be fully committed to allowing (and promoting) the right of self-determination, without exception. Therefore, the Indian res-

---

[287] The HRC has confirmed that reservations to human rights treaties that seek to restrict a peremptory norm are not permitted. See para 1, Human Rights Committee General Comment 12, Article 1 (twenty-first session, 1984). Further the International Law Commission attached to a jus cogens obligation a duty of abstention, which encompasses two different obligations: First, the duty not to recognize the unlawful situation; and second, not to render aid or assistance in maintaining the unlawful situation. See Report of the International Law Commission on the work of its fifty-third session: Commentaries to the draft articles on responsibility of states for internationally wrongful acts, April 23–June 1, and July 2–August 10, 2001, UN Doc A/56/10, commentary to Article 41, [1].

[288] In the landmark case, Reservations to the Convention on the Prevention and Punishment of the Crime of Genocide, the ICJ found that reservations are impermissible if they are against the object and purpose of the treaty. Advisory Opinion Concerning Reservations to the Convention on the Prevention and Punishment of the Crime of Genocide, International Court of Justice (ICJ), May 28, 1951, p. 24.

[289] See para. 1, "Human Rights Committee General Comments 12, Article 1" (twenty-first session, 1984 [emphasis added]).

[290] Ibid., para. 2.

ervation to Article 1 should be considered invalid; peoples within India may pursue the right to self-determination to the full extent permitted under international law.

## UDHR and Magna Carta, the Universal Declaration of Human Rights (1948)

By 1948, the United Nations' new Human Rights Commission had captured the world's attention. Under the dynamic chairmanship of Eleanor Roosevelt—President Franklin Roosevelt's widow, a human rights champion in her own right, and the United States delegate to the UN—the Commission set out to draft the document that became the Universal Declaration of Human Rights. Roosevelt, credited with its inspiration, referred to the Declaration as the international Magna Carta for all humanity. The United Nations adopted it on December 10, 1948.[291]

The Universal Declaration of Human Rights has inspired many other human rights laws and treaties throughout the world.

Discussions in the English-speaking world about the origins of rights invariably mention Magna Carta, in the context of forbidding detention without trial. For example, Article 9 of the declaration, relating to freedom from arbitrary arrest, detention, and exile, echoes the essence of clause 39 in the 1215 Magna Carta.[292] Following the adoption of the declaration by the United Nations General Assembly, the influence of the Magna Carta was acknowledged by Eleanor Roosevelt. She declared in a speech to the assembly that "this Universal Declaration of Human Rights may well become the international Magna Carta of all men everywhere."

---

[291] https://www.humanrights.com/what-are-human-rights/brief-history/the-united-nations.html.

[292] https://www.britannica.com/topic/Magna-Carta.

In Punjab, many Sikh political prisoners have been languishing in Indian jails since the 1980s. They are not informed of the charges filed against them, nor have they been brought to trial. Despite several agitations for their release, their fate is unknown. During the 1980s and 1990s, thousands of Sikhs in Punjab were arrested arbitrarily, detained from months to years without any charges filed against them and without any access to a judge or legal counsel.

To resolve their basic constitutional rights, Sikhs have tried to reach peaceful solutions by negotiations. Any reasonable demands by Sikhs on Punjabi Suba, Chandigarh, and Punjab waters have been answered with bullets, tortures, rapes, and lifetime imprisonments (life imprisonment until death on political issues), and last-minute cancellation of negotiated settlements. Before the well-planned and rehearsed attack on Golden Temple Amritsar in June 1984, Indira Gandhi reneged multiple times, and shortly before the planned announcement of negotiated settlements in early 1984 under pressure from the state governments of Haryana and Rajasthan.

Obviously in light of the above discussion, there remain limited choices for the people of Punjab regardless of their faith, color, or caste, an independent country of Punjab being one. For thousands of years, they have been suffering from the same chronic ailment—their foreign rulers having no interest in their welfare, except to some extent, the British, who did improve irrigation in Punjab and laid out a railway network. Now there is calling for them to stop it forever—legally, democratically, and peacefully and take control of their future and stop living in the past.

This topic has been discussed extensively under the heading "Self-Determination for the Sikh People."

# Self-Determination for the Sikh Peoples

International law provides all peoples with a right to self-determination. As a general rule, peoples should exercise their right to self-determination within the territory of their sovereign state, thus maintaining the existing territorial integrity. However, there are exceptions to this rule. Where a state is occupied, subjugated, and exploited by a foreign power, a right of secession may arise. Additionally where peoples are blocked from any meaningful exercise of their right to internal self-determination, a right of secession may arise as a last resort. This is because in both these situations, restoring or establishing an independent state becomes the only way of guaranteeing the rights of the people.

### United Nations on Right to Self-Determination

The United Nations Charter, Article 3, provides for the right to self-determination of the indigenous people who fulfill certain requirements. These requirements are discussed under the section "United Nations Requirements for Right to Self-determination."

### Article 3—UN Declaration on Rights of Indigenous People

Indigenous peoples have the right to self-determination. By that right, they freely determine their political status and freely pursue their economic, social, and cultural development (October 13, 2007).

Thomas Jefferson, with the Declaration of Independence in Philadelphia, Pennsylvania, USA, on Fourth of July 1776, affirmed the following resolution:

US Declaration of Independence, Fourth of July 1776

- We hold these truths to be self-evident, that all men are created equal, that they are endowed by their Creator with certain unalienable Rights, that among these are Life, Liberty and the pursuit of Happiness.
- That to secure these rights, Governments are instituted among Men, deriving their just powers from the consent of the governed.
- That whenever any Form of Government becomes destructive of these ends, it is the Right of the People to alter or to abolish it, and to institute new Government, laying its foundation on such principles and organizing its powers in such form, as to them shall seem most likely to affect their Safety and Happiness.
- Prudence, indeed, will dictate that Governments long established should not be changed for light and transient causes; and accordingly, all experience hath shown, that mankind is more disposed to suffer, while evils are sufferable than to right themselves by abolishing the forms to which they are accustomed.
- But when a long train of abuses and *usurpation*, pursuing invariably the same Object evinces a design to reduce them under absolute Despotism, it is their right, it is their duty, to throw off such Government, and to provide new Guards for their future security. (July 4, 1776)

Shortly after this Declaration of Independence, the United States of America got independence from the British. Many other countries in Europe and all over the world have achieved independence using this declaration as to the basis of their claim of right to self-determination.

## United Nations' Requirements for Right to Self-determination

The peoples wanting to exercise their right to self-determination need to fulfill *some or all* of the following UN charter requirements which are described below.

1. Common historical tradition
2. Racial and ethnic identity
3. Linguistic unity
4. Religious or ethnic affinity
5. Territorial connection
6. Common economic life

*The people of Punjab fulfill all these requirements.* Above all, Punjab was an independent country until 1849, when the British took control. Punjab had treaties with France and Britain. Moreover, India carried out the genocide of the Sikhs in 1984.

India has blocked and vehemently opposed the internal right to self-determination of the people of Punjab. All peaceful means and massive peaceful demonstrations for the exercise of the internal right to self-determination have been answered with bullets and unspeakable tortures and the Sikh Genocide.

That leaves the people of Punjab with the only choice of exercise of their external right to self-determination for the secession of Punjab from India and the recreation of an independent country as it was before 1849. Referendum 2020 is a peaceful, legal, and democratic method for achieving independence. Only in an independent country of Punjab, its people can attain their right to life, liberty, and pursuit of happiness.

## The Basis of the Pursuit of the Right to Self-Determination

The Sikhs are a minority religious community in India that forms a bare majority only in the northern state of Punjab. Since independence, they have suffered oppression at the hands of the Indian government in Delhi. Increasing militancy in the face of such oppression led to a brutal crackdown in Amritsar—the seat of Sikh spiritual and cultural life—in June 1984, which, in turn, led to the assassination of Indira Gandhi, India's then-prime minister, on October 31, of the same year. In response to the assassination, senior Congress Party officials and Indian Police organized and executed the massacre of Sikhs in Delhi and other parts of the country. From November 1–3:

> An estimated 8000 Sikhs, possibly much more, were slaughtered by rampaging mobs in the world's largest democracy. Some estimates put the figures as high as 30,000. Mass rapes and other forms of sexual violence accompanied the killings. Hundreds of Sikh Temples (gurdwaras) and homes were destroyed, and Hundreds of thousands of Sikhs were displaced. At that time, the Indian authorities explained the violence as the spontaneous reaction to the tragic loss of a much-loved prime minister. However, the evidence of a government-orchestrated massacre unleashed by politicians and cover-up with the help of the police, judiciary, and sections of the media tells the real story of a well-planned and systematically executed massacre of Sikhs.

The following section delineates the systemic massacres of the Sikh people by the Indian State:

A. India's violence against Sikhs:
- Indian Police attack on Golden Temple Amritsar (Darbar Sahib), July 4, 1955: An attack on peaceful demonstrators
- Operation Blue Star, June 1984: Indian Army invasion of Golden Temple Amritsar
- Operation Woodrose: Killing Sikh youth all over Punjab following Operation Blue Star

- Sikh Genocide (all over India), November 1984
- Hond-Chillar Massacre of Sikhs: November 1 and 2, 1984
- June 1985: Bombing of Air India Flight 182 from Toronto, 329 innocent people killed; India's brainchild
- Operation Black Thunder I, April 30, 1986: An attack on Golden Temple Amritsar
- Operation Black Thunder II, May 1988: Attack on Golden Temple Amritsar
- Chittisinghpura Massacre of Sikhs, March 2000, and more, too numerable to mention here.

B. India's enactment of cruel and black-draconian laws:
  - Unlawful Activities Prevention Act (UAPA) 1967, and its revisions
  - National Security Act, 1980 and its 1984 revision
  - The Punjab Disturbed Area Ordinance 1983
  - The Armed Forces (Punjab and Chandigarh) Special Powers Act 1983
  - The Terrorist Affected Areas (Special Courts) Act 1984
  - The Terrorist and Disruptive Activities (Prevention) Act (TADA), 1985-1995.

Under these acts, mere suspects could be arrested, detained for lengthy periods without any access to law and any charges filed against them. Their families were not informed about their whereabouts, condition, or status.

C. India carried out fake negotiations with Sikhs

Since 1947, when the Sikhs realized that India has betrayed them into a relationship of slavery and servitude, they tried to negotiate several issues affecting their rights with the Indian governments. Each time, the negotiations were carried out intransigently and in bad faith by India. Almost each time, India reneged shortly before the planned announcement of those negotiated resolutions, leading to the loss of trust the Sikhs had in India's claim to resolve the political and religious issues. Above all, India has been deliberately creating conflicts with Sikhs and then offering to negotiate, only to renege at the last hour.

D.  India has oppressed the Sikh people and blocked any meaningful exercise of their internal right to self-determination

In addition to the gradual destruction of the Sikh state's territorial integrity and Sikh national identity, the Sikh peoples have been subjected to systematic attacks and discrimination by Indian State actors. Since India's independence, Sikh communities have experienced regular acts of violence and attacks on their economic resources, religious rights, and the freedoms of speech, assembly, and association. The victims of these attacks have been consistently denied their constitutionally protected access to justice. The cumulative effect of such treatment amounts to serious and systematic oppression or subjugation of the Sikh minority in India. In this context, no meaningful exercise of internal self-determination is possible. Thus, the Sikh peoples are entitled to exercise the external right to self-determination.

## International Law Guarantees the Right to Self-Determination

The right to self-determination was cemented in Article 1 of the Charter of the United Nations of 1948 as one of the four founding purposes of the United Nations (hereinafter, UN). Article 73 of the UN Charter requires member states:

> To ensure, with due respect for the culture of the peoples concerned, their political, economic, social, and educational advancement, their just treatment, and their protection against abuses [...] and to develop self-government, to take due account of the political aspirations of the peoples, and to assist them in the progressive development of their free political institutions,

according to the particular circumstances of each territory and its peoples and their varying stages of advancement.[293]

Since the adoption of the UN Charter, the right to self-determination has been confirmed through international treaties and declarations.[294] Most significant are the International Covenant on Civil and Political Rights (the ICCPR) and the International Covenant on Economic, Social, and Cultural Rights (the ICESCR) of 1966 (enforce from 1976). Together referred to as the Bill of Rights, these two treaties are considered to be the cornerstone of international human rights law. Article 1 of both treaties states:

The International Court of Justice ("ICJ") has also confirmed the right to self-determination.[295] The ICJ first addressed the issue of self-de-

---

[293] UN Charter, Article 73.

[294] See, for example, UN General Assembly Declaration on the Granting of Independence to Colonial Countries and Peoples of 1960, "This Declaration states that: 'All peoples have the right to self-determination; by virtue of that right they freely determine their political status and freely pursue their economic, social, and cultural development.'" (UNGA Resolution 1514 (XV), December 14, 1960, Article 2).

See also, UN General Assembly Declaration on Principles of International Law concerning Friendly Relations and Cooperation among States in accordance with the Charter of the United Nations of 1970, "This Declaration states that: 'By virtue of the principle of equal rights and self-determination of peoples enshrined in the Charter of the United Nations, all peoples have the right freely to determine, without external interference, their political status and to pursue their economic, social and cultural development, and every State has the duty to respect this right in accordance with the provisions of the Charter.'" And, "Every State has the duty to promote, through joint and separate action, realization of the principle of equal rights and self-determination of peoples, in accordance with the provisions of the Charter [...]." (UNGA Resolution 2625 [XXV], October 24, 1970, Annex, Principle 5).

[295] Also known as the world court, the ICJ is the principal judicial organ of the UN with the mandate to settle legal disputes among member states and to issue advisory opinions.

termination in 1971 and praised the achievement of "self-determination and independence
of the peoples concerned."[296] In 1995, the ICJ
revisited self-determination in connection with a
dispute between Portugal and Australia over the
continental shelf adjacent to East Timor.[297] In
that case, the court found that: (i) the "assertion
that the right of peoples to self-determination,
as it evolved from the [UN] Charter and United
Nations practice, has an erga omnes character,
is irreproachable";[298] and (ii) the "principle of
self-determination of peoples [...] is one of the
essential principles of contemporary international law."[299]

---

[296] See Legal Consequences for States of the Continued Presence of South Africa
in Namibia (South West Africa) notwithstanding Security Council Resolution
276 (1970), Advisory Opinion," June 21, 1971, ICJ Reports 1971, para. 53, p.
19.

[297] East Timor (*Portugal v. Australia*), Judgment, 30 June 1995, ICJ Reports 1995,
p 90 (hereinafter, the 'East Timor Judgment').

[298] East Timor Judgment, para. 29. Obligations erga omnes are obligations a state
owes to the international community as a whole. "Barcelona Traction, Light and
Power Company, Limited," Judgment, February 5, 1970, ICJ Reports 1970, p.
3: "By their very nature and importance, such obligations are the concern of all
states and all states have a legal interest in their protection."

[299] East Timor Judgment, para. 29 (citing Namibia and Western Sahara Advisory
Opinions). In 2004, the ICJ was required to determine "the legal consequences
arising from the construction of the wall being built by Israel, the occupying
Power, in the Occupied Palestinian Territory." Recalling the UN Charter,
Resolution 2625, the International Covenants, and its own prior jurisprudence,
the Court reaffirmed the right to self-determination, its erga omnes character
and the duty of all states to promote the realization of the right. The ICJ
ultimately held that the wall was contrary to international law as it amounted
to a violation of the Palestinian people's right to self-determination. Legal
Consequences of the Construction of a Wall in the Occupied Palestinian
Territory, Advisory Opinion, July 9, 2004, ICJ Reports 2004, p. 136.

## India's Attempts to Block Punjab Independence Referendum Are Invalid

In July 2018, the government of India issued three demarches urging the UK authorities to ban a peaceful gathering by Sikh diaspora at Trafalgar Square in London for the twelfth of August 2018, named London Declaration of Punjab Independence Referendum 2020. In so doing, India's government has demonstrated that not only does it limit its citizens' freedom (right to life, liberty, free speech, and pursuit of happiness) at home, it is also aggressively pursuing to extend its repression internationally. By feeding false information to the foreign governments, India tries to link Sikhs with terrorism and separatism. When Sikhs are peacefully pursuing the right to self-determination and referendum vote in this regard, India is projecting it as secession and an attempt to break up India.

India has had six referenda of its own:

1. North-West Frontier Province Referendum, also called Khyber Pakhtunkhwa Referendum, was held in July 1947, to decide whether the North-West Frontier Province of British India would join the dominion of India or Pakistan upon the Partition of India. The polling began on July 6, and the results were made public on July 18. It went with Pakistan.

2. Sylhet, then a small Bengali-speaking Muslim-majority city surrounded by a Hindu-majority Assam, opted to join Bangladesh in 1947.

3. Junagadh, on the other hand, was a Hindu-majority princely state surrounded by India on all sides, headed by a *Nawab,* who wanted to secede to Pakistan. Pakistan even accepted the secession at one point. Still after an outcry from the people, the province was annexed to India, and a plebiscite was held in which a majority wanted to join India.

4. Pondicherry joined India without much fuss on the referendum front in 1954—the French territory had an extended

freedom movement. Still an overwhelming majority of the elected representatives opted to join India after that.

5. In Goa, the question of Portuguese Goa was knottier. Once Portugal decided to pack up, a Goa with a strong Konkan majority was given the option of either being absorbed into Maharashtra or becoming a union territory. Faced with being assimilated into a strong Marathi community, Goa chose the latter in a referendum in January 1967, but not before much drama between the two camps.

6. Sikkim, this referendum in 1975 brought Sikkim into India's fold. India and Sikkim had an arrangement that let India handle the tiny monarchy's defense and foreign affairs while staying out of its internal affairs. The 1975 vote was called by Sikkim's elected prime minister, Lhendup Dorji, whose government was in favor of abolishing the monarchy. A majority of the Sikkimese supported that decision, and the state officially joined India.

The British had Brexit in 2016 and allowed Scotland Referendum in 2014. However, India is vehemently opposing Punjab Independence Referendum 2020, an unofficial referendum for the exercise of the right to self-determination for the people of Punjab, and is labeling Sikhs as terrorists and separatists. India does not feel even a bit of embarrassment in asking the world community to oppose what these countries have already allowed to their citizens and what India has done herself. India wants to live by its own rules, even opposing the external right to self-determination of the nations by proposing to weaken the United Nations charter on the right to self-determination.

India has been a party to the International Covenant on Civil and Political Rights (the ICCPR) and the International Covenant on Economic, Social, and Cultural Rights (the ICESCR) since 1979. However, India registered the following reservation concerning Article 1 of both covenants.

Regarding Article 1 of the International Covenant on Economic, Social and Cultural Rights and Article 1 of International Covenant on Civil and Political Rights, the government of the Republic of India declares that the words "the right to self-determination" appearing [in this Article] apply only to the peoples under foreign domination and that these words do not apply to sovereign independent states or a section of a people of a nation which is the essence of the national integrity.

Undoubtedly concerned with the secessionist movements (notably Khalistan and Kashmir), India demanded a restricted interpretation of self-determination. In other words, when it came to the peoples within its territory, India sought to limit the right to self-determination to internal (rather than external) self-determination, no matter what the circumstances.

However, the Indian reservation to Article(s) 1 would be considered invalid under international law. The right to self-determination has attained the status of jus cogens. This means that (i) the right to self-determination exists above and beyond the ICCPR and ICESCR, and (ii) attempted derogation (either via ICCPR or ICESCR reservations or otherwise) is invalid.[300]

Furthermore, the ICJ (International Court of Justice) has ruled that a reservation to a treaty, contrary to its object and purpose, is not permitted.[301] In March 1984, when guiding the ICCPR and ICESCR, the UN Human Rights Committee observed that "The UN Human Rights Committee described the right as 'inalienable.' It noted that the 'corresponding obligations concerning its implementation are interrelated with other provisions of the Covenant and rules of international law.'" [302]

---

[300] The HRC has confirmed that reservations the human rights treaties that seek to restrict a peremptory norm are not permitted.

[301] In the landmark case, reservations to the Convention on Prevention and Punishment of the Crime of Genocide, the ICJ found that the reservations are impermissible if they are against the object and purpose of the treaty.

[302] For more details on right to self-determination, see annexure 1, "Self-Determination for Sikh Peoples: An Overview of the International Law."

## *World Leaders on Right to Self-Determination*

It's the human point of view of the identity of people and how they identify with a nation-state. If at some point they feel that the central government does not represent their interests and that they have an identity that they want to defend, according to the principle of self-determination, one should allow for a referendum because a referendum is an expression of people's choice and people's opinion. (Vaira Vīķe-Freiberga, two-time Latvian president, February 23, 2014)

I am logically in favor of a referendum. It would be the only legitimate way. (Jacques Chirac, former president of France [1995–2007] June 22, 2003)

We shall respect the right of self-determination of all peoples throughout the world. (Shinzo Abe, prime minister of Japan)

We believe that right makes might—that bigger nations should not be able to bully smaller ones; that people should be able to choose their future. These are simple truths, but they must be defended. (Barack Obama, US president, Septermber 4, 2014)

In its essence, the right of self-determination means that individuals and peoples should be in control of their destinies and should be able to live out their identities, whether within the boundaries of existing States or through independence. (Alfred De Zayas, human rights lawyer and former UN independent expert on the promotion of a democratic and equitable international order, October 11, 2014)

## *Overall Conclusion*

Sikhs have the right to self-determination under international law. With respect to the right to self-determination for Sikhs, international law provides a solid foundation for the following: First, Sikhs are "peoples" who enjoy the fundamental right to self-determination. Second, the right to self-determination is a peremptory norm of international law (or jus cogens) that may not lawfully be restricted or derogated from by the government of India. Third, whilst Sikhs (who are residents in India) should make every reasonable effort to exercise their right to self-determination within the territory of India, a right to secession may arise in certain exceptional circumstances. Fourth, international law does not prohibit referendums or unilateral declarations of independence.

With respect to the exceptional circumstances, international law recognizes (limited) categories of peoples who may be entitled to seek external self-determination, for example, through secession and independence. There is a good arguable case that Sikhs fall into two such categories, namely:

>   a. Those peoples under some type of foreign occupation who are subject to alien subjugation, domination, or exploitation.[303]
>   b. Those peoples denied the meaningful exercise of the right to self-determination internally (i.e., within India).[304]

The Sikhs need only fall into one of these categories to qualify for external self-determination.

---

[303] Quebec Secession Decision para. 133 and brief para. 25.
[304] Ibid., para. 134 and brief para. 25.

*The self-governing Sikh state was occupied and subjugated*: Section II(B) outlines how a sovereign self-governing Sikh Empire (a Sikh state) was attacked and occupied by foreign powers, namely, the East India Company and then the British Raj. It was then handed over to the newly independent India. Promises of self-governance and autonomy made by leaders of the Indian Congress Party during the struggle for independence have been broken. The Sikh state remains occupied to this day.

A process of alien subjugation, domination, and exploitation of the Sikh state began with British colonization and continues under the Republic of India. Despite assurances from Indian leaders that Sikhs would enjoy political, cultural, and religious autonomy within India, in practice, India took Sikh land and resources for itself and then proceeded to destroy Sikh national, religious, and cultural identity. The carving up of Sikh territory, diversion of its key economic resources, denial of religious freedoms, violation of fundamental civil and political rights, and regular pogroms on Sikh communities and holy sites across India demonstrates Sikh subjugation, domination, and/or exploitation by India. The Sikhs effectively swapped occupation and subjugation at the hands of the British for occupation and subjugation by India.

*India has oppressed the Sikh people and blocked their self-determination*: Since India's independence, Sikh communities have been subjected to regular acts of violence and attacks on their economic resources, religious rights, and freedom of expression. The powers of Punjabi representatives have been routinely superseded by those of the central government, particularly in response to calls for more autonomy and self-governance. On at least one occasion, the Sikhs have been victims of mass crimes bearing all the hallmarks of crimes against humanity and even genocide, perpetrated by Indian state actors and planned or encouraged by key figures within the ruling Congress Party. Victims of violence have been denied genuine justice and accountability.

All attempts to exercise the right to internal self-determination have effectively been blocked. They are met with state-backed violence and conveniently labeled as "terrorism."

*India's right to territorial integrity is not absolute*: The facts and analysis demonstrate that India, as a state, does not conduct itself "in compliance with the principle of equal rights and self-determination of peoples" and cannot claim to have "a government representing the whole people belonging to the territory without distinction of any kind." On the contrary, Indian state actors may have perpetrated against Sikhs the single most serious form of distinction possible, namely, acts of genocide. Accordingly the presumption in favor of territorial integrity does not apply with respect to the Sikh people.

For all the above reasons, there is a good arguable case that Sikhs may lawfully pursue external self-determination (for example, through secession and independence) as the only avenue available to them to achieve meaningful self-determination.

Courtesy: Global Diligence
Global Diligence LLP: international law and human rights compliance www.globaldiligence.com
By: Richard J Rogers: Global Diligence LLP
Alexandre Prezanti: Global Diligence LLP
Andrew Ianuzzi: Council Global Diligence LLP
http://www.globaldiligence.com; info@globadiligence.com
Global Diligence LLP Kemp House,
152 City Road London EC1V 2NX UK

# India's Dying Fake Democracy on Life Support

There have been numerous incidents of staged encounters by police, planned massacres of the minorities with the local, state, and central governments' connivance. These incidents have been taking place in India with a high degree of frequency and predictability of violence patterns since 1947. In almost all cases, the victims are either burnt to ashes with incendiary materials or hauled to unknown places.

Examples are several attacks on Golden Temple Amritsar, destruction of Akal Takhat, Sikh Genocide of November 1984, burning of dead bodies in a bonfire in Trilokpuri in Delhi in November 1984 to destroy the evidence. Ten commissions and committees were set up after the 1984 Sikh Genocide, all ignored. Justice B N Srikrishna Commission (investigating 1992–1993 Muslim massacre in Bombay) was disbanded by the Shiv Sena-led government in January 1996,[305] the recommendations of the commission have neither been accepted nor acted upon by Maharashtra government; the Indian government never released the report on Nellie massacre of Muslims in 1983, to mention a few.

In the majority of the massacres and state-sponsored terrorism, the victims are not identified, their families are never notified, nor are the bodies of the dead persons given to their families. No matter how atrocious, Mughal rulers gave the victims' dead bodies back to their families.

---

[305] https://indianexpress.com/article/india/babri-masjid-demolition-mumbai-riots-1992-srikrishna-commission-report-and-action-taken-4970003/.

In the Declaration of Independence on the Fourth of July 1776, Thomas Jefferson wrote, "All people are created equal and there are certain unalienable rights that governments should never violate. These rights include the right to life, liberty, and pursuit of happiness."

However, in India, the so-called world's largest democracy, all people are created *unequal* and have *unequal* rights. In India, both the government and its majority community are hand in glove to crush the minority population and turn India into Hindu-Rashtra (the Hindu country). The rights of the minority communities including Buddhists, Christians, Muslims, Sikhs, and others are at the mercy of one majority community.

Indian democracy is false and fake. Rules are applied arbitrarily and differently to different people. Judiciary, while trying to give fair verdicts, is not independent. The Indian Constitution framed in 1950 was drastically different in content from the one agreed upon and propounded before independence. It was averse to Sikh interests, and their representatives did not append their signature to this document. India has two constitutions: one written for the elite ruling party and the other unwritten, one for the minorities. India has no will or interest to apply the written constitution uniformly to be on the good side of one majority community to attract their votes, no matter what the composition of the ruling party at any particular time. As of January 2018 India's constitution has been amended 123 times.

From times immemorial, India has been a land of slavery and servitude under the rule of different foreign invaders who looted and plundered this region mercilessly. Under Brahaminical self-proclaimed religious superiority and their lack of will or concern about the wellness of the rest of the community, no organized force could emerge to fight the oppressors. East India Company, established in 1499, eventually took over India. A formidable force, Khalsa, was created by Guru Gobind Singh (the tenth Sikh guru) under the doctrine of "Wars must be won at any cost; defeat is not an option, and one must come out of any war victorious or dead." With this undefeatable spirit, Sikhs drove out the Mughals. Punjab was an independent country until 1849, when it fell to the British because of the treachery, deceit, and communal bias in the high command. Since India's independence and its partition in 1947, the successive Indian governments have turned the country into a state ruled by the elite few and suppressed the rights of the people.

The constitutional amendments, failure of implementation of the existing laws, ripping the judiciary of its powers, governmental control of news media, and lack of spine in the majority of the Indian masses and the press to stand up for their rights and of their fellow citizens, its majority community blindly pursuing the agenda of Hindu, Hindi, Hindustan, and Hindutva ideology have brought the country to the verge of breakup, which appears to be inevitable and the only viable solution.

Since Indian independence in 1947, the Indian government has killed hundreds of thousands of unarmed Sikh men, women, and children. During Operation Blue Star, Indian Army attacked Golden Temple Amritsar (Darbar Sahib, the holiest Sikh shrine) and thirty-seven other gurdwaras (Sikh houses of worship) in June 1984, killing thousands of unarmed pilgrims, their bodies never identified nor counted or given back to their families. The dead bodies were hauled away. There was no accurate account of the dead. As always, numbers are at the mathematical whim of the authority, adjusted up or down in the government's favor.

In November 1984, India carried out Sikh Genocide, killing more than thirty thousand Sikhs all over India (some by necklacing and violently gang-raping Sikh women) and rendering more than three hundred thousand homeless. In Operation Woodrose, following Operation Blue Star, India captured tens of thousands of Sikh youth and carried out the extrajudicial killing in fake police encounters. Indira Gandhi's government in the early 1980s declared the whole of Punjab as a disturbed area. It gave draconian powers to Punjab Police, allowing them to shoot who they wanted, when they wanted, and search where they wanted, to give them near-total freedom from the courts. Justice has been elusive as the Indian executive branch controls the judiciary. The genocide continues. Indian government carried out Operation Black Thunder I and II, attacking Harimandar Sahib and killing many more Sikhs.

Democracy is not free, and once acquired, it needs continuous nurturing. It requires social discipline, honoring the rights of others, and freedom of the press. It requires public participation and education. If India fails to confront the crises it now faces or slips deeper into authoritarianism, regional rebellion, religious strife, and political gangsterism, there will be those waiting to say that democracy was not compatible with Indian culture or that India was not ready for it.[306]

Words in the constitution do not necessarily deliver human rights or an independent judiciary. The power of ballot means little when party goons shoot their way into polling stations, and institutions cannot function for the public good when there is no accountability. India's successive political parties do not have the will, desire, or determination to uniformly enforce the law and order. Tolerance of violence against the minorities is the vote bank that keeps giving.

Mahatma Gandhi was shot dead in 1948 by Nathu Ram Godse, belonging to the Hindu nationalist party RSS. We do not know how much democracy he would have delivered had he lived longer. His cohort Jawahar Lal Nehru started dismantling the little democracy, if there was any starting in 1947. Indian Constitution labeled Sikhs as Hindus and included Buddhists and Jains in the same category. When asked why he had opposed the formation of Punjabi Suba (Punjab state, not Khalistan), Nehru answered, how could he give the power in the hands of the enemy (the Sikhs)?

According to the United States Commission on Religious Freedom, India is in gross violation of human rights and now has earned it a well-deserved place in the tier 1 category (the worst) of religious persecution. Along with the open and blatant violation of the rights of its minorities, India's successive governments have been supporting undemocratic and criminal behavior.

---

[306] Barbara Crossette, *India: Facing the Twenty-First Century* (Bloomington: Indiana University Press, 1993), xiii.

With time, India is becoming more and more a Hindu-centric one-religion country. It is dominated by the prevalence of antiminority sentiment. While there is no doubt that many Hindus disapprove of the current Hindutva agenda, they have not been able to be effective against the masses who hold the contrary opinion. Not surprisingly, majority of them do not see anything wrong with it.

In the 1960s, the late Swedish social scientist Gunnar Myrdal produced a monumental multivolume study of the problems and prospects for development in South Asia's new nations, with special emphasis on India, which is classified as a "soft state." In his exhaustive work *Asian Drama: An Inquiry into the Poverty of Nations*, Myrdal defined a soft state as one where policies are promulgated but never put into practice, laws are passed but not enforced, glaring inequalities are tolerated by the elite, and there is no social discipline.[307]

His views about India speak volumes of what has been going on in India. During President Trump's visit to India in early 2020, Indian Police silently watched many Muslims killed by the mobs in New Delhi. Their houses and places of worship were attacked. Many Indians celebrated the killing, and no one protested. In sharp contrast, the whole country and the news media were up in their arms when one police officer was killed by a Muslim. According to AP News on February 26, 2020, shops, houses, and masjids belonging to Muslims were set ablaze. They were protesting the new citizenship law that fast-tracks the naturalization for foreign-born religious minorities of all major faiths, except Islam.[308]

On December 10, 1948, the United Nations came up with the Universal Declaration of Human Rights. Out of thirty articles in this declaration, first five are: All humans are born free and have equal rights; everyone is entitled to all the rights and freedoms outlined in this declaration without distinctions of any kind; everyone has the right to life, liberty, and security of person; no one will be held in slavery or servitude; no one will be subject to torture, cruel,

---

[307] Barbara Crossette, *India: Facing the Twenty-First Century* (Bloomington: Indiana University Press, 1993), xviii.

[308] https://apnews.com/article/75fcfa1b92b991ccf4144fa6247e3e6c.

inhuman, or degrading treatment or punishment. Having voted in favor of this declaration, India has violated each one of these articles.

India signed the convention on October 14, 1997,[309] but has refused to ratify the United Nations Convention against torture and other cruel, inhuman, or degrading treatment (UNCAT-4, February 1985), which has been ratified by more than 130 other countries. India openly and decidedly caries out the tortures of Sikhs and others. India is one of only five countries that have not ratified the UNCAT. The others include Sudan, Brunei, and Haiti.[310]

The torture in police custody continues unabated till today. In the same week the world marked International Day in Support of Victims of Torture on June 26, 2020, a father-son duo in Tamil Nadu, who kept a shop open after COVID-19 curfew hours, died in custody, allegedly after being tortured at the hands of the Thoothukudi District Police. The police in the same district had, on May 22, 2018, shot dead thirteen people, who were among a crowd that had demonstrated for one hundred days without violence, seeking closure of Vedanta's highly polluting Sterlite Copper Unit. In two years, no one has been charged, and police impunity seems to continue.[311]

In the *New York Times* article by Suhasini Raj, on March 4, 2018, he reported that India denied visa requests from religious freedom monitoring groups. The members of the United States Commission on International Religious Freedom had planned a trip to India, scheduled to begin in April 2018, to assess religious liberty in the country. However, India has not issued visas to members of this commission.

The Central Intelligence Agency of USA (2018), in its latest World Factbook report, has categorized Vishwa Hindu Parishad (VHP) and Bajrang Dal as "militant religious organizations," and it

---

[309] https://www.prsindia.org/report-summaries/implementation-united-nations-convention-against-torture-0.

[310] https://thewire.in/rights/custodial-deaths-india-convention-against-torture.

[311] Ibid.

has referred Rashtriya Swayamsevak Sangh (RSS) as a Hindu nationalist organization. Mohan Madhukar Bhagwat is the pack's leader, the Sarsanghchalak, or the head of the RSS, the most radical and fanatic group. Its former activist Nathuram Godse assassinated Mahatma Gandhi in 1948.

If the CIA Factbook has finally taken note of India's three belligerent organizations, it was about time. During the 2002 Gujarat State massacre of Muslims, Indian prime minister Narendra Modi was then its chief minister, who did not take proper action to stop this massacre. He was denied a visa to the USA for several years. Massacres of Muslims, including the Hyderabad Massacre 1948, Nellie massacre 1983, Ayodhya massacre December 1992, and the Bombay massacre in 1992–1993 are a few other examples.

Since July 8, 2016, when popular Kashmiri youth leader Burhan Wani was assassinated, over 200 protesting Kashmiri youth were killed while over 3,500 Kashmiri youth and children have been blinded because of their faces and eyes were targeted with pellet guns by Indian forces.

*Hamdard*, a Punjabi weekly newspaper in its August 24, 2018, edition, reported that Bajrang Dal (named militant religious organization) has set up an award of Rs. 500,000 for bringing the head of Navjot Singh Sidhu MLA Punjab, just for hugging Pakistan army chief Kamar Javed at the time of the inauguration of new Pakistani prime minister Imran Khan, on August 21, 2018. No action has been taken against this organization.

According to *Caravan News* (April 14, 2018), Manish Chandela, BJP youth wing's leader, claimed the burning of Rohingya refugee camp in Delhi. An alleged member of BJP's youth wing has gone on Twitter claiming that he burnt the camp of Rohingya refugees on the Delhi-Noida border in the wee hours of Sunday (April 15, 2018). Around two hundred people—most of them women and children—were thrown under the open sky after the camp's destruction, and their meager belongings were burnt. He was not arrested nor was any action taken by his mother party, BJP. Again on April 16, at 5.42 p.m., Chandela posted on his Twitter handle, "Yes, we did it and we do again #Rohingya QUIT India." His account was deleted later that day.[312]

The ongoing violence in Shillong against Sikh settlers is not without precedent. In 1979, the Bengalis faced the locals' ire, and later in 1987, the Nepalis and Biharis were forced to flee town. The land occupied by the Punjabis, who were brought in by the British in the nineteenth century to work in the state as scavengers, has also been a source of tension for some time.

Nearly five million people in India's eastern state of Assam face the threat of deportation after a top government official said they have failed to provide documentation proving their families lived there since before 1971. The making of Prime Minister Narendra Modi's Hindu nationalist Bharatiya Janata Party, which came to power in Assam in 2016, has vowed to expel people who are not listed on the NRC (National Register of Citizens)

According to Corinne Abrams and Qasim Nauman,[313] in the *Wall Street Journal*, "More than 18 million people, or 1.4% of India's population, live in slavery. Out of 167 countries in the world, India has the highest number of people living in slavery." India has more people living in modern slavery than the population of the Netherlands, a new report estimates. Of the 167 countries surveyed, this South Asian country has the highest number of people living in slavery. "All forms of modern slavery continue to exist in India, including intergenerational bonded labor, forced child labor, commercial sexual exploitation, forced begging, forced recruitment into non-state armed groups, and forced marriage," the report said. "Among the sectors known to use slave labor in India were the construction, sex, agriculture, fishing, and manufacturing industries as well as domestic help and begging," the report said.

India is not leaving any stone unturned to stop the Punjab Independence Referendum 2020 for the self-determination of the

---

[312] https://www.newindianexpress.com/nation/2018/apr/20/bjp-youth-wing-leader-admits-to-burning-rohingya-camp-in-delhi-muslim-body-seeks-his-arrest-1804098.html.

[313] https://blogs.wsj.com/indiarealtime/2016/06/02/india-has-the-most-people-living-in-modern-slavery/.

people of Punjab. Punjab was an independent country before 1849, when the British conquered it and annexed it to its empire for administrative ease. In 1947, the British left Punjab to India as a result of improper decolonization. Punjabi people want to exercise the right of self-determination, which India is vehemently opposing. India has had six referendums of her own, those of Junagadh in 1948 and Sikkim in 1975 being noteworthy.

To hide its ugly acts, India has repeatedly denied Amnesty International and other NGOs to enter Punjab to gather firsthand information. Under the Terrorist Activities Disruptive (prevention Act) from 1985–1995, police had sweeping powers to detain anyone for twelve months without any charges filed against the detainees or required to present them before the court.

Most of the Indian media is also to blame, which has turned blind eyes and deaf ears to the endless murders of Sikhs and other minorities. News can be bought and can be downright manipulated with money. Indian media does face threats from the controlling government when the reporting exposes its wrongdoings. During the Sikh Genocide of November 1984, Indian media put fuel to the fire by making false statements like an announcement that trains full of dead Hindus are arriving in Delhi from Punjab, thus instigating mobs to kill more Sikhs.

Because India's majority population views Christians as outsiders, Christianity in India is in more danger than ever before. These radicals intend to cleanse the nation of both Islam and Christianity and employ violence to this end. Usually the converts to Christianity experience the worst persecution and are constantly under pressure to return to Hinduism. The law enforcement agencies continue to look away when religious minorities are attacked, indicating that violence may continue to increase in the coming years. Hindu India has already driven Buddhists out. It has nearly assimilated Jainism and Langayatism. The Muslims in India are under siege. According to *Max Arthur Macauliffe (1903),* Hinduism has embraced Sikhism in its folds; the still comparatively young religion is making a vigorous struggle for life, but its ultimate destruction is, it is apprehended, inevitable without state support.

> **India's Freedom of Religion Acts or "anti-conversion" laws are state-level statutes that have been enacted to regulate religious conversions. The laws are in force in Arunachal Pradesh, Odisha, Madhya Pradesh, Chhattisgarh, Gujarat, and Himachal Pradesh favoring conversions into Hinduism.**

The world has changed. India can no longer hide its ugly face and suppress the facts. India can lie and fabricate bundles of misinformation, but the ubiquitous availability of smartphones with cameras and cell phone video recordings instantly exposes the truth. The whole world now knows that India is a false and fascist democracy and how the killing, burning, and torturing of minorities go on.

Specifically in the case of Punjab, Sikhs have been pushed into agitations for the very same rights which are given to other people without asking, complicated by the opposition from the Hindu community of these demands, even though these demands have been for all the people of Punjab and not only for Sikhs. India has been playing the religious card all along to divide Hindus and Sikhs along the religious lines. Many different governments of Punjab have followed the same book: government by the few, accumulation of wealth and property at the cost of poverty of its people, unemployment, forced suicides of its farmers, and willfully allowing the central government to plunder its natural resources.

On June 25, 1975, Indira Gandhi declared an emergency to save her throne and political power.[314] It caused the democratic process and apparatus to collapse effortlessly by just one person. The question arises, with India being the largest democracy, why did people not come out in the streets and raise the hue and cry against this

---

[314] http://pucldemo.cusp.studio/writings/emergency-india-can-history-repeat-itself.

authoritarian declaration. Why did the legislature and the judiciary fall in line? Can it be interpreted that the majority of the Indian community does not care whether this declaration had even weakened their right to life, let alone the right to free speech? The majority community has never come to the side of persecuted minorities, but surprisingly they have also not come out to protect their own rights. The servitude and slavery under the foreign rules for about a thousand years may explain this ideology.

Serious attacks against the civil liberties of the people of India have been rampant since prime minister Narendra Modi came into power in 2014. According to the *Washington Post*,[315] "Democracy Dies in Darkness" (July 19, 2021), hundreds of phone numbers of India's politicians, activists, opposition leaders, and foreign diplomats have been discovered on the hack list, involving Pegasus assisted surveillance by India is considered controlled primarily by prime minister Modi and India's home minister, Amit Shah.

Pegasus is the name of the software developed by an Israeli company, NSO, named after its three founders. NSO has licensed Pegasus to more than forty countries in the world, including India. The purpose behind the use of the software is to gather intelligence information involving terrorists and criminal activities.

However, India has been using Pegasus to gather intelligence information on its citizens, opposition leaders, journalists, activists, foreign diplomats, and even supreme court justices.

The leaked list shared with the news outlets by Forbidden Stories, a Paris-based journalism nonprofit organization, and rights group, Amnesty International, showed the identities of people targeted in India, including politicians, dozens of journalists, businessmen, and even two ministers in the Modi's government.[316]

While several countries like France and Hungary have launched investigations into the Pegasus-assisted spy network, Modi's government has been reluctant to initiate such investigation, stating that all

---

[315] https://www.washingtonpost.com/world/2021/07/19/india-nso-pegasus/.

[316] https://www.aljazeera.com/news/2021/7/20/pegasus-project-india-modi-treason-spyware-snooping-scandal.

this is a part of anti-India propaganda, thus not worthy of investigation. Modi is afraid that such an investigation would expose his government's involvement in the serious violation of the civil liberties of the people of India.

Democracy in India is a facade since the state's power and resources are employed to serve a small elite comprising the rich, the politicians, and the bureaucrats. In short, the overwhelming majority of Indians do not identify with the democratic institutions and do not feel they have a stake in them. Or could it be that having been slaves for centuries, they have not understood democracy, or they have given up thinking that it would be a futile attempt since nobody listens or cares. It appears that they are not willing to pay the price to perpetuate and nurture the democracy, which was paid for by others to get them freed from foreign rulers. When minorities in India have demonstrated to get their democratic rights, an overwhelming proportion of the majority Indian community has always stood on the wrong side of the democracy, the Indian government.

In the case of Punjab, people came out on the streets and repeatedly demonstrated peacefully in numbers more than eighty-five thousand at times and demanded Punjabi Suba (Punjab statehood), the right which was given to other states without asking but denied to Punjabis. The Indian government responded with an attack on Golden Temple Amritsar on July 4, 1955, killing and injuring peaceful demonstrators by hundreds. To further repress Sikhs, the Indian government labeled Sikhs as traitors, antinationals, separatists, and terrorists. The same Sikhs who were heroes of yesterday were portrayed as criminals of the day. The spineless and biased, a large proportion of the Indian news media mindlessly propagated the anti-Sikh propaganda.

The party, which inherited power from the colonial rulers, was dominated by the elite, which had no genuine commitment to the people's welfare. The Indian Constitution reflects this reality. Any constitution, regardless of its contents, cannot accomplish the intended purpose if the administration applies it selectively and arbitrarily and twists it as if it were a worthless piece of paper. It is not the principle written on paper that matters, what matters is force and will to implement it, which are absent in Indian democracy.

Many Indians themselves debate if India is a fake democracy. However, India's majority community is ever so happy to see the minority communities deprived of democratic rights. Democracy is a system requiring a deep commitment to its values. In the face of the gravest of problems, it demands that a solution must be found without sacrificing or compromising its principles and values. This commitment was and is still absent in the rulers of independent India.

Indian government promulgated laws that no democracy can justify using against its people. In October 1983, Punjab was put under president's rule. A spate of laws followed this: Punjab disturbed Areas Act 1983, the Chandigarh Disturbed Area Act 1983, the National Security (Amendment) Acts 1984, the Armed Forces (Punjab and Chandigarh) Special Powers Act 1983, the Code of Criminal Procedures (Punjab Amendment) Act 1983, and finally the Terrorist Affected Areas (Special Courts) Act 1984.

Persecution of minorities under the draconian laws which started with the enactment of Preventive Detention Act of 1950, is continuing unabated both at the center and in the states, regardless of which political party is in power. At the time of the emergency, there were fewer weapons in the arsenal of Indira Gandhi than are available to the present-day rulers. No democracy has such draconian laws targeting its citizens, especially during a time of peace. An outstanding example is orchestrating attacks on Darbar Sahib (GTA) under the pretense of capturing a handful of alleged criminals without honestly trying the diplomatic solution to Punjab's political problem. When such laws are enacted in a democracy, and the state resorts to killing and detaining its citizens, it is always the consequence of the state serving an elite minority at the cost of the overwhelming majority. The repression is necessary to contain protests against the crimes committed by the state under the name of democracy.

Much before the emergency, Indira Gandhi realized that the judiciary's independence would impede her authoritarian ways. She insisted that Parliament had an absolute power to tinker with the constitution. She significantly weakened the judiciary. When the supreme court rejected this contention of her government, she retaliated by superseding three senior judges and appointing Justice A. N. Ray (who was then holding the fourth position in order of seniority), chief justice of India.

The present ruling party's parent organization is committed to having a Hindu Rashtra as the Muslim League was committed to having a separate Muslim nation. By their very nature, the theocratic states are antidemocratic because they cannot accept the equality of the citizens belonging to other religions. Democracy in India is in greater peril.[317, 318]

> The editor of India's prestigious English daily, Statesman, also agrees that Hinduism is killing India, implying that double-think, double-standards, double-cross is a way of life, with one set of rules to the high born and another to the lowly creatures. The Hindu mind does not see anything wrong with it. Therefore, our considered opinion is that for India to live, Hinduism must die.[319]

It may explain why many Hindus entertain the concept that Hinduism is a way of life, not a religion.[320]

As admitted by some prominent Hindus, Hinduism is not a religion, it is a way of life. Its emphasis is that the events are controlled by God, the suffering of its minorities is preordained, brought on by themselves, and the deliverance of the results of their deeds in their previous lives.

Worshiping animals and stones and justification of killing defenseless humans defies logic. It is double talk, double-crossing,

---

[317] Prof. Prabhakar Sinha, July 1, 2015, tags: "Emergency."

[318] http://pucldemo.cusp.studio/writings/emergency-india-can-history-repeat-itself.

[319] V. T. Rajshekar, *Dalit: The Black Untouchables of India*, 3rd ed. (Gyan Publishing House, 2015), 68.

[320] https://www.hinduwebsite.com/hinduway.asp.

and double personality to the level of psychopathic behavior. On the one hand, it is worship, and on the other, it is deep-rooted hate of minorities and some of its own who disagree. One can explain this behavior based on the will to protect and preserve this system of belief having recognized its vulnerability and unsustainability. Any violence is justifiable in this psychopathic-sociopathic mind. Hindus' feeling of humiliation by the foreign invader is justifiable. However, before that, the Hindu rulers had persecuted Buddhists and Jains. Now they are persecuting Sikhs, Muslims, and Christians. They have learned nothing from history.

Keshav Hedgewar (1889–1940) founded the Hindu militant organization Rashtriya Swayamsevak Sangh (RSS) in 1925 in Nagpur. He propagated the concept of the Hindu state. He was anti-Muslimism and anti-Gandhi. He was succeeded by S. Golwalker, who was followed by Babasaheb Deoras. Together they propagated fascist propaganda and targeted social workers among the Hindus during calamities like earthquakes, famines, and partition.[321] Among the RSS supporters are included: Atal Behari Vajpayee, L. K. Advani, Murli Manohar Joshi, Uma Bharti, and Narendra Modi, who was chief minister of Gujarat and supervised the Muslim massacres of 2002 in his home state of Gujarat, after the Godhra train incident.[322]

Shiv Sena's Bal Thackeray, admirer of Adolf Hitler, started the movement called Maharashtra for Maharashtrians, aimed at ousting South Indians from Bombay. Besides Shiv Sena, there are Bajrang Dal (youth wing of BJP) and Vishva Hindu Parishad, who defy the government and the courts to carry out their agenda. The RSS agenda is anti-Sikh, anti-Muslim, and anti-Christian and anti-Hindus who disagree with them. The minorities are suppressed to the level that they dare not speak. Any attempt to raise their voices is met with severe retribution risking their lives. Without outside help, it may go on for the foreseeable future.

Democracy in India is in greater peril. The ruling party is determined to unabashedly serve the rich at the cost of farmers, workers,

---

[321] Khushwant Singh, *The End of India* (Penguin Books, 2003), 11.
[322] Ibid.

and the rest of the people. Protests are inevitable. It is not likely that an authoritarian party's government would choose the people over the few rich elites. If it chooses its benefactors, severe repression is the only course open to the government against popular protests. The present ruling party is committed to authoritarianism, has committed cadres modeled after fascist organizations, and has great support among the people due to its communal appeal. However, ultimately, it is the people who have the last laugh, as is evident from the fates of all tyrants.[323, 324]

Article 19 of the Indian Constitution refers to speedy trials. Nevertheless, detainees languish in jails for years at a time. Article 21 states that you cannot keep a person in custody for more than twenty-four hours. There are many cases of illegal custody for more than three years. Some have been in custody for life. They have not been tried in court. Multiple peaceful demonstrations by Sikhs have failed to get them released. All these demonstrations, no matter how large, are unheeded. India is frequently in violation of its constitution. If Sikhs say that they have no faith in the Indian Constitution or the political system, are they to blame? The laws are arbitrary, enforced discriminately. *Indian Police* run the country of India and enjoy immunity. They are tools of the politicians to oppress people and harm and harass their political opponents.

Under the Children Act 1960 or the East Punjab Children Act 1976, boys younger than sixteen years old and girls below the age of eighteen cannot be detained either at a police station or in a regular jail, but the authorities paid no heeds to these laws with several children jailed. A CBI officer confessed, "These are all fine ideas for newspapers and preachers. We had on our hand suspected terrorists and would-be terrorists."[325] Human rights organizations brought these acts of inhumanity to the notice of senior-most administrators, including the governor. However, no relief was granted till Kamladevi Chattopadhyay, the well-known social worker, finally approached the

---

[323] Prof. Prabhakar Sinha, July 1, 2015, tags: "Emergency."

[324] http://pucldemo.cusp.studio/writings/emergency-india-can-history-repeat-itself.

[325] Gobind Thukral, "Atrocities on Sikh Children," *India Today*, September 30, 1984.

supreme court, which ordered their release.[326] However, there were more children in the Ludhiana Jail than Kamladevi knew about and got released. To avoid revealing their illegal detention, the superintendent of the jail transferred some of them to the Nabha Jail, where already a few such children had been kept, thereby increasing their number to eight. They remained unrescued.[327]

Unfortunately, India's majority community rewards those politicians who promote antiminority, violence and massacres, overwhelmingly reelect them, and protect them. Similarly the majority community cheers the police atrocities and unspeakable tortures of the people belonging to other religions or races and never objects to police excesses and minorities' extortions.

On April 28, 2020, United States Commission on International Religious Freedom recommended putting India on the blacklist. USCIRF, on April 28, 2020, released its annual report documenting significant developments in 2019 and making recommendations to enhance the United States government's promotion of the freedom of religion and belief in 2020. The report recommends putting India on the blacklist. It has also recommended designating India as a country of particular concern for engaging in and tolerating systematic ongoing and egregious religious freedom violations as defined by the International Religious Freedom Act.

In its report, the US Commission has also recommended to the US government to:

> Impose targeted sanctions on India government agencies and officials responsible for severe violation of religious freedom by freezing these individuals' assets and or barring their entry into the United States under human-rights related financial and visa authorities, citing specific religious freedom violations.

---

[326] Ibid.

[327] Ram Narayan Kumar and Georg Sieberer, *Sikh Struggle* (Delhi, 1991), 291.

According to the March 2021 annual report on global political rights and liberties, India's status as a free country has changed to "partly free." Civil liberties in India have been in decline since PM Narendra Modi came to power in 2014, said Freedom House in its report, "Democracy under Siege." It said the change in India's status is part of a global shift in the balance between democracy and authoritarianism. US-based Freedom House, a nonprofit organization that researches political freedom and human rights, added that the number of countries designated as "not free" was at its highest level since 2006. [328]

---

[328] https://www.bbc.com/news/world-asia-india-56249596.

# Economic Viability of Independent Punjab

Punjab, as a country, has a high potential of becoming a role model for the other countries for their right to life, liberty, and pursuit of happiness. Punjab is a combination of a diverse population and natural resources. Sikhs in Punjab have a slight majority, thus eliminating the possibility of an authoritarian rule, about which the Hindu community of Punjab is concerned.

The people of Punjab have serious concerns about the economic viability of independent Punjab. They want to know about their economic future, health, education, and relations with the neighboring counties. They think Punjab is too small and landlocked. These are valid questions. In this section, the author explains answers to all those questions and addresses their concerns.

The constitution will administer Punjab based on the federal structure of the empire of Maharaja Ranjit Singh and the guidance of the international laws and the United Nations Charter. Any constitution is a piece of paper in the absence of the ruling party's desire to honor and implement it.

The independence of the judiciary is key in administering justice and equal rights. The effectiveness of the United States of America's Constitution lies in the strength of its independent judiciary. Even a local judge has the power of stopping and delaying the administration's (president's) agenda. In an appeal, the case will have to run through the judicial system to the top, to the supreme court, to reach the final verdict. No one person or group of persons has the power to implement their agenda if the people deem it inappropriate or unreasonable.

An important reason for America's success is its immigrant population. Even the newly arrived legal immigrants feel America is their country as much as the born Americans. They work hard, follow the law, and merge into the mainstream of the American population. Another important reason for America's success is its female workforce. Women comprise about half of the US workforce. They are educated, feel empowered, and refuse to be subjected to social abuse. They are willing to take on any challenge in politics and the country's economic, scientific, and social fabric.

Punjabi women are strong and willing to take the challenge. They have the same potential as Western women, given the opportunity. Only an independent Punjab can provide them with the necessary ingredients to unleash their power.

An independent Punjab would be an economically viable state. It was a sovereign state until 1849, when it came under British rule. Maharaja Ranjit Singh ruled over Punjab from 1799–1849. Before that, it was an area of twelve sovereign regions called misls (confederacies). Maharaja Ranjit Singh consolidated these misls into one cohesive country and further expanded his rule far and wide. Punjab has an abundance of water resources, fertile land, and hardworking people. The most important ever-inexhaustible resource of Punjab is its people. For centuries, they have been held back by foreign invaders and hostile forces. Since 2005, Punjab's economy has been on a downward spiral because of the Indian governments' detrimental economic policies. Moreover, the Punjabis are hardworking people and will make Punjab an economically thriving country. Punjab holds an abundance of natural water, one of the most precious commodities in the world in the near future.

Punjab constitutes about 1.54 percent of India's landmass. It produces enough agricultural products to feed 40 percent of India's population of 1.38 billion people. The agriculture industry in Punjab is now under Indian control, subjected to the manipulation of fertilizer and food prices, making it disadvantageous to the farmers. Water and electricity supply have been diverted to neighboring states in violation of riparian rights. Punjab has a relatively well-developed infrastructure. It has an extensive network of roads and railways. The state has one of the lowest poverty rates in India.

### Agriculture and Industry

Punjab's highly fertile land is suitable for growing wheat, rice, corn, fruits, sugarcane, vegetables, which is why Punjab has been termed the granary or the breadbasket of India. More than 80 percent of Punjab's land is cultivated, and farming is the leading occupation. The major crops are wheat, maize (corn), rice, pulses (legumes), sugarcane, and cotton. Among the livestock raised are buffalo and other cattle, sheep, goats, and poultry.

The state has an essentially agrarian economy with lower industrial output as compared to other states. A prominent feature of Punjab's industrial landscape is its small-size industrial units. The principal industries include the manufacture of textiles, sewing machines, sporting goods, starch, fertilizers, bicycles, scientific instruments, electrical goods, machine tools, sugar, and pine oil processing.

### Textile Industry

The state produces nearly 25 percent of the best-quality cotton in India. Despite several advantages, the major disadvantage is that it has only 1.5 percent of the spindle capacity of India. Dera Bassi and Ludhiana are known as Manchester of India. Batala is one of the leading cities in northern India in manufacturing steel casting and mechanical machinery. Cotton mills are located at Abhor, Malout, Phagwara, Amritsar, Khakar, Mohali, and Ludhiana.

### Sugar Industry

Sugar mills in Punjab are located at Batala, Gurdaspur, Bhogpur, Phagwara, Nawanshahr, Zira, Morinda, Rakhra, Dhuri, Fazilka, Nakodar, Dasua, Budhewal, Budhladha, Mukerian, Tarn Taran, Ajnala, Faridkot, Jagraon, and other cities.

## Dairy Industry

The primary source of milk and other dairy products in the state is buffalo. The state ranks at the top in the country in the availability of milk, after Haryana and Gujrat.

## Power

The energy for the state of Punjab is provided by hydropower and thermal plants. Among them are the Guru Gobind Singh Super Thermal Plant, Guru Nanak Dev Thermal Plant at Bathinda, Guru Hargobind Thermal Plant in Lehra Mohabbat. The common pool projects are the Bhakra Nangal Complex, the Dehar Power Plant, and the Pong Power Plant. Punjab gives out about 51 percent of the power generated from Bhakra Nangal Complex and 48 percent of the Pong Project's power. Growth in Punjab has been lower than the national average after 2005.[329]

## Punjab Is Landlocked

In the world, forty-four countries are landlocked. Africa includes fifteen landlocked countries; Asia has twelve; Europe has fifteen, and South America has two. Being landlocked is not a problem. Many other landlocked countries are smaller than Punjab. The average gross domestic product (GDP) per capita for the world is approximately $15,000 (USD). Of the world's landlocked countries, only a few, such as Switzerland and Austria, have higher GDPs per capita than this average. The average of all landlocked countries is about $13,000.

Punjabis, being hardworking people, have the potential of exponential economic growth with a much higher GDP than the above average. Foreign investments, treaties, and international trade would greatly enhance the standard of living of the people of Punjab.

---

[329] http://documents.worldbank.org/curated/en/273301504174310304/
Punjab-Poverty-growth-and-inequality.

### Punjab Is Not Too Small

With its 50,362-square-kilometer area, Punjab occupies 1.54 percent of India's total geographical area.[330] Punjab is bigger than a large number of countries in the world. Area wise, Punjab ranks 126th out of 194 countries on the list of countries by size. It is bigger than Slovakia, Dominican Republic, Estonia, Denmark, Netherlands, Switzerland, Israel, Palestine, Kuwait, and the state of Puerto Rico, Lebanon, Jamaica, and many others. It is economically viable on its own. It possesses much-needed natural resources like water and electricity and has productive land and is currently feeding about 40 percent of India's 1.38 billion people.

Punjab, as a country, would be financially independent and able to thrive. In addition to agriculture, the food processing and dairy industries will take off. Manufacturing would be revived which has been ignored and driven out of the state by the successive state and Indian governments. The producers will have the whole world as an open market for all their products.

### Defense and Foreign Relations

Sikhs are renowned for their bravery and martial skills. They fought in World War I and World War II. They drove out the Mughals, freeing India from centuries of slavery. They made more than 80 percent of the sacrifices to get India liberated from the British. Importantly Punjab would be a buffer state between Pakistan and India, reducing the risk of future wars and a nuclear conflict between the two archrivals. Once a free country, Punjab would develop diplomatic relations with foreign nations.

---

[330] https://www.allaboutsikhs.com/punjab/geographical-overview-of-punjab.

# How India Is Taking Land Away from the Farmers

Farmers from all over India, and most significantly from Punjab and Haryana States, are vehemently opposing the three new farm bills enacted in 2020. These farmers have pitched in for a lengthy fight and are determined to continue their campaign until all three bills are annulled. In the harsh cold weather, away from home, under the open sky, they are determined to reverse these bills. These bills violate the Indian Constitution; since agriculture is a state issue, the Indian government has overstepped its authority.

In 2020, the Indian government passed the following three bills:

1. Farmers Produce Trade and Commerce (Promotion and Facilitation) Bill, 2020
2. Farmers (Empowerment and Protection) Agreement on Price Assurance and Farm Services Bill, 2020
3. Essential Commodities (Amendment) Bill 2020

Under the Promotion and Facilitation Bill, *mandis* (market system) will be eliminated. The Empowerment and Protection Bill section of the farm bill covers contract farming with corporate entities. The Essential Commodities section has eliminated the restrictions on hoarding. Hoarding was disallowed in 1955 to prevent black marketing. Lifting the restriction on hoarding will promote price gouging, affecting farmers and nonfarmers alike.

In layman's terms, these bills may be interpreted as the promotion of private corporations to take control of the food products and facilitation of this process by the government. The government would empower corporations and also protect them from any litigation during this process. Permitting hoarding of essential commodities is for price manipulation to the advantage of the hoarders. All three bills are pitched against marginal, small, and medium-sized farmers, and eventually the general public.

The central government argues that these three bills are necessary to encourage private sector investments from domestic and foreign corporations to enhance production, processing, storage, transportation, and marketing of agricultural products. However, these farm bills are intended to dominate the agriculture business by handing over the agribusiness to private corporations and centralizing control of this business. Indian government wants to do so in face of the fact that farming in Punjab and Haryana is highly efficient, and the marketing system is fully developed.

The government has hastily passed these three bills without consulting the states or the farmer unions or any experts on the matter. The Farmers (Empowerment and Protection) Agreement on Price Assurance and Farm Services Act 2020 was enacted by Lok Sabha, on September 17, 2020, and Rajya Sabha, on September 20, 2020. The voting in Rajya Sabha was done on Sunday by a show of hands, a crude method of voting. Sunday voting is highly unusual in the Indian Parliament. Inherently these bills are unconstitutional since the power to make laws on agriculture matters lies with the states. The speed with which the bills have been passed without due process is a clear indication that the Modi government did not want to give the opposition parties any meaningful chance to have their voice heard. In Punjab, the farmers are the warrior class willing to challenge the attacks on their land, rights, and religion. This bill is a backdoor method to weaken the Sikhs of Punjab since they form a vast majority of the farmers.

The system of landownership was started by Banda Singh Bahadur, a renowned Sikh warrior (being the first one to establish Sikh rule). He passed the ownership of the land conquered from the Mughals to the tillers starting in 1709. The land parcels have been passed on to the next generations for centuries. This system has worked efficiently. Even a farmer owning a few acres of land feels independent as he is not dependent on others for livelihood. There is no plausible argument in the favor of this act, other than central control of farmers through depriving them of their ancestral land.

Farmers, the owners of their ancestral land, are feeling threatened. They are peacefully protesting in adverse circumstances like harsh cold weather just to protect the ownership of their meager landholdings. The average landholding in Punjab is less than five acres. They have been attacked with dirty water cannons and road blockades. Determined to achieve their cause, they have manually cleared the roads of heavy vehicles and boulders.

There is no provision in these acts on the continuity of minimum support price (MSP). The farmers are rightfully concerned that these three bills will eliminate MSP, and corporations will control farming and grain and food prices. These bills will eliminate the current law against food hoarding and lead to the black marketing of the food products. Food prices will increase in off seasons. The produce prices paid to farmers would decrease because of the lack of the mandi system and the loss of MSP. Farmers are concerned that even though initially, they may get better prices, removal of the current mandi system and MSP would eventually lead to the loss of the ownership of land since they would no longer get the fair price for their products, resulting in lower income and inability to pay off loans on land.

Most of the farmers hold a few acres of land. Even such a small parcel of land can support a good-size family. The land in Punjab and Haryana being fertile, farmers often get two to three crops a year.

The current mandi system works efficiently. Although the current system is somewhat rigged against the farmers, it still is the best they have. Even now the farmers are forced to accept a lower price with excuses that their products are wet or not of high quality. This system has been working for hundreds of years. Under the current system, farmers take their products to a nearby mandi close to home, sell them at close-to-prevailing prices without unnecessary delay. They also have a personal relationship with the buyers (merchants, also called *arhtyias*) and can borrow money instantly, in times of urgent needs, in a matter of hours without any collateral. With the mandi system gone, they will be at the mercy of corporate officials whose bosses, sitting hundreds or thousands of miles away, call the shots. Farmers would lose any negotiating power. They do not have the time, system, or capability to take their products from place to place. They would, thus, be forced to sell their products at a lower price when corporations play hardball. Lowered grain prices mean lower profit and inability to pay off loans resulting in loss of land.

In case of a dispute, the corporations will be in the driver's seat. Small and medium-sized farmers, having limited knowledge and economic power, will be at disadvantage to negotiate reasonable contracts with powerful corporations. For the same reason, the mechanism for contract resolution between a farmer and a corporation or a trader is heavily loaded against the farmers who, for lack of time, expertise, and economic resources, would be hesitant to initiate a formidable task against big corporations. The act provides for a three-level-dispute settlement mechanism by the conciliation board, subdivisional magistrate, and appellate authority. It bypasses the traditional judicial court system for conflict resolution.

With respect to Punjab, since 1947, the Sikhs have been bearing the brunt of the Indian governments' assault on their land (Punjab trifurcated in 1966), natural resources (India diverted Punjab waters and is controlling its hydroelectric power), and attacks on their religion (June 1984 Indian Army invasion on Darbar Sahib, the Golden Tempe Amritsar complex, with the destruction of Akal Takhat, the highest temporal seat for Sikhs) and the 1984 Sikh Genocide. Unlike the last straw that broke the camel's back, this bill is a devastating blow and an existential threat to the Sikhs, compelling them to seek secession from India.

Several members of the Sikhs for Justice (SFJ), a human rights advocacy group based in New York, have been charged as terrorists just for supporting Punjab farmers. SFJ has been promoting the independence of Punjab through a referendum vote. SFJ has been providing monetary assistance to the farmers who are at risk of losing their land as their loans are in default. There is a high rate of suicide among Punjab farmers because of their inability to pay back loans. The police have been using brutal force to silence the farmers, depriving them of their constitutional right to demonstrate in the capital city of Delhi.

The farmers do not feel the need for these bills, nor do they think these would do them any good. They have a clear understanding that these bills would have devastating effects on their livelihood and survival. Despite lengthy and peaceful protests by hundreds of thousands of farmers, and diaspora Sikhs blocking Indian Consulates in the USA, UK, and Canada, the government is not budging, anticipating that the farmers, after months of agitation, will get sick and tired and go home. So far, the farmers are determined to push their cause. The main reason they have been successful so far is that they have astutely kept the politicians out, who, in the past, have always betrayed them. One with stronger determination would win.

Prolonged and powerful protests by farmers around Delhi borders failed to get any response from the Modi government. Several negotiations between leaders of farmers' unions and the Indian government failed to produce any results. The Indian government refused to budge and paid no heed to the ongoing farmers' protests.

However, India took serious notice when more than thirty-five thousand Sikhs showed up for the Punjab Independence Referendum 2020 voting on October 31, 2021, at Queen Elizabeth II Center in Central London, UK. This shook up Modi's government. On the advice of India's intelligence agencies that the Sikh drive for secession is real and strong, the Modi government abruptly made the declaration to annul the highly contentious farms laws, hoping to prevent farmers from joining the independence campaign. He announced to withdraw three farm laws on November 19, 2021, while addressing the nation on the occasion of Guru Nanak's Gurpurb (birthday).

# Punjab Analysis and Conclusion

## Analysis

Since the independence of India in 1947, the relationship between Sikhs and the government of India has been tense and untrustworthy at best. At times, it has been confrontational. Other times, it has been downright warlike. An in-depth look into the history and events that have molded this relationship can shed light on the genesis of this uncomfortable and untenable situation.

Before 1947, Sikhs were promised religious freedom and an autonomous state in the north of India, where they would enjoy the glow of freedom. It was based on the promises made to them that Sikhs, under what was considered an unofficial referendum of their own, decided to go with India. Even though they had suspicions about India's promises, they decided upon assurances given by Jawaharlal Nehru and Mahatma Gandhi that they would honor their words. However, shortly after August 15, 1947, it became apparent that the trio—Jawaharlal Nehru, Mahatma Gandhi, and Sardar Patel—had, from the beginning, a sinister design to entrap the Sikh nation and then perform its boa constriction. The Indian Constitution, framed in 1950, was drastically different in content from the one agreed upon and propounded before independence. It was averse to the Sikh interests, and their representatives did not append their signature on this document.

India has two constitutions: one written one for the elite ruling party and the other unwritten one for the minorities. India has no interest, will, or desire to apply the written constitution uniformly. It is simply a tool for the persecution of minorities—to be on the

287

good side of one majority community to attract votes no matter what the composition of the ruling party is at any particular time. The concept and the process of the persecution of minorities to grab the vote bank of the majority community has stood the test of time. As of January 2018, India's constitution has been amended 104 times. The latest amendment became effective on January 14, 2019, giving more powers to the central government and weakening the judiciary.

In August 1947, Hindus got India, Muslims got Pakistan, and the Sikh slavery got a new master: India. The Sikhs made a political miscalculation by going with India based on promises made by the Congress leadership. They failed to get any written document from the British or from the Congress Party to nail down those promises.

The first installment of the devastation of Sikhs caused by this relationship came in the form of a massacre of more than six hundred thousand Sikhs and the displacement of millions during a few days of August 15, 1947. This was unplanned and poorly managed and is one of the most horrific mass migrations of people in human history.

Starting in 1948, India started carving areas out of Punjab, finally leading to the formation of the state of Punjab in 1966—ten years after the other states were established, having an area of fifty thousand square kilometers—about one-tenth of its original size before partition. The water resources of Punjab have been illegally diverted to the adjoining states.

Indian police attacked Darbar Sahib and unarmed Sikhs on July 4, 1955, killing two hundred and injuring thousands who were peacefully demanding Punjab statehood and not the country of Punjab (Khalistan). During the Nirankari massacre of the Sikhs on April 13, 1978, in Amritsar, thirteen Sikhs were gunned down, and none of the sixty-two Nirankaris charged were punished, all done with the connivance of the state and the central government.

When Sant Jarnail Singh Bhindranwale protested the injustice to Sikhs, he was called a terrorist and separatist. The once amicable relation between Hindus and Sikhs was turned venomous by Arya Samaj and the biased Hindu-Indian press controlled by Congress and subsequent Hindu ruling parties. Lavleen Kaur, a Sikh journalist, stated that the police would capture Bhindranwale's men and beat them mercilessly without any record of their arrest or any charges filed against them. According to Khushwant Singh, a Sikh historian, Bhindranwale was falsely blamed for violence in Punjab, which was the Indian government's clandestine plan to secure Hindu vote by claiming itself as Hindu savior.

Indian government promulgated black-draconian law like the Unlawful Activities Prevention Act-UAPA (1967), Maintenance of Internal Security Act (1971), National Security Act (1980), Punjab disturbed Area Ordinance (1983), Armed Forces (Punjab and Chandigarh) Special Powers Act (1983), Terrorist Affected Area Act 1984 (Special Courts Act), TADA (1985-1995), POTA (2002-2004), and multiple revisions to UAPA. Under these acts, the Sikhs were denied the due process of law, arresting them without charges and detaining them in jails for prolonged periods without trial while their families were not informed of their whereabouts.

Before Operation Blue Star and Operations Black Thunder I and II, the Indian government supplied weapons by truckloads to Sikh militants. Indian intelligence agents penetrated Sikh organizations and convinced them to escalate the demand for Khalistan, putting words in their mouths. Not satisfied by the RAW, Indira Gandhi created a new agency called the Third Agency to plan Operation Blue Star. The Third Agency was accountable only to Indira Gandhi.

Indira Gandhi declared emergency rule in Punjab in 1988 and suspended the right to life of the people in this state. Fake police encounters were the primary means of extrajudicial killings of the Sikhs by the government.

Operation Blue Star, Operation Woodrose, and Operations Black Thunder I and II were the means used by the Indian government for massacring Sikhs. In November 1984, the Sikh genocide was conducted all over India, leading to the killing of more than thirty thousand Sikhs and violent gang rapes of Sikh women with the connivance of the then ruling Congress Party and prominent politicians. For Sikhs, Indian democracy ceased to exist in June 1984, November 1984, and actually right from the start in 1947. India's constitution refused to recognize Sikhism as a separate faith in 1950. In the early nineties, the government of India allocated Rs. 4,500 crore (a crore equals ten million) to pay bounties for the heads of the Sikhs. The Indian Constitution is applied arbitrarily and selectively to the Sikhs not only failing to protect their rights but also severely curtailing those rights by enacting black laws.

Overseas, India is not leaving any stone unturned and has thousands of intelligence agents interfering in Sikh religious and political activities. Their goal is to portray Sikhs as terrorists and defame them internationally. However, the Sikhs are fighting back vigorously. Many Sikhs Gurdwaras have denied Indian agents access to the gurdwara stages.

There has been an established and highly predictable pattern of sinister behavior toward the Sikhs by the successive Indian governments regardless of their political makeup. Sikhs have realized that these patterns are not spontaneous or unplanned. The ultimate goal of India is to weaken Sikhs, their identity, their religion, their language, and the Punjab economy, reducing Sikh people to a subservient society and thus assimilating and subsuming Sikhism into the vast interior of Hinduism.

India hastily and improperly pushed three farm bills into law in September 2020 under which the farmers are at risk of losing control and ownership of their land. This is yet another backdoor effort by the Indian government to turn the state of Punjab further into a deeper state of slavery, servitude, and poverty.

The tiny state of Punjab covers barely 1.54 percent of India's landmass, and Sikhs comprise about 1.8 percent of the Indian population. However, it has the dubious honor of hosting more troops, paramilitary forces, and police than ever maintained by foreign rulers—Mughals and the British during peacetime. More Sikhs have been killed in free India in seventy-four years since 1947 than the number of all the freedom fighters killed in this land in two hundred years preceding August 15, 1947. This validates the argument that in India, the Sikh masses are repressed, persecuted, and face an existential threat.

The campaign for the independence of Punjab in itself has nothing to do with the breakup of India. It is to reestablish the sovereign country of Punjab. India's reference to this campaign as acts of terrorism and separatism is designed to justify the repression and persecution of Sikhs and further fuel the anti-Sikh sentiment in India. India's breakup would be its own creation, the direct result of its actions against the minorities and minority religions. To save India, it is pursuing a path of self-destruction. The concept of Hindutva is dead on its start to nowhere because people are willing to die to protect their religion, identity, and language. Silencing their voices by repression does not convey their complicity. The origin of four religions in this geographical area (Buddhism, Jainism, Langayatism, and Sikhism) confirms that India's majority community's belief system (faith) is not sustainable. It has led to thousands of years of slavery, servitude, and human suffering.

Punjab's demographics and its natural resources have been at risk since 1947. Now the Sikhs in particular and Punjabis in general have to decide if they want to continue the status quo of slavery under India or change the course of history for the better by going the way of independent Punjab. The challenge to the people of Punjab, regardless of their race or religion, is whether they want to brighten the future of their coming generations or stay marred in their hopeless trust in the Indian system of governance, which has repeatedly failed them.

After finally realizing that Sikhs can never get justice and human equality in India, they are right in conducting a peaceful campaign to reclaim their lost sovereignty. Several different Sikh Jathebandies (organizations) have been active in the struggle for the sovereignty of Punjab at various times. More than 150,000 Sikhs have paid the ultimate price for the independence of Punjab by sacrificing their lives and enduring unspeakable tortures and genocidal violence. Currently, Sikhs for Justice and the Council of Khalistan are at the forefront of this campaign.

The Punjabi Hindus ought to break their silence on Sikh genocide and torture and the killing of innocent, unarmed Sikh men, women, and children. Their silence and inaction on the issue of the freedom of Punjab invite more violence. Punjab is the country of Punjabis. Punjabis want to reclaim their sovereignty. Their experiment in going with India for seventy-four years, since 1947, has cost them life, liberty, and an uncertain future. Punjabis must learn from their mistakes. For Punjabis, an independent Punjab is the only option. Failing this, all of them, regardless of their religion, would have to endure an uncertain future because India's governance system would always favor mainland India at the cost of Punjab and its people.

Sikhs are campaigning for the independence of Punjab (Khalistan) by exercising their right to self-determination for the same reasons India got freedom from the British Raj. They are seeking independence by exercising their right to self-determination by a referendum vote—no different from the referendums India utilized to attach Junagadh in 1948 and Sikkim in 1975. Sikhs uniquely qualify and fulfill all the requirements for exercising the right to self-determination. Additionally, Sikhs are being subjected to ongoing genocidal violence in India. Above all, they are facing existential threat in India as described in detail in this book.

The people of Punjab need an independent political system of their own. Since 1947, they have had the choice between the frying pan and the fire. Punjab needs to rid itself of this kind of leadership. Revolutions throughout history have brought freedom and prosperity. Referendum 2020 is the Punjabis' revolution. However, this revolution is different in being legal, democratic, and peaceful.

These alarm bells keep tolling the warning signals of the impending future genocidal violence in India against the minorities. Therefore, every Punjabi must agree with him/herself that each of them has an equal stake in the country of Punjab regardless of their religion or belief. They must also realize that the religion of their fellow Punjabis is their own business. To exert superiority of one over the other is inhuman and has also been detrimental to them all as far back as the arrival of the Arians about 3,500 years ago and beyond.

Freedom and justice are fundamental human rights. Subjecting people to slavery and servitude in any form is not only a violation of their fundamental human rights but also evil and savage. Punjab is occupied by India and treated as its colony. Punjabis have what it takes to liberate their country from Indian occupation.

## *Conclusion*

In the light of the above background; no possibility of justice or human equality; India's Hindutva (making India a Hindu country) agenda; ongoing tortures, massacres, and rapes of minority women; open agenda of the genocide of Sikhs; and hidden agenda of econocide of the people of Punjab, Punjabis would be wise to get Punjab liberated from never-ending slavery. Punjabis stopped Alexander the Great at Beas River, defeated the formidable Mughal Empire, and forced the British to vacate India. Liberating Punjab from India, though no less arduous, is an achievable goal. International law is on their side. India never has—and never would—consider Punjab as its part. India would always treat Punjab as its colony. Punjabis must understand that their master, India, is different from all others; it is cunning and treacherous, being disguised as a friend. They can win this war by a legal, peaceful, and democratic process by a referendum vote called Punjab Independence Referendum. An independent Punjab will be a solution where everyone benefits—the people of Punjab, India, and Pakistan.

# Timeline of Sikh History from 1947

- 1948, carving of Punjab began

    In 1948, the province of Himachal Pradesh was carved out of twenty-eight princely states controlling the foothills of western Himalayas, with further four southern hill states carved out of East Punjab. The further territory was reallocated to Himachal Pradesh in November 1956, when the latter became a union territory in the 1956 States Reorganization Act.

- 1950, Indian Constitution adopted, January 26, 1950

    The constitution of India was adopted on January 26, 1950. It is considered a "bag of borrowings" because it borrowed many provisions from the constitutions of France, Germany, the USSR, Japan, the USA, and the UK. Indian Constitution labels Sikhs as Hindus and is called a soft document as it does not protect the rights of minorities and is applied arbitrarily at the whim of the ruling party.

- 1953, Dr. B. R. Ambedkar in Rajya Sabha on September 2, 1953

    Dr. Ambedkar, on September 2, 1953, stated that even though he played a major role in framing India's Constitution, he disapproved of the final version. He stated that he would be the first person to burn it out. He disapproved of the argument that recognizing the rights of minorities will harm Indian democracy. He stated that the greatest harm will come by injuring the minorities.

- 1955, the States Reorganization Commission Report

  The commission, in its 1955 report, rejected the demand for a Punjabi-speaking state. The explanation for the denial of statehood of Punjab was the preservation of unity and secularism of India. But it seems that denial of the rights of minorities and tribal people was projected as a way to preserve the democracy of India.

- 1955, Indian Police attacked Darbar Sahib on July 4, 1955

  On July 4, 1955, Indian Police attacked the peacefully protesting Sikhs demanding Punjabi Suba. The police entered Darbar Sahib (Golden Temple Amritsar), killing about two hundred persons, injuring three thousand, and arresting many more thousands.

- 1958, Punjabi Suba Conference

  The first Punjabi Suba Conference was held on October 12, 1958, under the leadership of Sant Fateh Singh. Election to the SGPC was held in January 1960, on the issue of Punjabi-speaking state. Master Tara Singh bagged 132 out of 139 seats.

- 1960, the Children Act 1960

  Under the Children Act, 1960, or the East Punjab Children Act 1976, the boys younger than sixteen and the girls below the age of eighteen years cannot be detained either in a police station or in a regular jail, but the authorities paid no heed to these laws, stating that these laws are just for the books.

- 1966, a crippled Punjabi Suba was created

  Punjabi Suba (state) was established in 1966. However, it was made into a permanently ineffective sub-state. Under the provision of the Punjab Reorganization Act (1966), the powers of control, administration, maintenance, distribution, and developments of the waters and the hydel powers of Punjab rivers were vested in the central government. It violated the riparian rights of Punjab but honored the same rights for Haryana when the control of Yamuna waters remained under the exclusive jurisdiction of the Haryana government. Chandigarh, the capital of the state of Punjab, was converted into a union territory and not given exclusively to Punjab in violation of the basis of the formation of the states on a linguistic basis.

- 1967, enactment of UAPA

  The object of this bill was to make powers available for dealing with activities directed against the integrity and sovereignty of India. The bill was passed by both the Houses of Parliament and received the assent of the president on December 30, 1967.

  The UAPA has been amended several times. TADA was applied from 1985–1995. It was allowed to elapse in 1995, but most of its provisions were incorporated into POTA. The Prevention of Terrorism Act (POTA), 2002, was an act passed by the Parliament of India on March 26, 2002, to strengthen antiterrorism operations. It was repealed on September 21, 2004, because of its misuse by the government against its people and opposition parties. After POTA was withdrawn, most of its provisions were incorporated into UAPA.

  In July 2019, the ambit of UAPA was expanded. It was amended, allowing the government to designate an individual as a terrorist without trial. Before this, only organizations and not individuals could be declared terrorists.

- 1971, maintenance of Internal Security Act

  The Maintenance of Internal Security Act (MISA) was a controversial law passed by the Indian Parliament in 1971, giving the administration of Prime Minister Indira Gandhi and Indian law enforcement agencies very broad powers—indefinite preventive detention of individuals, search and seizure of property without warrants, and wiretapping.

- 1973, Anandpur Sahib Resolution

  This document was adopted unanimously by the working committee of the Shiromani Akali Dal at a meeting held at Anandpur Sahib on October 16–17, 1973, and came to be known as the Anandpur Sahib Resolution. It was endorsed in the form of a succession of resolutions at the Eighteenth All India Akali Conference of the Shiromani Akali Dal in Ludhiana, on October 28–29, 1978.

The resolution included both religious and political issues. It asked for recognizing Sikhism as a religion separate from Hinduism. It also demanded that power be generally devolved from the central to state governments and more autonomy for Punjab.

- 1975, Indira Gandhi declared emergency on June 26, 1975

Former President Fakhruddin Ali Ahmed, on the orders of then-Prime Minister Indira Gandhi, proclaimed a national emergency across India in 1975, which lasted for twenty-one months. Thus, elections were suspended, and civil liberties were curbed. Most of Gandhi's political opponents were imprisoned, and the press was censored. The emergency also saw the violation of human rights. This period saw the forced mass-sterilization campaign spearheaded by Sanjay Gandhi. The emergency period is considered one of the most controversial times in independent India's history.

Originally at the beginning, a national emergency could be declared based on "external aggression or war" and "internal disturbance" in the whole of India, or a part of its territory, under Article 352. Such an emergency was declared in India in the 1962 war (China war), the 1971 war (Pakistan war), and the 1975 internal disturbance (declared by Indira Gandhi).

During a national emergency, many fundamental rights of Indian citizens can be suspended. The freedoms under the right to freedom are automatically suspended. By contrast, the right to life and personal liberty cannot be suspended, according to the original constitution. However, during the emergency declared by Indira Gandhi in June 1975, the government decided to suspend even the right to life and personal liberty.

The constitution's Fifty-Ninth Amendment Act, 1988, empowered the central government to impose an emergency in Punjab when deemed necessary. Under the amendment, the president's rule can be extended up to three years, increased from one year under the previous amendment. This time, the emergency was applied to Punjab only.

- 1978, Nirankari massacre of the Sikhs, April 13, 1978

  Nirankaris, with the connivance of the Punjab government, killed thirteen unarmed Sikhs in Amritsar, who wanted to persuade the Nirankaris to stop blasphemy against Sikhism and disparaging remarks about the Sikh gurus. Sixty-two Nirankaris were charged. All were acquitted by a Haryana court when the case was tried out of the state of Punjab.

- 1978, Babbar Khalsa was established

  Babbar Khalsa International, better known as Babbar Khalsa, founded in April 1978, by Sukhdev Singh Babbar and Talwinder Singh Parmar, is a Sikh freedom fighter organization whose main objective is to create an independent country, Khalistan.

  It operates in Canada, Germany, the United Kingdom, and some parts of India.

- 1978, Indira Gandhi sent to jail, December 20, 1978

  Indira Gandhi was briefly imprisoned in 1978 for official corruption and fraud during the 1971 elections.

- 1980, National Security Act of 1980

  Under the National Security Act, a person is liable to be jailed without disclosure of reason, without a trial, and without redress for two years in Punjab.

- 1982, Dharam Yudh Morcha was launched

  In 1982, Sant Bhindranwale launched the Dharam Yudh Morcha (religious political movement). These were peaceful protests to support the implementation of the Anandpur Sahib Resolution. During these peaceful demonstrations, thousands of Sikhs courted arrest. Despite the government's attempts to malign Sant Bhindranwale, he rekindled in the minds of Sikhs the noble teachings of their gurus. He emphasized that neither the Sikhs oppress others nor should they live under oppression.

Due to the rise of Congress and state-sponsored terrorism, hundreds of Sikhs were killed in staged encounters by the Indian security forces. Many Sikhs, feeling helpless, turned to the message of Guru Gobind Singh Ji, who, after losing most of his family, said in his now-famous words echoed by Sant Jarnail Singh Bhindranwale, "When all other peaceful means have failed, only then, it is right and just to take sword in hand."

- 1982, construction of SYL Canal, April 8, 1982

On April 8, 1982, Indira Gandhi formally launched the construction of the canal in the Kapoori village of Punjab. On April 23, the Punjab government issued a white paper hailing the agreement. As per terms reached under the Punjab accord, a tribunal was to be set up to investigate the river water claims of Haryana, Punjab, and Rajasthan. The Akali Dal came back to power in Punjab in October 1985, and on November 5, 1985, the newly elected Punjab Legislative Assembly repudiated the 1981 agreement (proposed legislation for conferment of ownership rights on tenants). The Ravi and Beas Waters Tribunal (also known as Eradi Tribunal after its chair V. Balakrishna Eradi) was constituted on April 2, 1986. On January 30, 1987, the tribunal upheld the legality of the agreements of 1955, 1976, and 1981. It also increased shares of both Punjab and Haryana, allocating them 5 MAF (million acre-feet) and 3.83 MAF, respectively. It also noted that while the canal's portion had been completed in Haryana, the portion in Punjab was not and urged that it be completed expeditiously. The Akali Dal government in Punjab, under Surjit Singh Barnala, started the construction of the canal by 1990. However, it kept dithering on its completion.

The Punjab portion of the canal has not been completed and has been mired in court fights.

On July 12, 2004, the Punjab Legislative Assembly passed the *Punjab Termination of Agreements Act, 2004*, which abrogated all its river water agreements with neighboring states. The president of India then referred this bill to the supreme court in the same year.

The court began hearings on the bill by the Punjab Assembly on March 7, 2016. On March 15, 2016, the Punjab Legislative Assembly unanimously passed the *Punjab Satluj Yamuna Link Canal Land (Transfer of Proprietary Rights) Bill, 2016*, proposing to return the land that had been acquired from owners for building the SYL Canal. The land was subsequently transferred to its owners.

- 1982, Sikhs denied entry into Delhi during the 1982 Asian Games

  Every Sikh traveling to Delhi was stopped, searched, humiliated, and insulted in the presence of others by the Haryana Police. Cars were checked, trains were stopped, and buses were detained to get the Sikh passengers down for thorough scrutiny. Even eminent persons like Air Chief Marshal Arjan Singh, Lt. Gen. Jagjit Singh Aurora, and Swaran Singh, former central minister, were stopped and searched despite their telling who they were.

- 1983, the Punjab Disturbed Area Ordinance 1983

  This was repealed and replaced with the Armed Forces (Punjab and Chandigarh) Special Powers Act.

- 1983, the Armed Forces (Punjab and Chandigarh) Special Powers Act, December 8, 1983

  Under this act, any commissioned officer, warrant officer, noncommissioned officer, or any other person of equivalent rank in the armed forces may, after giving such due warning as he may consider necessary, fire upon or otherwise use force, even to the cause of death, against any person who is acting in contravention of any law or order, prohibiting the assembly of five or more persons or the carrying of weapons or of things capable of being used as weapons or of firearms, ammunition, or explosive substances.

- 1984, Operation Blue Star, June 5, 1984

  Operation Blue Star was a preplanned and well-organized ghastly invasion of the holiest Sikh shrine, Darbar Sahib (Golden Temple Amritsar) by the Indian Army in June 1984, resulting in the death of more than ten thousand Sikh men, women, and children—mostly pilgrims. Before the attack, Punjab came to a standstill, all news media, transportation, and telecommunication were cut off. More than seventy thousand army personnel were brought in and spread all over Punjab. The Sikh regiments were moved away from Punjab. The border with Pakistan was sealed. The details of this horrific attack and the events leading to it are discussed under the chapter "Operation Blue Star."

- 1984, Special Courts Act, July 14, 1984

  Also called the Terrorist-Affected Areas Act (Special Courts Act), was promulgated on July 14, 1984. The act was passed to provide speedy trials for certain offenses. The state of Punjab and the union territory of Chandigarh were declared as "terrorist affected" areas. Under this act, anyone who has committed almost any crime could be tried. Cases could be tried under the camera (protection of open trial is denied), witnesses can remain anonymous, there was a denial of anticipatory bail and bail in bailable cases. The trial could be moved to a distant place, away from where the alleged case had occurred, making it difficult for the defendant and his/her lawyers.

- 1984, Sikh Genocide in India in November 1984

  Following the assassination of Prime Minister Indira Gandhi by her two Sikh bodyguards on October 31, 1984, the then-ruling party of India (the Indian National Congress), also known as Congress (I), organized and orchestrated attacks targeting Sikhs, a religious minority, throughout India. The personalized attacks were on the lives, homes, businesses, personal property, and places of worship of Sikhs in India. They were carried out with impunity and in a meticulous and malicious manner, resulting in the loss of thousands of lives. More than thirty thousand Sikhs were killed in this brief yet tragic period. Most of the victims were helpless and burnt alive in front of family members and neighbors. Hundreds of Sikh women were raped. Countless Sikh temples or places of worship, known as gurdwaras, were burnt to the ground. Sikh properties, homes, and businesses were looted, ransacked, and destroyed. Over three hundred thousand (300,000) Sikhs were uprooted and displaced during the melee.

- 1984, Hondh-Chillar and Pataudi massacre of the Sikhs on November 2, 1984

  Thirty-eight people, including women and children from Hond-Chillar village in Rewari district of Haryana State, were burnt alive in a local gurdwara, on November 2, 1984, two days after former Prime Minister Indira Gandhi was assassinated by her Sikh bodyguards. A similar killing of Sikhs happened in the nearby village of Pataudi.

- 1984, Operation Woodrose

  Operation Woodrose was a military operation carried out by the Indira Gandhi-led Indian government in the months after Operation Blue Star to "prevent the outbreak of widespread public protest" in the state of Punjab. The government arrested all prominent members of the largest Sikh political party, the Akali Dal, and banned the All India Sikh Students Federation, a large students' union. At the same time, the Indian Army conducted operations in the countryside during which thousands of Sikhs—mostly young men—were detained for interrogation and subsequently tortured.

- 1984, World Sikh Organization was established

  The World Sikh Organization (WSO) was formed after an international gathering of Sikhs on July 28, 1984, at Madison Square Garden in New York City, New York, which included several thousand people from the United States, Canada, Great Britain, and several countries in the Far East. The organization was formed with two branches: WSO Canada and WSO America, with headquarters in Ottawa and New York.

- 1984, World Sikh News was started in December 1984

   In December 1984, a bilingual newspaper, the *World Sikh News*, was launched from Stockton, California, to "project the voice of Sikhs across the world" and highlight "Sikh participation in America's social and cultural life." It was started by Dr. Gurinder Singh Grewal, MD, its president, and Narinder Singh Somal, its secretary. The *World Sikh News* was a supporter of the WSO but was not officially linked with this organization in any way, and operated independently.

- 1986, Khalistan flag hoisted at Akal Takhat on January 26, 1986

   The widows of Sant Bhindranwale, Bhai Amrik Singh, and Gen. Subeg Singh were honored, and the Khalistan flag was hoisted at Akal Takht during the *Sarbat Khalsa Samagam* (large gathering of Sikhs) held in Amritsar in January 1986.

- 1986, Sarbat Khalsa Assembly, January 26, 1986

   Sarbat Khalsa elected and inaugurated the five members of Panthak Committee at Harmandar Sahib, Amritsar, to decide on behalf of the Sikhs. The committee went on to declare Khalistan on April 29, 1986.

- 1986, Khalistan Commando Force (KCF) was established

   On January 26, 1986, Sarbat Khalsa elected a Panthak Committee at Akal Takhat, and KCF was formalized as its official military wing.

- 1986, Original Panthak Committee formed, January 26, 1986

   On this day, a five-member Panthic Committee, consisting of Gurbachan Singh Manochahal, Wassan Singh Zaffarwal, Dhanna Singh, Aroor Singh, and Gurdev Singh Usmanwala was formed for guiding the Sikh Panth.

- 1986, declaration of Khalistan on April 29, 1984

  On April 29, 1986, an assembly of separatist Sikhs at the Akal Takht made a declaration of an independent state of Khalistan, and several rebel militant groups in favor of Khalistan subsequently waged a major insurgency against the government of India.

- 1986, Operation Black Thunder I, April 30, 1986

  After the Khalistan declaration on April 29, 1986, from Akal Takhat, the Indian government attacked Darbar Sahib on April 30, 1986. About three hundred National Security Guard commandos, along with seven hundred Border Security Force troops, stormed into the Golden Temple complex and captured about three hundred Sikhs. This operation was approved by Surjit Singh Barnala, the then-chief minister of Punjab, and lasted eight hours. A force of nearly two thousand paramilitary police completed a twelve-hour operation to regain control of the Golden Temple at Amritsar from several hundred Sikh radicals. The police stated that almost all the major radical leaders managed to escape.

- 1986, Khalistan Liberation Force (KLF)

  Khalistan Liberation Force is a freedom fighter group and is part of the Khalistan movement to create a Sikh homeland, Khalistan, via armed struggle. The KLF appears to have been a loose association of scattered Khalistani groups. The KLF Jathebandi was founded by Aroor Singh and Sukhvinder Singh Babbar in 1986. Its notable activities included the 1991 abduction of the Romanian diplomat Liviu Radu and the killing of SSP Gobind Ram.

- 1987, Gurbachan Singh Manochahal formed BTFK

  In 1987, Gurbachan Singh Manochahal, a member of the original Panthak Committee, formed his own Bhindranwale Tiger Force for Khalistan (BTFK).

- 1988, Operation Black Thunder II, May 9, 1988

  Indian government forces attacked Harmandar Sahib on May 9, 1988, which led to the killing of about two hundred Sikhs. Planning for Operation Black Thunder II was started in early 1988, in Manesar (Aravali hills), forty kilometers from Delhi, by National Security Guard (NSG) under patronage from the home minister rather than the Ministry of Internal Security. A large model of the Darbar Sahib complex was prepared. The practice was carried out at the high school in Tauru and in a college in Nuh, Haryana. Both these schools had structures that resembled the parikarma (perimeter) of Darbar Sahib. Regular visits to Darbar Sahib were carried out clandestinely by members of Special Action Group (SAG), who started growing beards to disguise their operation.

- 1986, Council of Khalistan was established in the USA in October 1986

  Dr. Gurmeet Singh Aulakh was appointed its first president, who started working for the independence of Khalistan by lobbying in the US Congress. He worked till the last day of his life, when he met his maker in 2017. He died as a result of the complications of colon cancer. Dr. Bakhshish Singh Sandhu, MD, was appointed (unanimously elected) his successor in a meeting of the advisers of the Council of Khalistan held at Sikh Cultural Society Gurdwara Sahib, Richmond Hill, New York, on October 7, 2017.

- 1985, TADA enacted on May 23, 1985

  Terrorist and Disruptive Activities (Prevention) Act, commonly known as TADA, was an Indian antiterrorism law that was in force between 1985 and 1995 (modified in 1987) under the background of the Punjab insurgency and was applied to the whole of India. It came into effect on May 23, 1985. It was renewed in 1989, 1991, and 1993, before being allowed to lapse in 1995 due to increasing unpopularity after widespread allegations of abuse.

  It gives a thorough definition of terrorism:

  > Whoever with intent to overawe the Government as by law established or to

BAKHSHISH SINGH SANDHU, MD

strike terror in the people or any section of
the people or to alienate any section of the
people or to adversely affect the harmony
amongst different sections of the people
does any act or thing by using bombs, dyna-
mite or other explosive or inflammable substances or lethal weapons or poisons or nox-
ious gases or other chemicals or by any other
substance (whether biological or otherwise)
of a hazardous nature in such a manner as
to cause, or is likely to cause the death of, or
injuries to, any person or persons or loss of,
or damage to, or destruction of, property or
disruption of any supplies or services essential to the life of the community, or detains
any person and threatens to kill or injure
such person to compel the Government
or any other person to do or abstain from
doing any act, commits a terrorist act.

- 1988, Fifty-Ninth Constitutional Amendment

  The Constitution (Fifty-Ninth Amendment) Act,
  1988, empowered the central government to impose an
  emergency in Punjab when deemed necessary. Under the
  amendment, the president's rule can be extended up to
  three years, increased from one year under the previous
  amendment.

- 1988, Punjab deliberately flooded

  In 1988, Punjab had its most disastrous floods when
  all the rivers in Punjab overflowed, killing and displacing
  thousands of people. In four days, from September 23–26,
  634 mm rainfall fell in the Bhakra area. This was the biggest flood in Punjab's history as it disrupted the lives of
  over 34 lakh people.

  Accusing fingers were soon pointed at the Beas
  Bhakra Management Board which was held responsible for

306

triggering off the devastation by releasing—without adequate warning—the waters which, overnight, turned the Beas and Sutlej into Punjab's rivers of sorrow. Much of the loss of life and crops along the Beas and Sutlej River basins could have been averted if the discharges from the Bhakra and Pong Dams had been spread out over a longer period.

- 2000, Chittisinghpura massacre of Sikhs on March 20, 2000

    In March 2000, on the eve of the arrival of President Clinton in India, thirty-six Sikhs were murdered by Indian Forces, in cold blood, in Chittisinghpura (Chiti-Singh-Pura), a small village two and a half hours' drive from Srinagar.

- 2002, POTA was enacted

    The Prevention of Terrorism Act, 2002 (POTA), was an act passed by the Parliament of India in 2002, to strengthen antiterrorism operations. The act was passed due to several terrorist attacks that were being carried out in India and especially in response to the attack on the Parliament. The act replaced the Prevention of Terrorism Ordinance (POTO) of 2001 and the Terrorist and Disruptive Activities (Prevention) Act (TADA) (1985–1995) and was supported by the governing National Democratic Alliance. The act was repealed in 2004 because of its misuse by the politicians for personal gains.

- 2007, Sikhs for Justice was established in 2007

    In a meeting held in New Jersey, Sikhs for Justice (SFJ) was established with seven founding members: Bakhshish Singh Sandhu MD of Pennsylvania, Avtar Singh Pannu, Charanjit Singh, Bibi Balvir Kaur—all three of New York—and Baljinder Singh Brar of New Jersey, Gurpatwant Singh Pannun of New York, being its legal adviser, and Dilvar Singh Sekhon of New Jersey, as an auxiliary supporter.

- 2009, Arun Jaitley, BJP member, stated the 1984 Delhi massacre of Sikhs as state-sponsored, December 2009

- 2009, SFJ held a conference and march at Capitol Hill, Washington, DC, in November 2009

More than two thousand supporters marched from Lafayette Park to Capitol Hill to mark the twenty-fifth anniversary of the massacre of more than thirty thousand Sikhs in eighteen states and 110 cities across India. A conference was held at the end of the march at Capitol Hill.

- 2010, Delhi High Court dismissed Sajjan Kumar's plea to squash charges against him, July 2010

  Delhi High Court dismissed Sajjan Kumar's plea to squash various charges, including that of murder, against him.

- 2010, civil complaint filed against Congress Party leader Kamal Nath, April 2010

  SFJ filed a civil complaint in the US Federal Court for the Southern District of New York, according to the Alien Tort Claims Act and Torture Victims Protection Act, against former member of Parliament and Congress Party leader Kamal Nath for his role in the 1984 anti-Sikh violence.

- 2011, India placed on US watch list, April 2011

  India was placed on the watch list of the United States Commission on International Religious Freedom for continuous incidents of religious violence and impunity for the perpetrators from such acts of violence.

- 2012, SFJ filed a civil case against Parkash Singh Badal in Wisconsin, August 2012

  SFJ filed a complaint under ATCA and TVPA in the US Federal District Court of Wisconsin, against Parkash Singh Badal, the then-chief minister of Punjab, on charges of commanding and controlling a police force that committed widespread torture on Sikh political activists in Punjab.

- 2013, SFJ filed a case against Indian Prime Minister Manmohan Singh in Washington, DC

  The Sikhs for Justice, a New York-based human rights organization, filed a civil case against Prime Minister Manmohan Singh at the US District Court for the District of Columbia, before he arrived in the United States, for his role in crimes against humanity, perpetrated upon the Sikh community in India, which issued a summons to appear before it within twenty-one days after receiving the summons.

The suit alleged that Singh's culpability began in 1991, when he took over as India's finance minister. Mr. Singh approved and financed the infamous practice of cash rewards to members of security forces for killing Sikhs through extrajudicial means, often in staged and fake encounters, to curb the Sikh rights movement in Punjab. More than $200 million were disbursed as cash rewards for the extrajudicial killings.

- 2013, Sikhs from all over the world protested in Geneva, Switzerland, on November 1, 2013

  Some fifteen thousand Sikhs stood in front of the United Nations Headquarters in Geneva, Switzerland, on November 1, 2013. They came from all over the world, including United Kingdom, United States, Germany, France, Italy, Holland, Switzerland, Belgium, India, Australia, Canada, Japan, Spain, Portugal, Austria, and Middle Eastern countries. Their message was loud and clear—demanding justice for Sikhs and the independence of Punjab. It was an unforgettable experience that was witnessed by the author himself. Sikh men and women, clad in orange turbans and *chunnies* (chunny is a head cover for Sikh women) were visible as far as one could see, shouting, "We want justice. We want Khalistan."

- 2013, SFJ petitioned UN OHCHR to investigate November 1984 Anti-Sikh Violence

  Sikhs for Justice filed a petition with more than a million signatures before the UN Office of the High Commissioner for Human rights to intervene and investigate November 1984 anti-Sikh violence.

- 2013, court case filed against Sonia Gandhi in New York

  Sikhs for Justice (SFJ) filed a lawsuit in 2013 against Sonia Gandhi for allegedly shielding and protecting Congress Party leaders accused of inciting violence against the Sikh community after the assassination of then-Prime

Minister Indira Gandhi. The three-judge panel affirmed the district court's order that it lacked subject matter jurisdiction over plaintiffs' claims because "all the relevant conduct took place outside the United States," in India.

- 2014, civil complaint filed against Indian prime minister, Narendra Modi, September 2014

  SFJ filed a civil complaint against Narendra Modi in September 2014, in the US Federal Court, for the Southern District of New York, under the Torture Victims Protection Act (TVPA), for his role in the 2002 massacre of Muslims in the state of Gujarat.

- 2015, SFJ filed a criminal complaint in Toronto, Canada, against Indian prime minister, Narendra Modi

  In April 2015, SFJ filed a criminal complaint in Toronto, Canada, against Narendra Modi for his role in the 2002 massacre of Muslims in the state of Gujarat, India, while Modi was head of the government of Gujarat.

- 2015, Sarbat Khalsa Assembly

  Sarbat Khalsa (Global Assembly of Sikhs) met on November 10, 2015, in the village Chabba in District Amritsar, where several resolutions were passed, including the reaffirmation of the independence of Punjab Khalistan. About six hundred thousand Sikhs from all over the world attended the event.

- 2015, Paramjit Singh Pamma detained in Portugal under red alert, December 18, 2015

  Before his arrest by Interpol in Portugal, on December 18, 2015, Pamma was living in the UK after being granted political asylum in 2000. Pamma, along with his family, was staying at a hotel in Portugal when he was detained. He was released, successfully following extensive efforts by Gurparwant Singh Pannu, the legal adviser for SFJ. A case was filed against Punjab Police constables who were dispatched from Punjab to bring Pamma back. Once they learned of the case against them, they eloped in a hurry, leaving their belongings in their hotel rooms.

- 2016, SFJ filed a criminal complaint in Toronto against Capt. Amrinder, chief minister of Punjab, in April 2016
- In April 2016, SFJ filed a criminal complaint (private prosecutor) in Toronto against Capt. Amrinder Singh (chief minister of the state of Punjab, India) on charges of torture.
- 2016, SFJ filed a case against Indian prime minister, Narendra Modi, in Canada in April 2016
- 2017, SFJ installed Referendum 2020 billboards in Punjab, July 2017

   Punjab Police filed a sedition case against the Sikhs for Justice team for putting up these billboards.
- 2017, India placed in tier 2 of religious persecution list

   In August 2017, the US Commission on International Religious Freedom (USCIRF) ranked India's persecution severity at tier 2, along with Iraq and Afghanistan. Over the past seven years, India has risen from number 31 to number 10 on Open Doors World Watch List, ranking just behind Iran in persecution severity, indicating worsening records of religious persecution in India.
- 2018, SFJ delegation met the United Nations officials on January 15, 2018

   SFJ members met the United Nations officials for human rights violations of the Sikhs in India and denial of the necessary medical treatment to Jathedar Jagtar Singh Hawara in Tihar Jail.
- 2018, London Declaration of Punjab Independence Referendum 2020, August 12, 2018

   More than fifteen thousand Sikhs gathered at the Trafalgar Square, London, on August 12, 2018, from all over the world to join the historical event of the London Declaration for the Independence of Punjab. All efforts of the Indian government to stop this declaration failed miserably.
- 2018, CIA classified VHS and Bajrang Dal as militant and RSS as a Hindu nationalist organization

US Central Intelligence Agency has classified Vishva Hindu Prashid and Bajrang Dal as militant religious outfits and RSS as a Hindu nationalist organization.

The militant Hindu organizations like the BJP, RSS, VHS, Shiv Sena, and Bajrang Dal argue that Hindutva alone can be the basis of India's unity. It is considered in some Hindu circles that the Hindutva agenda is a Hindu sphinx. Unless stopped in time, it could have tremendous destructive power. The minorities are determined to confront it.

- 2019, Sikhs burnt Indian tricolor flag on January 26, 2019, in front of the Indian Embassy in Washington, DC

  Sikhs for Justice, a pro-Khalistan human rights advocacy group based in New York, burnt India's tricolor flag right across the Indian Embassy building in Washington, DC, on Massachusetts Avenue, on Saturday, January 26, 2019, India's Republic Day. Sikhs have burnt India's tricolor flag multiple times in different places, including the UK, USA, and Canada, highlighting their rejection of India's constitution.

- 2019, SFJ held a conference on June 6, 2019, at Lincoln Memorial, Washington, DC

  More than four thousand Sikhs from all over the world gathered at the Lincoln Memorial to further the cause of independence of Punjab Khalistan. Lincoln Memorial was specifically chosen as President Lincoln ended slavery in America.

- 2019, SFJ team was invited as a special guest on the Fourth of July celebration in Washington, DC, by the Trump team

  Gurpatwant Singh Pannun, Dr. Bakhshish Singh Sandhu, and Jagjit Singh (a.k.a. Baba Jagga) joined the celebrations.

- 2019, India banned Sikhs for Justice, July 10, 2019

  Sikhs for Justice was banned on July 10, 2019 by the government of India under the Unlawful Activities (Prevention) Act, UAPA, on cookbook charges of anti-India activities. Sikhs for Justice filed an appeal to this ruling. On

January 9, 2020, the tribunal, headed by Delhi High Court Chief Justice DN Patel, upheld the ban on pro-Khalistan group Sikhs for Justice. The tribunal constituted, under the Unlawful Activities (Prevention) Act, stated that the activities of Sikhs for Justice were "disruptive" and threatened the "sovereignty, unity and territorial integrity of India." The defense's several documents to refute the charges went unheeded.

- 2019, a caravan of about fifty eighteen-wheeler trucks went around Houston all day with truck-size posters of "Go Back, Modi" on September 20, 2019

  Sikhs for Justice arranged this caravan of fifty trucks, with a huge poster covering the flat sides and the back of the trucks with "Go Back, Modi" posters. SFJ volunteers from all over the US and Canada participated in this caravan and worked for weeks to get the trucks ready with posters and Khalistan flags. It was quite a show. It was well covered by the US news media.

- 2019, Kashmiris filed a lawsuit against Modi in Houston Court, on September 19, 2019

  The summons was issued Thursday, September 19, on a civil complaint filed by two unnamed Kashmiris settled in the US through an organization called the Kashmir Khalistan Referendum Front. This lawsuit was filed by a collaboration between SFJ and Kashmiris. SFJ legal adviser, Gurpatwant Singh Pannu, provided legal expertise. According to *The Houston Chronicle*, the lawsuit, filed in the federal district court of the Southern District of Texas by the Kashmir Khalistan Referendum Front and two individuals identified as Ms. TFK and Mr. SMS, sued Modi, Home Minister Amit Shah, and the Indian Army's Lt. Gen. Kanwal Jeet Singh Dhillon for allegedly carrying out extrajudicial killings, causing wrongful death, battery, emotional distress, crimes against humanity upon Kashmiris.

- 2019, SFJ organized Go Back, Modi, Rally in Houston, September 22, 2019

An event called Go Back, Modi, Rally was arranged and managed by the SFJ. While several thousand people gathered inside the NRG football stadium to listen to Prime Minister Narendra Modi at the mega Howdy Modi event in Houston, Texas, about fifteen thousand gathered outside the stadium to protest against the event, including Sikhs, Kashmiris, Muslims, and people from the United States of America.

- 2019, Geneva Convention against genocides in Kashmir and Punjab and submission of reports to the UN, November 1, 2019

  SFJ arranged for an international conference in Geneva, in front of the United Nations Headquarters, on November 1, 2019 in commemoration of the victims of the 1984 Sikh Genocide and kick-start the voter registration for the Punjab Independence Referendum 2020. Earlier, on the same morning, the SFJ delegation met the UN officials to stop the ongoing genocide of Sikhs and Kashmiris.

- 2019, Sikh for Justice opened 'Punjab Independence Referendum 2020 voter registration worldwide, except for Punjab

  SFJ opened voter registration for Punjab Independence Referendum 2020 all over the world, except for Punjab, on November 1, 2019.

- 2020, India downgraded to tier 1, from tier 2, for worsening religious persecution in Modi India

  As of April 2020, the United States Commission on International Religious Freedom placed India in tier 1 because of minority persecution, along with countries like China, North Korea, Pakistan, and Saudi Arabia. This is the first time that USCIRF has placed India in its top tier of violators and recommended that the State Department list it as a country of particular concern. This development follows a serious deterioration of religious freedom in India over the past several years since Modi came into power.

- 2020, Sikh for Justice wrote a Letter to China's president on June 1, 2020

   Sikh for justice has sent a letter to the president of China, that the Sikhs living around the world, who want the freedom of Punjab from India, support China's stand against India.
- 2020, award set for Khalistan flag hoisting at Lal Kila, Delhi

   Sikhs for Justice declared an award of $125,000 for anyone who would hoist the Khalistan flag at Lal Kila, Delhi, on or before August 15, 2020.
- 2020, Sikhs for Justice provided financial support to the people of Punjab

   SFJ provided financial support for the COVID-19 victims in Punjab, along with Rs. 3,500 monthly, for three months, to any farmer whose loan is in default and owns less than five acres of land in Punjab. This amount was later increased from Rs. 3,500 to Rs. 5 000. SFJ declared an award of $125,000 to anyone hoisting the Khalistan flag at Lal Kila (Red Fort), New Delhi, $2,500 at any government building, and $250 at any Panchayat Ghar (local municipality) office.
- 2020, India blocked forty websites of Sikhs for Justice, July 5, 2020
- The government of India blocked forty websites of SFJ on July 5, 2020. These websites were created to propagate the message of voter registration for the unofficial Punjab Independence Referendum.
- 2020, *rail roko* ("stop the trains") launched by Sikhs for Justice on September 13, 2020

   "Stop the rails" call given by Sikhs for Justice was phenomenally successful in Punjab. It was an astounding success, almost no trains left the railway stations in Punjab on this day.
- 2020, SFJ hired one thousand ambassadors for voter registration

SFJ announced hiring one thousand ambassadors for Rs. 7,500 each for voter registration for the Punjab Independence Referendum 2020 in Punjab, from September 21–October 21, 2020.

# Journalists and Human Rights Activists on Operation Blue Star

A team of doctors...examined 400 corpses, including women and 15 to 20 children, all under five and a two-month-old baby...dead including scores of young Sikhs shot from close range with their hands tied behind their backs. (Associated Press, June 13, 1984)

A warrant was out for the arrest of an Indian Journalist who provoked displeasure by doing his job too well. Brahma Chellaney of the Associated Press was in Punjab last June when Prime Minister Indira Gandhi ordered the attack on Sikh extremists occupying Golden Temple Amritsar. ("The Truth on Trial—In India, *The New York Times*, October 23, 1984)

An army which wants to destroy a nation destroys its culture. That is why the Indian army burnt the Sikh Reference Library. (Mark Tully and Satish Jacob, *Amritsar: Mrs. Gandhi's Last Battle*)

Thousands of people have disappeared from Punjab since the siege of Sikh's Golden Temple here seven weeks ago. In some villages, men between 15–35 have been bound, blindfolded, and taken away. Their fate is unknown. (Mary Ann Weaver, *London Sunday Times*, July 22, 1984)

On a day of pilgrimage when thousands had gathered at the Golden Temple, army tanks moved into the Temple complex, smashing into the sanctum, and shooting everyone in sight. Those left were prevented from leaving the building, many wounded were left to bleed to death and when they begged for water, army Jawans (soldiers) told them to drink the mixture of blood and urine on the floor. Four months later no list of casualties or missing persons had yet been issued. (Amrit Wilson, *New Statesmen*, November 16, 1984)

On Saturday, medical workers in Amritsar said soldiers had threatened to shoot them if they gave food or water to Sikh pilgrims wounded in the attack and lying in the hospital. (Christian Science Monitor, June 1984)

The army which had suffered a heavy toll in three days of battle went berserk and killed every Sikh who would be found inside the Temple complex. They were hauled out of the rooms, brought to the corridors on the circumference of the Temple, and with their hands tied behind their back, were shot in cold blood. (Ram Narayan Kumar and Georg Sieberer, *Sikh Struggle: Origin, Evolution and Present Phase*, pp. vii, 396)

In the Akal Takhat built by Guru Hargobind and the supreme seat of Sikhs, the stench of death still lingered. It seemed inconceivable that this was the holiest shrine of a major religion—the equivalent of Vatican and Canterbury Cathedral, 1991. (David Graves, *The Telegraph London*, June 15, 1984)

Army unit acted in total anger and unwittingly shot down all suspects rounded up from Golden Temple complex. (Joshi Chand, *Bhindranwale: Myth and Reality*, 1984)

Thus the Operation Blue Star will go down in the history as one of the biggest massacres of unarmed civilians by the organized military force of a nation. (CKC Reddy, et al., *Army Action in Punjab: Prelude and Aftermath*, 1984)

India's crime of 1984 began with its assault on, and the massacre at, the Golden Temple and dozens of other Gurdwaras across India in the first week of June 1984 and continued with nationwide government-sponsored pogroms of November 1984. In many ways, the crimes continue, not just in the cover-up and sheltering the criminals, but in actual outrages by the government and its minions to date. (Professor Cynthia Keppley Mahmood, researcher on Sikh issues at the University of Notre Dame)

The Indian Army went into Darbar Sahib not to eliminate a political figure or a political movement but to suppress the culture of a people, to attack their hearts, to strike a blow at their spirit and self-confidence. (Joyce Pettigrew, *Sikhs of Punjab: Unheard Voices of State and Guerrilla Violence*, 1995, p. 8)

The Operation Blue Star was not only envisioned and rehearsed in advance, meticulously and in total secrecy, it also aimed at obtaining the maximum number of Sikh victims, largely devout pilgrims unconnected with political agitation. The facts speak for themselves. (Ram Narayan Kumar, Georg Sieberer, *The Sikh Struggle: Origin, Evolution, and Present Phase*, 1991)

# Relevant Quotes

It (Hinduism) is a boa constrictor of the Indian forests. When a petty enemy appears to worry it, it winds around its opponent, crushes it in its folds, and finally causes it to disappear in its capacious interior... Hinduism has embraced Sikhism in its folds; the still comparatively young religion is making a vigorous struggle for life, but its ultimate destruction is, it is apprehended, inevitable without state support. (Max Arthur Macauliffe 1903)

Hinduism has always been hostile to Sikhism whose Gurus powerfully and successfully attacked the principle of caste which is the foundation on which the whole fabric of Brahminism has been reared. The activities of Hindus have, therefore, been constantly directed to undermine Sikhism both preventing children of Sikh fathers from taking Pahul and reducing professed Sikhs from their allegiance to their faith. Hinduism has strangled Buddhism once a formidable rival to it and it has already made serious inroads into the domain of Sikhism. (D. Petrie, assistant director, Criminal Intelligence, government of British India, intelligence report of August 11, 1911)

In future, the Congress shall accept no constitution which does not meet with the satisfaction of Sikhs. (The Lahore session of the Congress Party, December 31, 1929)

The brave Sikhs of Punjab are entitled to special considerations. I see nothing wrong in an area set up in the North of India wherein, Sikhs also can experience the glow of freedom. (Jawahar Lal Nehru, *Lahore Bulletin*, January 9, 1930)

I ask you to accept my word and the resolution of Congress that it will not betray a single individual much less a community. Let God be the witness of the bond that binds me and the Congress with you (Sikhs). When pressed further Gandhi said that Sikhs would be justified in drawing their swords out of the scabbards as Guru Gobind Singh had asked them to if Congress would renege on its commitment. (Mohandas Karamchand Gandhi, *Young India*, March 19, 1931)

In 1940 Dr. Vir Singh Bhatti demanded the formation of Khalistan. (Dr. Vir Singh Bhatti)

In 1942, Master Tara Singh demanded the Azad (sovereign and independent) Punjab. (Master Tara Singh)

You have seen the Hindus as co-slaves and you will know when they will be your masters and You (Sikhs) their slaves. (Janab Mohammad Ali Jinnah, Quid-e-Azam, the father of Pakistan)

Sikhs as a community are a lawless people and a menace to the law-abiding Hindu community. The deputy commissioners should take special measures against them. (An official circular of the government of India, October 10, 1947)

Master Tara Singh saw me on return from Delhi, and, seemed concerned at the approaching departure of the British. He demanded Khalistan, with the transfer of population, or a new state from Jammu to Chenab, in which Sikhs would not be oppressed. (Sir E. Jenkins, governor of Punjab, April 15, 1946)

*Mulak Hindu Ka, Raj Tikri ka* (trio, Jawaharlal Nehru, V. B. Patel, and Chandu Lal Trivedi), Guru (the Lord) Rakha Bhai Sikre ka. (Sirdar Kapoor Singh, Indian Civil Services, national professor of Sikhism)

Kya Main Taaqat Dushman (the enemy, Sikhs) ke haath main de dun (How can I give the power in the hands of Sikhs). (Jawahar Lal Nehru)

The individual known to common Indian masses as chacha (uncle), the so-called messiah of peace and secularism, was the main architect of anti-Sikh policies and practices, in India and abroad. (Dr. Harjinder Singh Dilgeer)

Physical death I do not fear, death of conscious is a sure death. (Sant Jarnail Singh Bhindranwale)

I don't give a damn if the Golden Temple and the whole Amritsar are destroyed, I want

Bhindranwale dead. (Indira Gandhi to Gen. Vaidya during Operation Blue Star)

We have broken the back of Sikhs and will get them elsewhere. (M. M. K. Wali, Indian foreign secretary, June 7, 1984 [Canadian Broadcasting Corporation, Radio 740, as it happens])

Sikh Nation declared independence on April 29, 1986. (Sarbat Khalsa at Darbar Sahib Complex)

Sikh Nation declared Independence of Punjab-Khalistan on October 7, 1987 forming the sovereign country of Khalistan. (The Council of Khalistan, Washington, DC)

You do not know the might of our armed forces. We will eliminate 10,000 Sikh youth and the world will know nothing about it. (Chander Shekhar, former prime minister of India, CK, October 21, 1991)

To preserve the unity of India, if we have to eradicate 2 crore (20 million) Sikhs, we will do so. (Balram Jakhar, a former Indian cabinet minister)

The world's largest democracy is tyranny willing to commit any act of brutality or terrorism to maintain its corrupt occupation of Khalistan...showing the American public that India's claim of being a democracy is more disinformation. (Dr. Gurmeet Singh Aulakh, former president of Council of Khalistan, *The Washington Post*, April 25, 1994)

For Sikhs to safeguard their religion, unique identity, and language independence of Punjab-Khalistan is their only option.

Denial and Obstruction of Justice are Crimes Against Humanity. (Bakhshish Singh Sandhu, MD, president of Council of Khalistan, January 26, 2020)

# Annexure 1

## Resolution by US Congress on Right to Self-Determination For Punjab

US Congress on Right to Self-determination for the People of Punjab, October 5, 1990

On October 5, 1990, Hon. Mr. Faleomaraga introduced H. Con. Res. 380 Concurrent Resolution:

Expressing the sense of the Congress that the people of the province of Punjab in India should be allowed to determine its political status.

Whereas Congress is concerned about the violence in the Province of Punjab, India.

Whereas the violence in Punjab appears to be related to a desire by the majority of the residents to obtain fundamental human rights, which are denied to them.

Whereas the denial of basic human rights has increased under the current Indian government.

Whereas the Government of India is not permitting internationally recognized human rights organizations, such as Amnesty International, to determine the validity of the claims of violation of human rights in Punjab.

Whereas the elections in Punjab have been repeatedly postponed which have the effect of denying the residents of Punjab the inalienable right to select their political leaders and determine the political status of the region: Now, therefore, be it

Resolved by the House of Representatives (the Senate concurring), that it is the sense of the Congress that the people of the Province of Punjab, India, like people of all nations, have the right to self-determination and should be allowed to decide their future through a plebiscite sponsored or supervised by the United Nations.

# Annexure 2

## US Congress on Right to Self-determination for Punjab, 1994

House of Representatives,
Washington, DC, October 7, 1994
Hon. Bill Clinton,
President of the United States,
Washington, DC.

We, the undersigned Members of Congress, ask You to persuade the Indian government through the State Department to:[331]

1. Recognize the right of the Sikh Nation to pursue its right to self-determination peacefully.
2. Allow a plebiscite in Punjab, Khalistan under the United Nations' auspices so that Sikhs can peacefully decide for themselves their political future.

---

[331] *US Congress on the Sikh Struggle for Khalistan: Volume One, 1985–1998* (International Sikh Organization, 2013), 316–321.

If the Indian government refuses to consent to these basic concerns, we urge you to

1. Cut all direct U.S. aid to India.
2. Withdraw U.S. support for loan programs to India in the IMF and the World Bank.
3. Bring the issue of freedom for Khalistan and India's brutality against Sikhs to the United Nations and ask for international sanctions against the Indian government.

Mr. President, it is time that the United States sends a message to the Indian government. In the name of freedom and democracy, we beseech you to act immediately.

Sincerely,

Peter Geren, John T. Doolittle, John J. Duncan, Jr., Peter King, William J. Jefferson, Dan Burton, Gary Condit, Gerald Solomon, William O. Lipinski, Chris Cox, Phil Crane, Collin C. Peterson, Arthur Ravenel, Jr., Christopher Shays, Dana Rohrabacher, Charles Wilson, Randy "Duke" Cunningham, Richard Lehman, Tom Bliley, Dick Zimmer, Robert K. Dornan, Dean A. Gallo, George Miller, Roscoe Bartlett, Jack Fields, Robert T. Matsui,

Esteban E. Torres, Wally Herger,
Ken Calvert, Richard,
Pombo, Edolphus Towns, Lincoln Diaz-Balart,
James H. Quillen, Scott L. Klug, Bill Paxton.

# Annexure 3

---

## HR 1425
## Human Rights in India Act[332]

A BILL
April 6, 1995

To suspend United States development assistance for India unless the President certifies to the Congress that the Government of India has taken certain steps to prevent human rights abuses in India.[333]

*Be it enacted by the Senate and House of Representatives of the United States of America in Congress assembled,*

---

[332] H. R. 1425, the Human Rights in India Act, was introduced to the US House of Representatives, 104th Congress, First Session, on April 6, 1995, by Republican Representative Dan Burton. Of particular concern to Dalit activists, who have long labored for congressional recognition of the human rights violations perpetrated in India against the Dalits, is item 10 (in the Indian Constitution, the Untouchables or Dalits are referred to as Scheduled Castes). According to Dr. Velu Annamalai, this may be the first time that the plight of the Dalits has found a place in US Congressional records. Dr. Annamalai's assistance in provision of a copy of H. R. 1425 is gratefully acknowledged. Citations follow as per H. R. 1425/briefing packet.

[333] V. T. Rajshekar, *Dalit: The Black Untouchables of India*, 3rd ed. (New Delhi: Gyan Publishing House, 2015), 99–104

SECTION 1. SHORT TITLE

This Act may be cited as the "Human Rights in India Act"

SEC. 2. FINDINGS

Congress finds the following:

(1) In India, tens of thousands of political prisoners, including prisoners of conscience, are being held without charge or trial under special or preventive laws.[334]

(2) The special and preventive detention laws most frequently cited by human rights organizations are the Terrorist and Disruptive Activities (Prevention) Act (TADA) of 1987, the National Security Act of 1980, the Armed Forces (Punjab and Chandigarh) Special Powers Act of 1983, the Armed Forces (Jammu and Kashmir) Special Powers Act of 1990, and the Jammu and Kashmir Public Safety Act of 1978.[335]

(3) These laws provide the military and police forces of India sweeping powers of arrest and detention with broad powers to shoot to kill with virtual immunity from prosecution.[336]

---

[334] "Amnesty International Report 1994," p. 157, para. 1 and 5.
"Human Rights Watch World Report 1995," p. 155, para. 2.
[335] "Amnesty International Report 1994."
"INDIA: Torture and Deaths in Custody in Jammu and Kashmir," Amnesty International, January 1995.
"INDIA: Human Rights Violations in Punjab: Use and Abuse of the Law," Amnesty International, May 1991.
[336] "INDIA: Torture and Deaths in Custody in Jammu and Kashmir," Amnesty International, p. 46, para. 3.

(4) These laws contravene important international human rights standards established under the International Covenant on Civil and Political Rights, to which India is a party, such as the right of liberty and security, the right to a fair trial, the right of freedom of expression, and the right not to be subjected to torture or arbitrary arrest and detention.[337]

(5) Throughout India, political detainees are often held for several months, and in some cases a year, without access to family, friends, or legal counsel.[338]

(6) Throughout India, the torture of detainees has been routine, and scores of people have died in police and military custody as a result.[339]

(7) Throughout India, scores of political detainees have "disappeared" and hundreds of people are reported to have been extrajudicially executed by military and police forces.[340]

(8) In Punjab, the Punjab Government encouraged extrajudicial executions by offering bounties for the killing of mil-

---

[337] "INDIA: Torture and Deaths in Custody in Jammu and Kashmir," Amnesty International, p. 46, para. 3; p. 48, para. 1.

[338] "INDIA: Human Rights Violations in Punjab: Use and Abuse of the Law," Amnesty International, May 1991, p. 49, para. 3.

[339] "Amnesty International Report 1994," p. 157, para. 1.

[340] "Amnesty International Report 1994," p. 157, para. 2.

itants and paid over 41,000 in bounties between 1991 and 1993.[341]

(9) Abuse by the military and police forces of India is particularly widespread in the states of Punjab, Assam, Manipur, Nagaland, and the portion of the disputed territory of Jammu and Kashmir under the control of the Government of India.

(10) Many victims come from underprivileged and vulnerable sections of society in India, particularly the scheduled castes and tribes.[342]

(11) The establishment of the National Human Rights Commission by the Government of India is an important first step toward improving the human rights record of India.[343]

(12) However, many human rights organizations are deeply concerned about the severe limitations placed on the powers, mandate, and methodology of the National Human Rights Commission.[344]

(13) In 1994, the decision by the Government of India to allow the International Committee of the Red Cross to provide limited humanitarian assistance in the portion of the disputed territory of Jammu and Kashmir

---

[341] "State Department's Human Rights Report for 1993," India section, p. 1,340, para. 4.

"Amnesty International Report 1994," p. 158, para. 1.

[342] "Amnesty International Report 1994," p. 157, para. 5.

[343] "Amnesty International Report 1994," p. 157, para. 11.

[344] "Human Rights Watch World Report 1995," p. 156, para. 5.

under the control of the Government of India was an important first step in providing international humanitarian organizations greater access to troubled areas of India.

(14) However, in 1994, the Government of India continued to prohibit several international human rights organizations from conducting independent investigations in the portion of the disputed territory of Jammu and Kashmir under the control of the Government of India and provided only limited access to such organizations to other states such as Punjab, Assam, Manipur, and Nagaland where significant human rights problems exist. [345]

(15) In India, armed opposition groups have committed human rights abuses.[346]

(16) Several human rights organizations have called on such armed opposition groups to respect basic standards of humanitarian law which require that individuals not taking part in hostilities should at all times be treated humanely. [347]

SEC. 3. LIMITATION ON DEVELOPMENT ASSISTANCE FOR INDIA UNLESS CERTAIN STEPS ARE TAKEN BY THE GOVERNMENT OF INDIA TO IMPROVE HUMAN RIGHTS IN INDIA

---

[345] "Human Rights Watch World Report 1995," p. 156, para. 5.
    "Amnesty International Report 1994," p. 159, para. 12.
[346] "Amnesty International Report 1994," p. 157, para. 1.
[347] "Amnesty International Report 1994," p. 160, para. 3.

A)   LIMITATION.—The President may not provide development assistance for India for any fiscal year unless the President transmits to the Congress a report containing a certification for such fiscal year that the Government of India meets the following requirements:[348]

1)   The Government of India has released all prisoners of conscience in India.

2)   The Government of India ensures that all political prisoners in India are brought to trial promptly and fairly, or released, and have prompt access to legal counsel and family members.

3)   The Government of India has eliminated the practice of torture in India by the military and police forces.

4)   The Government of India impartially investigates all allegations of torture and deaths of individuals in custody in India.

5)   The Government of India has established the fate or whereabouts of all political detainees in India who have "disappeared."

6)   The Government of India brings to justice those members of the military and police forces responsible for torturing or improperly treating prisoners in India.

7)   The Government of India permits citizens of India who are critical of such

---

[348] "Amnesty International Report 1994," p. 159, para 7.

a Government to travel abroad and return to India.[349]

8) The Government of India ensures that human rights monitors in India are not targeted for arrest or harassment by the military and police forces of India.

9) The Government of India permits both international and domestic human rights organizations and international and domestic television, film, and print media full access to all states in India where significant human rights problems exist.

B) REQUIREMENT FOR CONTINUING COMPLIANCE.—Any certification with respect to the Government of India for a fiscal year under subsection (a) shall cease to be effective for that fiscal year if the President transmits to the Congress a report containing a determination that such Government has not continued to comply with the requirements contained in paragraphs (1) through (9) of such subsection.

c) Waiver.—The limitation on development assistance for India contained in subsection (a) shall not apply if the President transmits to the Congress a report containing a determination that providing such assistance for India is in the national security interest of the United States.

---

[349] "State Department Human Rights Report for 1994," India section, p. 1,228, para. 2.

D) Definitions.—As used in this section:

    1) DEVELOPMENT ASSISTANCE.—The term "development assistance" means assistance under chapter 1 of part l for the Foreign Assistance Act of 1961 (22 U.S.C. 2151 et seq.).

    2) India.—The term "India" includes the portion of the disputed territory of Jammu and Kashmir under the control of the Government of India.

E) Effective date.—The prohibition contained in subsection s

    shall apply with respect to the provision of development assistance beginning 9 months after the date of the enactment of this Act.

# Annexure 4

## United States Must Support Human Rights and Freedom for Sikhs of Khalistan

(Document)
Congressional Record—Extensions
Wednesday, April 9, 1997
105th Congress, 1st session
143 Cong Rec E164
Ref: Vol. 143, No. 41
Title: United States Must Support Human Rights and Freedom for Sikhs Of Khalistan
Hon. Peter t. King[350] of New York in the House of Representatives
Wednesday, April 9, 1997

"...The United States must support human rights and democracy throughout the world. Our Nation is a beacon of hope for the people seeking self-determination and freedom. The people of Khalistan deserve that support"

---

[350] *U.S. Congress on the Sikh Struggle for Khalistan: Volume One, 1985–1998* (International Sikh Organization), 124–125.

## The U.S. responds to Indian oppression of Sikhs

Tuesday, April 15, 1997

105th Congress, 1st Session, 143 Cong Rec E 663

Ref: Vol. 143, No.44

Title: Happy 2298th Birthday Khalsa Panth

In response to the continued subjugation of Sikhs in Khalistan,[351] Congress has just introduced legislation, House Concurrent Resolution 37 (H. Con. Res. 37), which recognizes and supports the Sikh nation's right to national self-determination. The bipartisan resolution, co-sponsored by Gary Condit (D-CA) and Dana Rohrabacher (R-CA), urges the implementation of an international sponsored plebiscite so that Sikhs themselves could decide, by free and fair vote, whether or not they want to remain with India.

If India is the democracy that it claims, then it should allow the people of Khalistan to decide for themselves whether or not they want to be a part of India, just as the U.S. has done with respect to Puerto Rico and Canada has done with respect to Quebec.

Please join us in celebrating this auspicious holiday of the Sikh Nation, it is a time of feasting and festivity. However, please also remember that there are millions of Sikhs in our homeland Khalistan who do not have much to celebrate. Moreover, think about them the next time you read something about the world's largest democracy And call your Member of Congress and ask

---

[351] *U.S. Congress on the Sikh Struggle for Khalistan: Volume One, 1985–1998* (International Sikh Organization), 120–124.

them to cosponsor H. Con. Res. 37—because everyone deserves the kind of freedom that we enjoy in the U.S.

Happy 298th Birthday to Sikh Nation.

# Annexure 5

---

## Christians Attacked in India

Hon. John t. Doolittle Of California In the House of Representatives
Tuesday, March 2, 1999

Mr. Doolittle. Mr. Speaker, James Madison, the primary author of the U.S. Constitution, warned about "the tyranny of the majority." The modern state of India is an example of that about which Madison warned us. Between Christmas and New Year, several Christian churches, prayer halls, and missionary schools were attacked by extremist Hindu mobs affiliated with the parent organization of India's ruling Bharatiya Janata Party (BJP).

The Washington Post reported on January 1 that ten such attacks occurred the week between Christmas and New Year's Day. Six people were injured in one of these attacks. The Vishwa Hindu Parishad (VHP), or World Hindu Council, appears to be responsible for the attacks. The BJP is the political wing of the VHP.

The Hindu militants are upset that Christians are converting low-caste Hindus. Their frustration does not justify acts of vio-

lence. Christian activists report that there were
more than 60 recorded cases of church and Bible-
burning, rape, and other attacks in 1998 alone,
including the recent rape of four nuns. The VHP
called the rapists "patriotic youth."

In 1997 and 1998, four priests were murdered. In the fall of 1997, a Christian festi-
val was stopped when the police opened fire.
There is a pattern here. However, Christians
are not the only victims of India's tyrannical
"democracy."

Muslims have seen their most revered
mosques destroyed; Sikhs have seen their most
sacred shrine, the Golden Temple in Amritsar,
attacked and remain under occupation by
plainclothes police. Their spiritual leader, the
Jathedar of the Akal Takht, Gurdev Singh
Kaunke, was tortured and killed in police custody. Although there is a witness to this murder,
no action has been taken against those responsible. Is this the secular democracy of which
India is so proud?

The United States is the beacon of freedom
to the world. As such, we cannot sit idly by and
watch India trample on the religious freedom of
its minorities. We should put this Congress on
record in support of peaceful, democratic freedom movements in South Asia and throughout
the world.

The United States recently allowed Puerto
Rico to vote on its status; our Canadian neighbors
held a similar referendum in Quebec. When do
the Sikhs of Khalistan, the Muslims of Kashmir,
and the other people living under Indian rule
get their chance to exercise this basic democratic
right? Will we support democratic freedom for

the people of South Asia, or will we look away while the tyranny of the majority continues to suppress fundamental rights like freedom of religion?[352]

---

[352] https://en.wikisource.org/wiki/Christians_Attacked_in_India.

# Annexure 6

---

## The Punjab Disturbed Areas Act, 1983 Act No. 32 of 1983

An Act to make better provision for the suppression of disorder and for the restoration and maintenance of public order in disturbed areas in Punjab.[353]

Be it enacted by Parliament in the Thirty-fourth Year of the Republic of India as follows:—

1.  Short title, extent, and commencement.—
    (1) This Act may be called The Punjab Disturbed Areas Act, 1983.
    (2) It extends to the whole of the State of Punjab.
    (3) It shall be deemed to have come into force on October 7, 1983.
2.  Definition.—In this Act, "disturbed area" means an area that is for the time being declared by notification under section 3 to be a disturbed area.
3.  Powers to declare areas to be disturbed areas.—The State Government may, by notification in the Official Gazette, declare

---

[353] http://legislative.gov.in/sites/default/files/A1983-32.pdf.

that the whole or any part of any district of Punjab as may be specified in the notification, is a disturbed area.

4. Power to fire upon persons contravening certain orders.—Any Magistrate or Police Officer not below the rank of Sub-Inspector or Havildar in case of the Armed Branch of the Police may, if he is of opinion that it is necessary to do so for the maintenance of public order, after giving such due warning, as he may consider necessary, fire upon, or otherwise use force, even to the causing of death, against any person who is acting in contravention of any law or order for the time being in force in the disturbed area, prohibiting the assembly of five or more persons or the carrying of weapons or of things capable of being used as weapons or of fire-arms, ammunition or explosive substances.

5. Powers to destroy arms dump, fortified positions, etc.—Any Magistrate or Police Officer not below the rank of a Sub-Inspector may if he thinks that it is necessary so to do, destroy any arms dump, prepared or fortified position or shelter from which armed attacks are made or are likely to be made or are attempted to be made or any structure used as a training camp for armed volunteers or utilized as a hide-out by armed gangs or absconders wanted for any offense.

6. Protection of persons acting under sections 4 and 5.—No suit, prosecution, or other legal proceedings shall be instituted except with the previous sanction of the 1 [Central

Government] against any person in respect of anything done or purporting to be done in exercise of the powers conferred by sections 4 and 5.

7. Repeal and saving.—(1) The Punjab Disturbed Areas Ordinance, 1983, is hereby repealed.

(2) Notwithstanding such repeal, anything done, or any action taken under the said Ordinance shall be deemed to have been done or taken under the corresponding provisions of this Act.

1. Subs. by President Act 2 of 1989, s. 2, for "State Government" (w.e.f. 3-4-1989).

# Annexure 7

---

## The Armed Forces (Punjab and Chandigarh) Special Powers Act, December 8, 1983[354]

An act to enable certain special powers to be conferred upon members of the armed forces in the disturbed areas in the State of Punjab and the Union territory of Chandigarh.

Be it enacted by Parliament in the Thirty-fourth Year of the Republic of India as follows:—

1. **Short title, extent, and commencement**:—
   (1) This Act may be called The Armed Forces (Punjab and Chandigarh) Special Power Act,1983.
   (2) It extends to the whole of the state of Punjab and the Union territory of Chandigarh.
   (3) It shall be deemed to have come into force on the 15th day of October 1983.

2. **Definitions**:—In this act, unless the context otherwise requires:—
   (a) "Armed forces" means the military forces and the air forces operat-

---

[354] https://www.vakilno1.com/bareacts/laws/the-armed-forces-punjab-and-chandigarh-special-powers-act-1983.html.

ing as land forces and includes any other armed forces of the Union so operating.

(b)     "Disturbed area" means an area that is for the time being declared by notification under section 3 to be a disturbed area.

(c)     All other words and expressions used herein, but not defined and defined in the Air Forces Act, 1950, or the Army Act, 1950, shall have the meanings respectively assigned to them in those Acts.

3.     **Power to declare an area to be a disturbed area:—**

If in relations to the State of Punjab or the Union Territory of Chandigarh, the Governor of that State or the Administrator of that Union territory or the Central Government, in either case, is of the opinion that the whole or any part of such State or Union territory, as the case may be, is in such a disturbed or dangerous condition that the use of armed forces in aid of the civil power is necessary, the Governor of the State or the Administrator of that Union territory or the Central Government, as the case may be may, by notification in the Official Gazette, declare the whole or such part of that State or Union territory to be disturbed area.

4.     **Special power of the armed forces:—**

Any commissioned officer, warrant officer, non-commissioned officer, or any other person of equivalent rank in the armed forces may, in a disturbed area,—

(a)  if he is of opinion that it is necessary so to do for the maintenance of public order, after giving such due warning as he may consider necessary, fire upon or otherwise use forces, even to the causing of death, against any person who is acting in contravention of any law or order for the time being in force in the disturbed area prohibiting the assembly of five or more persons or the carrying of weapons or of things capable of being used as weapons or firearms, ammunition or explosive substances;

(b)  if he is of opinion that it is necessary so to do, destroy any arms dump, prepared or fortified position or shelter from which armed attacks are made or likely to be made or are attempted to be made, of any structure used as a training camp for armed volunteers or utilized as a hideout by armed gangs or absconders wanted for any offense.

(c)  Arrest, without a warrant, any person who has committed a cognizable offense or against whom a reasonable suspicion exists that he has committed or is about to commit a cognizable offense may use such force as may be necessary to effect the arrest;

(d)  Enter and search, without a warrant, any premises to make any such arrest as aforesaid or to recover any person believed to be wrongfully restrained or confined or any property reasonably suspected to be stolen property or any arms, ammunition, or explosive substances believed to be unlawfully kept in such premises, and may for that purpose use such forces as may be necessary, and seize any such property, arms ammunition or explosive substances;

(e) Stop, search and seize any vehicle or vessel reasonably suspected to be carrying any person who is a proclaimed offender, or any person who has committed a non-cognizable offense, or against whom a reasonable suspicion exists that he has committed or is about to commit a non-cognizable offense, or any person who is carrying any arms, ammunition or explosive substance believed to be unlawfully held by him, and may, for that purpose, use such forces as may be necessary to effect such stoppage, search or seizure, as the case may be.

5. **Power of search to include powers to break open locks, etc:—**

Every person making a search under this Act shall have the power to break open the lock of any door, almirah, safe, box, cupboard, drawer, package, or another thing if the key thereof is withheld.

6. **Arrested person and seized property to be made over to the Police:—**

Any person arrested and taken into custody under this Act and every property, arm ammunition or explosive substance or any vehicle or vessel seized under this Act, shall be made over to the officer-in-charge of the nearest police station with the least possible delay, together with a report of the circumstances occasioning the arrest, or, as the case may be, occasioning the seizure of such property, arm, ammunition or explosive substance or any vehicle or vessel, as the case may be.

7. **Protection of a person acting in good faith under this Act:—**

No prosecution, suit, or other legal proceedings shall be instituted, except with the previous sanction of the Central Government, against any person in respect of anything done or purported to be done in exercise of the powers conferred by this Act.

8. **Repeal and saving:—**
   (1) The Armed Forces (Punjab and Chandigarh) **Special Powers Ordinance**, 1983, is hereby repealed.
   (2) Notwithstanding such repeal, anything is done, or any action taken under the said Ordinance shall be deemed to have been done or taken under the corresponding provisions of this Act.

# Annexure 8

## The Hindu Caste System

The caste system has been prevalent in the Indian subcontinent for thousands of years. According to this system, Hindus are divided into four main categories: Brahmins, Kshatriyas, Vaishyas, and the Shudras. It is noteworthy that the Dalits are not included in any of these four categories; they are outside of the Hindu caste system, thus being the most unprivileged of all. Dalits have been intentionally deprived of education or landownership, thus finding it difficult to make significant socioeconomic progress or switch the caste category.

At the top of this pyramid system are the Brahmins, who are mainly teachers and intellectuals. Second from the top are the Kshatriyas, or the warriors and rulers. The third place is assigned to the Vaishyas, or the traders. At the bottom of the pyramid are the Shudras, who do all the menial jobs. The main castes have been further divided into thousands of subcastes, depending upon the kind of work they are supposed to perform.

The system grants many privileges to the upper castes while promoting repression of the lower castes by privileged groups. The caste system is inherently undemocratic and violates basic human rights. It promotes inequality and deprives the unprivileged of their rights and the opportunity to advance themselves. The system has been so prevalent for so long that many of the Dalits and Shudras feel proud of their inheritance and have been unable to realize that their basic human rights have been abridged. With the migration of the people from the villages to the urban areas, the effect of the caste system has been declining but is still prevalent in rural areas.

# Appendix

## *Images*

Destruction of Akal Takhat by Indian Army in June 1984

Cleanup of dead bodies from Darbar Sahib after
the Indian Army Invasion in June 1984

Sikh properties set on fire during November 1984 Sikh Genocide in Delhi

Bodies of Thirty-seven Sikhs, massacred in Chattisinghpura in
March 2000 on the arrival of former President Clinton in India

Image of destruction of Darbar Sahib (GTA)
by India army invasion in June 1984

## Additional Images

Images of Sikhs killed by police torture and fake encounters may be accessed under the reference http://shaheed-khalsa.com/genocide.html.

# Abbreviations

---

AISSF—All India Sikh Student Federation
BJP—Bharatiya Janta Party
BSF—Border Security Force
CBI—Central Bureau of Investigations
CID—Criminal Intelligence Division
CRPF—Central Reserve Police Force
DGP—Director general police
DIG—Deputy inspector general
DSP—Deputy superintendent police
GTA—Golden Temple Amritsar
ICCPR—International Covenants on Civil and Political Rights
ICESCR—International Covenant on Economic, Social and
    Cultural Rights
IPS—Indian Police Services
MISA—Maintenance of Internal Security Act
NSA—National Security Agency
NSG—National Security Guard
POTA—Prevention of Terrorism Act
RAW—Research and Analysis Wing
SHO—Station House Officer
SGGS—Sri Guru Granth Sahib (the Sikh Holy Scripture)
SGPC—Shiromani Gurdwara Parbandhak Committee
TAAA—Terrorist Affected Area Act (Special Courts Act)
TADA—Terrorist and Disruptive Activities (Prevention) Act
UAPA—Unlawful Activities (Prevention) Act
UDHR—Universal Declaration of Human Rights
UNCAT—United Nations Convention against Torture

# Glossary

---

**Akal Takhat**: The highest temporal seat of the Sikh people

**Amritdhari**: A baptized Sikh, one who has taken amrit

**Ardas**: The Sikh prayer

**Bandh**: A total closure of all businesses, government offices, transportation, and educational institutions

**Crore**: Ten Million

**Darbar Sahib**: The holiest Sikh shrine, also known as Golden Temple Amritsar or Harmandar Sahib

**Doaba**: Region of Punjab between two rivers, Sutlej and Beas

**Gurdwara**: A Sikh house of worship

**Guru Granth Sahib (Sri Guru Granth Sahib)**: The Sikh Holy Scripture

**Jathebandhi**: A group of people for a certain cause

**Khalsa**: An order of baptized Sikhs

**Khalsa Panth**: The Sikh people; the Sikh nation

**Kirpan**: Sword; one of the five Sikh symbols (means a weapon of kindness)

**Khalistan**: A sovereign country of Punjab; independent Punjab

**Lakh**: One hundred thousand

**Malwa**: An area of Punjab, south of Sutlej

**Majha**: An area of Punjab between Beas and Ravi Rivers

**Misl**: An independent Sikh Confederacy

**Panth**: The Sikh nation; the Sikh people

**Sarbat Khalsa**: General assembly of the Sikh nation; no minimum number required

**Sat Sri Akal**: Sikh salutation, meaning "truth is eternal"

**Satnam**: True name, referring to God

**Sewa (kar-sewa)**: Volunteer, collective work for a common cause

**Shahid**: Martyr

**Thana**: Police station

**Waheguru**: Almighty God

**Zafarnama**: Means the "Declaration of Victory" and is the name given to the letter sent by the tenth Sikh guru, Shri Guru Gobind Singh Ji, in 1705 to the emperor of India, Aurangzeb

# Selected Bibliography

Brass, Paul R. "The Politics of India." *A New Cambridge History of India*. Cambridge: Cambridge University Press, 1990.

Dhillon, Gurdarshan Singh. *India Commits Suicide*. Singh and Singh Publishers, 1992.

Dhillon, Gurdarshan Singh. *Truth About Punjab: Shiromani Gurdwara Parbandhak Committee Amritsar White Paper*, 1996.

International Sikh Organization. *U.S. Congress on the Sikh Struggle for Khalistan: Volume One, 1985–1998*, 2013.

Jaijee, Inderjit Singh. *Politics of Genocide: Punjab 1984–1994*. Baba Publishers, 1995.

Kaur, Jaskaran. *Twenty Years of Impunity: The November 1984 Pogroms of Sikhs in India*. 2nd ed. Ensaaf, 2006.

Kashmeri, Zuhair and Brian McAndrew. *Soft Target: How the India Intelligence Service Penetrated Canada*. James Lorimer and Company, 1989.

Kumar, Ram Narayan and Georg Sieberer. *Sikh Struggle: Origin, Evolution and Present Phase*. Delhi: Chanakya Publications, 1991.

Mahmood, Cynthia Keppley. *Fighting for Faith and Nation*. Philadelphia: University of Pennsylvania Press, 1996.

Mcleod, Hew. *Sikhism*. Penguin Books, 1997.

Pettigrew, Joyce. *Sikhs of the Punjab*. Zed Books Ltd., 1995.

Rajshekar, V. T. *Dalit: The Black Untouchables of India*. 3rd ed. Gyan Publishing House, 2015.

Sandhu, Ranbir Singh. *Struggle for Justice: Speeches and Conversation of Sant Jarnail Singh Bhindranwale*. Sikh Education and Religious Foundation, 1999.

Singh, Pav. *1984: India's Guilty Secret*. Kashi House, 2017.

Singh, Jagjit. *Percussions of History: Sikh Revolution in the Caravan of Revolutions*. The Nanakshahi Trust, 1981.

Singh, Khushwant. *The End of India*. Penguin Books, 2003.

Singh, Lt. Col. Partap. *Khalistan: The Only Solution; Bleeding Punjab*. 1991.

Tully, Mark and Satish Jacob. *Amritsar: Mrs. Gandhi's Last Battle*. Rupa Publications, 1985.

# About the Author

Bakhshish Singh Sandhu, MD, is a human rights activist who has dedicated his life to protect and promote human rights. He is a staunch supporter of the fact that all people are created equal, and they should have equal access to the right of life, liberty, and pursuit of happiness, as our forefathers had envisioned.

He is a cofounder of Sikhs for Justice (SFJ), a human rights advocacy group, based in New York. SFJ is heading the campaign for the independence of Punjab Khalistan by the exercise of the right to self-determination of the people of Punjab by peaceful, legal, and democratic means. He is the current president of the Council of Khalistan, an organization seeking reestablishment of the sovereignty of Punjab.

He is the founder of Khalsa Global Reach Foundation, Inc., whose goal is empowering people to achieve their best by improving access to education for the socioeconomically disadvantaged children in the world. Since education is the best equalizer in any society or country in the world, his emphasis is on improving the affordability of education. He is a cofounder of the nonprofit charitable organization called Khalistan Food For All, whose main objective is to support the United Nations World Food Program to feed the hungry and end hunger by 2030.

CPSIA information can be obtained
at www.ICGtesting.com
Printed in the USA
BVHW040751081022
648999BV00004B/16